DOUBLE TALK

DECONSTRUCTING MONOLINGUALISM IN CLASSROOM SECOND LANGUAGE LEARNING

Virginia M. Scott
Vanderbilt University

Series Editors
Judith Liskin-Gasparro
Manel Lacorte

Prentice Hall
Boston   Columbus   Indianapolis   New York   San Francisco   Upper Saddle River
Amsterdam   Cape Town   Dubai   London   Madrid   Milan   Munich   Paris   Montreal   Toronto
Delhi   Mexico City   Sao Paulo   Sydney   Hong Kong   Seoul   Singapore   Taipei   Tokyo

Publisher: Phil Miller
Executive Editor: Bob Hemmer
Marketing Manager: Denise Miller
Production Manager: Fran Russello
Art Director: Jayne Conte
Cover Designer: Bruce Kenselaar
Full-Service Project Management: Aparna Yellai, GGS Higher Education Resources,
   A Division of Premedia Global, Inc.

Text Font: 10/12 Garamond

Many of the designations by manufacturers and seller to distinguish their products are claimed as
trademarks. Where those designations appear in this book, and the publisher was aware of a
trademark claim, the designations have been printed in initial caps or all caps.

Library of Congress Cataloging-in-Publication Data

Scott, Virginia Mitchell.
   Double talk : deconstructing monolingualism in classroom second language learning / Virginia
M. Scott.—1st ed.
      p. cm.
   Includes bibliographical references and index.
   ISBN-13: 978-0-205-68688-9
   ISBN-10: 0-205-68688-5
   1. Languages, Modern—Study and teaching. 2. Second language acquisition. I. Title.

PB36.S36 2010
418.0071–dc22

2009031040

Prentice Hall
is an imprint of

www.pearsonhighered.com

ISBN 10: 0-205-68688-5
ISBN 13: 978-0-205-68688-9

I dedicate this book to Gay, who listens to all my language stories.

TABLE OF CONTENTS

ACKNOWLEDGMENTS

The inspiration for *Double Talk* comes from my earliest memories of living in France, Madagascar, Kenya, Denmark, and the United States. In all of these countries I heard and spoke other languages—French, English, Swahili, Danish, Swedish, Norwegian, German, Dutch, Spanish, and Italian. My life has always been populated with multilingual people—family, friends, colleagues, and students—who play with words and tell stories about their language experiences. Your stories have humbled me, filled me with admiration, and made me laugh. Thank you.

The language stories of Michael, Emma, Felix, Jeanne, Bill, Sarah, Julien, Sharon, and countless others have enriched my understanding of the many ways people navigate language worlds. Thank you.

Graduate students Eva Dessein and Ingrid Schwab read and commented on early versions of *Double Talk*. Rachel Nisselson, Louis Betty, Robert Watson, Daniel Ridge, David Mora, and Rachel Early have listened, asked questions, and kept us all from engaging in double-talk. Haleh Kadivar, who majored in French and neuroscience, shared her knowledge of gray matter. Thank you.

Bob Terry read early versions of *Double Talk* and reminded me of what is true and what needs to be reworded. Thank you.

Judith Liskin-Gasparro and Manel Lacorte were always an e-mail away, keeping me on track. They are offering an important contribution to our profession by serving as the first editors of the new Prentice Hall series in applied linguistics. Thank you.

After reading the proposal for *Double Talk*, Bob Hemmer told me his story of living in a bilingual household. He believed in this book's possibilities to inspire others. Thank you.

The production editor, Aparna Yellai, working from her office in India, has made this experience truly global. We have communicated for several months across many time zones, and her patience and good cheer have been a daily gift. Thank you.

Vivian Cook's notion of multicompetence is the most compelling theory about language development and use I have encountered. He has generously allowed me to appropriate this term to describe multicompetent second language learners in *Double Talk*. Thank you.

Catherine Snow and Doug Knight have cheered me on in English, French, Italian, Norwegian, and German. (Griao.) Thank you.

Anne Christensen, Jørn Heldrup, Tania, and Thomas keep Danish alive in my head and only occasionally make fun of me. Thank you.

My parents, John and Beatrice Mitchell, took us all over the world and were confident we would learn every new language and fit in easily. Our home was filled with multinational people for as long as I can remember. Thank you.

Lauren, Ian, Se Jin, Elizabeth, Joshua, Susannah, Jordan, and Destiny have added Korean, Catalan, Pulaar, and Wolof, as well as colorful variations of American English, to the languages of our household. All kinds of sounds and songs can be heard at our family gatherings. Thank you.

Gay and I tell stories at the same time. This double talk is not confusing to us; we get twice as much said. She is the best friend I have ever had. Thank you.

Finally, I thank the readers of *Double Talk* who will certainly continue to explore ways to empower second language learners of all kinds to discover the world through the lens of another language.

PREVIEW

"SORRY. I DON'T REMEMBER MUCH."

AN OPENING LANGUAGE STORY

Recently I was watching a college soccer game with my friend whose daughter was on the team. The man sitting next to me on those cold bleachers, making friendly small talk, asked me what I do. "I am a French teacher," I answered. He seemed impressed and uttered some clichéd French phrase, and then admitted apologetically that he had studied French for 3 years but really didn't remember much. I had heard this kind of confession many times before, so I smiled and said nothing. In the past, I would have countered with "You might not have had the right teacher" or "You probably remember more than you realize." This time I sat in the cold and let his words—familiar words—sink in. Rather than put this exchange out of my mind as I have done with others in the past, I decided to focus intentionally on what he said and its implications about the seeming futility of our professional enterprise. The unsettling fact is that our students spend a short time with us in the classroom—a semester, a year, sometimes more—but later, in casual conversation, most of them probably laugh nervously and say they don't remember much.

Do teachers in other fields have this experience? Do their former students say openly that they forgot everything from U.S. history, anthropology, or philosophy class? In all probability, students *do* forget much of what they learned in these other kinds of classes, but they are unlikely say so because they perceive these academic subjects to be different from learning a foreign language. For many students, studying a foreign language means learning grammar to be able to understand, speak, read, and write another language. They perceive studying another language to be concrete learning and skill development. The goals of a U.S. history class might also include learning certain dates and facts, but students may also perceive other implicit objectives such as engaging them in critical inquiry and problem solving to prepare for other kinds of life endeavors. For example, students may forget the date of the Boston Tea Party but might remember something about its significance—that it was a protest, that it had something to do with taxation without representation, that it changed the way the American colonies interacted with their distant British rulers. The details and the facts of this historical event are, it seems to me, less important than the principles students may internalize about power, fairness, and human rights. The man next to me at the soccer game was a lawyer and, if I had asked, might have been able to tell me how learning about the Boston Tea Party had influenced his thinking. I don't know what he might have said if I had asked how studying French had influenced his career, shaped his identity, or contributed to his understanding of others. I didn't ask him because I assumed he was remembering his French studies in terms of verb conjugations and vocabulary lists; I presumed he was thinking that he wouldn't fare very well if he were to travel to a Francophone country and had to interact with native speakers. Looking back, it is clear he was thinking of French as a set of lost skills; he was apologizing for his lack of competence in French—his deficiencies.

My conversation with Soccer Dad (I never knew his name) served as a catalyst in my thinking about how we define our work as foreign language teachers and, by extension, how our students experience what we do. Do we spend class time training our students to understand, speak, read, and write the target language with native-like proficiency? Do we work to create opportunities for students to experience and appreciate the target culture(s) through film, song, and a variety of informative or creative readings? Do we strive to prepare students to perform successfully on standardized tests? Do we equip them for life in a multilingual, 21st-century world? And, perhaps most important, do our students experience success, or do they become like the soccer dad for whom learning a foreign language in a classroom felt difficult, potentially useless, and mostly forgettable? To avoid perpetuating this all-too-familiar response from our former students we must rethink what we do and why. Ultimately, foreign language teachers in the United States must define learning goals in terms that are both tangible and realistic so that *all* students—not just the very few who are talented language learners—have a sense that studying a foreign language is one of the fundamental features of being a member of a global community.

By the time most of our students come into our foreign language classes, they are well beyond the sensitive period for language learning.[1] In other words, for most students, learning a second language is not a spontaneous process but rather a deliberate and often challenging one. Despite this reality, many of us define learning goals in terms that are based on developing accurate, native-like proficiency in the target language. Drawing on theories and research in second language acquisition that validate the importance of input and interaction, we often design activities to help our students develop the necessary level of proficiency in the target language so they are able to move on to more interesting things, such as reading authentic texts and speaking perceptively about relevant topics. The harsh reality is, however, that most students achieve limited proficiency in the target language and do not have opportunities to engage in more challenging kinds of academic activities. Learning goals defined in these terms are therefore inadequate and restrictive. This simple truth should serve as a reality check for our profession—a profession that claims to open up the world to its students. Foreign language study should be an affirming experience for all students and not just for a privileged few; it should enable students to use their knowledge of the second language to gain access to other world views.

This lofty aspiration requires a radical change in the way we think about learning and teaching foreign languages in a classroom in the United States. By *change*, I do not mean simply revising our approaches to teaching grammar or reconsidering the value of input and interaction. Rather, I am proposing a transformation in our overarching goals for American students in the 21st century that involves a fundamental rethinking of classroom language use.

Specifically, I want to challenge the emphasis on target language use that has characterized foreign language classroom teaching practice for more than four decades. I want to make a case for an approach that recognizes that various media—particularly television and the Internet—have already made the multilingual, multicultural world in which we live available to most students in the United States. Although they may not be consciously aware of it, students who navigate this digital reality (often continuously) have begun to equip themselves with the necessary tools to function in a multilingual world. Linguistic isolation is a thing of the past and language use means something new. Above all, I would contend that monolingualism in the strictest sense is no longer a reality in the American experience.

Even though monolingualism may no longer be a valid way to describe the American experience in general, the foreign language classroom is still principally operating according to a monolingual standard. In other words, monolingualism is the point of departure for second language learning, and successful foreign language teaching moves learners from a monolingual (English) state to some degree of bilingual functioning. Regardless of the overarching theoretical framework (cognitive or social), the underlying goal is to move the foreign language learner away from monolingualism and toward bilingualism. Achieving some level of bilingual functioning is clearly a valid goal of foreign language instruction; however, it is ironic that becoming bilingual often means engaging primarily in a monolingual encounter with the target language. Although many foreign language teachers recognize that English is present in their classrooms—and may even use English as the main language of instruction—they generally believe that a monolingual approach is the best way to promote proficiency in the target language. In fact, good teaching practice is often defined by the degree to which a teacher can keep classroom interaction in the target language. Moreover, it implicitly places the focus of instruction on developing monolingual target language competence.

Using a monolingual standard to promote a bilingual reality is inherently problematic. First, and most obvious, English (the common language of students in an American classroom) is ever-present in the foreign language classroom, although it may be zealously discouraged. Teachers resort to English for all kinds of reasons—from carrying out discipline in the classroom, to giving directions, to explaining difficult concepts. Likewise, students use English whenever possible regardless of how motivated they may be to develop their proficiency in the target language. This inconsistency between implicit goals that support a target language approach and the reality that native and target languages coexist arbitrarily in the classroom is rarely discussed among foreign language teachers.[2] Second, foreign language learning and teaching has been implicitly founded on the notion that monolingualism and bilingualism are two distinct definitions of language functioning. Teachers and learners generally misunderstand what it means to be bilingual and falsely assume that people are monolingual until they have reached an advanced level of proficiency in a second language. This binary understanding of language functioning, with monolingual at one end and bilingual at the other, is a theoretical construct that is outdated at best. Third, and most important, a monolingual foreign language classroom does not provide a realistic vision of our multilingual world. Very few (if any) people today can claim that they have never seen a person, Web site, movie, magazine, or sign in another language. The fact that foreign language learning in the classroom setting is not informed by the ways real people use language in real-life settings is sufficient reason to rethink our traditional monolingual framework.

What would it mean to rethink this monolingual approach? Above all, it would require that we face head-on the *double-talk*, or deliberately ambiguous talk, regarding the role of the native language in foreign language learning and teaching. Rather than adhere to a target-language-only approach, we must articulate learning goals that draw on the ways first and second (and third) languages can be involved in promoting second language competence. What I am proposing (however silly it may sound) is that we should take the dash out of *double-talk* and explore *double talk*, or multiple-language use in the foreign language classroom.

DOUBLE TALK WITHOUT THE HYPHEN

When I decided to listen to what Soccer Dad said to me—to really listen—I realized that foreign language teachers rarely pay attention to these kinds of stories because they occur outside the realm of the classroom. Foreign language teachers focus mainly on what goes on in the classroom—a mostly closed environment over which we have some control. Within this sheltered space we can devote our energies to creating rich learning opportunities for students; we can also avoid thinking about students who are not always successful and who leave our classrooms with a sense of failure. In an effort to account for broader and more diverse experiences, *Double Talk* includes language stories from beyond the classroom to focus our attention on several key topics that can inform thinking about teaching in the classroom.

To bring these topics into focus, *Double Talk* draws on six real-life stories of second language use. These seemingly disparate language stories—referred to as "snapshots"—are personal in that they describe my experiences as well as those of my friends, colleagues, and students. Rather than offer a comprehensive approach to language teaching and learning, they provide examples of ways people use a second language in ordinary circumstances to help us re-envision our goals for foreign language learners. In other words, these personal observations offer foreign language teachers—both novice and experienced teachers—an opportunity to reflect critically on a variety of issues related to foreign language teaching. An analysis of each of these language stories, together with its pedagogical implications, provides a forum for discussion that circumvents evasive (hyphenated) double-talk.

Chapter 1 tackles the issue addressed above, namely the role of English in the foreign language classroom. Analyzing a logo on a T-shirt announcing that "monolingualism can be cured," I propose that monolingualism is a theoretical construct rather than a description of real language use. Moreover, I argue that, in the context of foreign language learning, a monolingual target language approach does not provide realistic models of the kinds of multilingual language use that learners are likely to encounter in the world. Multilingual classrooms that embrace linguistic and cultural diversity can serve to promote mulitilingual, multicultural learner identities and create empowered second language users.

Chapter 2 sets the stage for understanding bilingual functioning. I introduce Emma, a bilingual 3-year-old child who, when she first saw my dog, exclaimed, "Regarde le dog, Maman. Il est si cute!" This chapter describes code-switching, or the alternating use of two or more languages in a single conversation event. This spontaneous, rule-governed language phenomenon occurs among people of all ages who speak more than one language, and is considered an indicator of bilingual functioning. Moreover, research in bilingual studies shows that there are many different definitions of *bilingual* and that no one has the same level or same type of proficiency in two (or more) languages. This discussion of bilingualism and code-switching serves to confront our biases against multiple language use in the foreign language classroom.

Chapter 3 addresses the issue of language loss. My own story as an English–French bilingual who acquired Danish as a child and then "forgot" it when I moved away from Denmark serves to illustrate that different features of language are more susceptible to loss than others. Theories about child first (and second) language acquisition, adult second language development, and memory and language processing offer insights into ways people acquire and lose a language. Ultimately, I propose that words are more resistant to loss than grammar in adult second language learning. In addition, I argue that developing an awareness of the role of memory systems can serve to promote second language maintenance.

Chapter 4 builds on the distinction between words and grammar outlined in Chapter 3 and focuses on the importance of words in second language use. The story of Sarah, who barely remembers the French she learned in college 25 years ago, tells of her successful use of words and short utterances to interact with merchants in a French market. Although she is adept at learning new words, she feels as though grammatical language remains beyond her reach. Various theories about the evolution of human language, studies on primate and child language, and theories on the conceptual representation of words in a second language highlight the differences between learning words and learning grammar. Furthermore, Sarah's story calls attention to the ways that grammatical language may emerge from language use.

Chapter 5 underscores the limitations of focusing on grammar to develop competence in a second language. The story of Julien, a French high school exchange student who spent a summer with our family, illustrates that learning grammatical paradigms can inhibit real language use. Despite his apparent knowledge of many English grammatical structures, Julien was incapable of doing much more than listing the infinitive, past tense, and past participle forms of verbs: "Eat, ate, eaten; go, went, gone." This chapter reviews theories that have shaped our understanding of the role of grammar in second language learning, ultimately proposing that we must reconceptualize our definition of grammar and the ways we teach second languages.

Chapter 6 tells the story of Sharon, whose brief multilingual encounter with a Japanese woman in France proves to be the highlight of her short trip. Her experience sets the stage for exploring second language learning that avoids isolationist thinking and promotes cross-cultural literacy. In particular, I argue that foreign language teaching in the United States must be re-envisioned so that learners at all levels of study have opportunities to engage in substantive, text-based interactions with the target language and culture.

There is no question that *Double Talk* is an ambitious project that tackles a wide range of topics. Bilingual studies, the evolution of language, neurolinguistic theories, identity construction, and child language acquisition are among the many topics I address. However, as indicated earlier, this book is not an attempt to outline a specific approach to second/foreign language teaching. Rather, it offers new ways to think about issues that are problematic for classroom teachers. Code-switching, language loss, impoverished language use, and deficient language learners are among the issues foreign language teachers might wish to avoid. However, the stories, theories, and pedagogical recommendations outlined in *Double Talk* are inspired by my firm belief that learning a second language will play an increasingly important role as we face the complex political, economic, and ecological challenges of the 21st century. People of all languages and cultures will need to talk to each other and, more importantly, be sensitive to the many ways that people construe and convey meaning. However, the emergence of new superpowers and the shifting roles of the old national languages of the West (French, German, Spanish) demand that we re-envision the goals of foreign language learning and approaches to second/foreign language teaching. Foreign language teachers in the United States—especially those who teach traditional Western languages—can no longer afford to rely on theoretical paradigms of the past to inform the future. Specifically, I believe we need to rethink our monolingual attitude about second language learning and adopt a multilingual approach that is representative of real language use in the world today. To enact this change we must deconstruct our traditional notions of monolingualism in order to empower learners with the necessary confidence to function in a multilingual world.

THE THEORETICAL FRAMEWORK FOR *DOUBLE TALK*

Although relatively new to the field of applied linguistics, dynamic systems theory (DST) and other related frameworks (e.g., complex systems theory, chaos/complexity theory, and emergentism) offer compelling new ways to think about second language development.[3] DST involves the study of systems "in which systems are studied as a whole rather than with a focus on their parts" (de Bot, 2008, p. 166). Within this framework, language is viewed as a holistic, complex system that emerges from the interactions of various components, including subsystems of the language itself (e.g., phonological, lexical, syntactical, pragmatic), systems within individual learners (e.g., cognitive and affective dimensions), and systems external to the learner (e.g., communities and cultures). In other words, language development is a nonlinear, dynamic process that changes over time. As N. C. Ellis (2008) notes:

> Cognition, consciousness, experience, embodiment, brain, self, communication and human interaction, society, culture, and history are all inextricably intertwined in rich, complex, and dynamic ways in language. (p. 232)

Even though this dynamic understanding of language is principally applied to research exploring first and second language development, it has much to offer to the practice of foreign language teaching. Of particular interest is Cook's (2002a, 2007) theory of multicompetence, defined as the knowledge of two languages in one mind. This theory maintains that people who know more than one language have a distinct compound state of mind that is not equivalent to two monolingual states. In other words, multicompetence underscores the idea that bilingual people have a single language system comprised of two interconnected language systems. Dynamic models of multilingualism (e.g., Herdina & Jessner, 2002; Jarvis & Pavlenko, 2008) draw on Cook's notion to explain cross-linguistic interaction, such as code-switching and language transfer. Applied to second/foreign language learning, this holistic view validates the role of a person's native language in second language development and use. By extension, it opposes inhibiting the use of a person's native language during second language processing and use.

In addition to the notion of multicompetence, Cook (1999, 2002a) proposes the idea of a "multicompetent L2 [second language] user" who uses a language other than his or her native language at any level for any purpose. Rather than employ an idealized, monolingual native-speaker standard as a model for second language use, Cook's L2 user model accounts for unique, individual language use. Moreover, it validates second language use at various stages of development. Although the idea of multicompetence has been a topic of interest among applied linguists for the past several years (e.g., Byrnes & Sprang, 2003; de Bot, Lowie, & Verspoor, 2005; Dewaele & Pavlenko, 2003; Herdina & Jessner, 2002; Jarvis & Pavlenko, 2008; Kramsch & Whiteside, 2007), it is notably absent in the scholarship of foreign language pedagogy. That is, goals for foreign language learners are often still articulated in terms of achieving native-like proficiency in the target language rather than in terms of multicompetent second language use. In order to operationalize the notion of multicompetent second language use in the foreign language classroom, I use the term *multicompetent second language learner*.[4] In *Double Talk* I argue that learning goals designed to develop multicompetent second language learners can offer us fundamentally different ways of thinking about second/foreign teaching. In particular, this term can serve to re-envision learners as potentially competent second language users rather than as deficient native speakers. Accordingly, each chapter of the book concludes with a set of guiding principles designed to foster the development of multicompetent second language learners who are prepared to function as multicompetent second language users.

Above all, *Double Talk* seeks to relate theoretical views of second language development to classroom practice. That is, the research perspectives are designed to inform foreign language teaching in tangible ways. The various topics in the book—monolingualism, bilingualism, language loss, lexical usage-based approaches, emergent grammar, and multilingualism—are discussed through the lens of dynamic systems theory and Cook's complementary notion of multicompetence. Rather than view these theories as alternatives to existing theories of second language acquisition (i.e., cognitive and social theories), I consider them interconnected and mutually informative. In fact, I consider foreign language teaching itself to be a dynamic system—both a single teacher's practice and the entire professional enterprise. As such, foreign language teaching is a process that is shaped and informed by various theoretical frameworks as well as by teachers, students, administrators, and language policy makers. All of these elements conspire in *Double Talk* to offer new ways of thinking about foreign language teaching in the 21st century.[5]

THE IDIOSYNCRASIES IN *DOUBLE TALK*

The language stories, research perspectives, and pedagogical discussions in *Double Talk* relate specifically to the foreign language classroom in the United States. Although many of the principles may have applications elsewhere, I have confined my references to the unique qualities and challenges of learners in American classrooms. Because this book describes the American foreign language classroom setting, the term *native language* always refers to English—the common language of most students in the American foreign language classroom. The terms *second language* and *foreign language* are used to refer to two different settings. *Second language* is a generic term that describes any language experience that is distinct from first language. Given the diversity of learners in American classrooms today, I assume that a single classroom may have students with many different language backgrounds and therefore different first and second languages. *Foreign language* is used to describe the classroom experience in which students are learning a particular target language.

In addition, the reader will find relatively few acronyms in *Double Talk*; I use the terms *L1* and *L2* only when citing the work of others. Other acronyms, such as *DMM* (dynamic model of multilingualism) and *CLT* (communicative language teaching) are used to conform to the research citations that make frequent reference to them.

It is worth noting that the language stories and examples in *Double Talk* come from Western national languages—French, German, and Spanish. In the chapter on language loss, I cite examples from Danish—a language I learned as a child. Although I fully recognize the importance of studying less commonly taught languages, such as Arabic, Chinese, Hebrew, Korean, and Japanese, I believe that the approach I endorse has general applicability. In other words, although my examples may come from more traditionally taught Western languages, I am convinced that the principles outlined in *Double Talk* are relevant to any foreign language teaching context.

Finally, the most distinctive (and perhaps destabilizing) feature of the prose in *Double Talk* is the alternating use of the pronouns *she* and *he*. In chapters that draw on a language story in which the person is female I use *she*; likewise, when the person in the story is male I use *he*. There are occasions, however, where I alternate between the two. I have chosen to avoid references such as *s/he* or *he/she*.

DOUBLE TALK AT A GLANCE

Each chapter of *Double Talk* includes eight principal sections:

1. **Overview:** This brief section provides a summary of the theoretical perspectives and the content of the chapter.
2. **Snapshot:** Using mostly first-person narration, the snapshots are language stories from my own experience that have served as catalysts for my rethinking of foreign language learning and teaching. These stories create a context for exploring how two (or more) languages can function in second language development.
3. **Research Perspectives:** This section reviews research in fields that are not always traditionally related to foreign language teaching and learning. This research and its theoretical underpinnings serve to illumine ways in which the language phenomena presented in the snapshots offer important insights into foreign language learning and teaching.
4. **Perspectives for the Classroom:** Drawing on the stories in the snapshot and the relevant research, this section outlines the practical implications for the foreign language classroom. At the end of this section there are specific references to principles designed to foster the development of multicompetent second language learners.
5. **Your View:** Each chapter is punctuated by five or six boxes labeled "Your View," designed to elicit critical reflection on the material presented.
6. **Concluding Propositions:** Three concluding propositions summarize the theoretical and practical approach outlined in each chapter.
7. **Suggested Readings:** This section provides a list of readings pertinent to the subjects discussed in each chapter.
8. **Researching Your Own Language Stories:** At the end of each chapter there are two suggestions for further research based on the critical reflection called for in "Your View."

Notes

1. Most specialists in language development agree that there is a period of time in a young child's life when language can be learned nearly effortlessly. Although there is no consensus about the length of this sensitive period, it is generally understood to end at puberty. Chapter 2 includes a detailed description of the sensitive period for language learning.

2. The potential role of English (the L1) in the foreign language classroom is garnering attention among applied linguists (Atkinson, 1993; Belz, 2002; Cook, 1999, 2001; Levine, 2003, 2004; Scott & Huntington, 2006; Scott & de la Fuente, 2008; Storch & Wigglesworth, 2003); however, these theories and research have yet to have a significant impact on general classroom practice.

3. See, for example, the Summer 2008 volume of *The Modern Language Journal*, which includes contributions from de Bot; N. C. Ellis; Larsen-Freeman & Cameron; Van Geert; and Verspoor, Lowie, & Van Dijk.

4. Informal correspondence with Vivian Cook has confirmed my sense that the term *multicompetent second language learner* is a valid construct and is applicable to the foreign language learning setting.

5. I have been particularly inspired by Diane Larsen-Freeman's (1997, 2003, 2007) idea that chaos/complexity theory may offer a more pluralistic way to frame our understanding of second language development.

CHAPTER **1**

"Monolingualism can be cured!"

OVERVIEW

Monolingual is a word used to describe a person who knows or speaks only one language. More than just a descriptive term, however, it is often a label that implies certain judgments about a person or a group of people. It may be used to describe people who are provincial, unsophisticated, or uneducated; it may also refer to a country, such as the United States, where a large number of people have limited opportunities to interact with people of other language backgrounds. Regardless of how it is used, the word monolingual generally suggests a negative or deficient state of being. Although some people may be satisfied, or even take pride in being monolingual, the label can serve as an obstacle for those who want to learn a second language. In fact, for many people in the United States the idea of learning a second language is perceived as a monumental undertaking that is likely to result in limited success. For people in many other regions and countries of the world, however, second language learning is seen as a normal way of life. "Adults in these contexts continue learning additional languages throughout their lives; neither age nor aptitude is considered [an] important [factor] in the learning process" (Pavlenko, 2002, p. 298). The real world, as described by Doughty and Long (2003), is no longer monolingual:

> Second language acquisition—naturalistic, instructed, or both—has long been a common activity for a majority of the human species and is becoming ever more vital as second languages themselves increase in importance. In many parts of the world, monolingualism, not bilingualism or multilingualism, is the marked case. The 300–400 million people whose native language is English, for example, are greatly outnumbered by the 1–2 billion people for

whom it is an official second language. Countless children grow up in societies where they are exposed to one language in the home, sometimes two, another when they travel to a nearby town to attend primary or secondary school, and a third or fourth if they move to a larger city or another province for tertiary education or for work. (Doughty & Long, p. 4)

In large part, the fact that Americans frequently consider second language learning a daunting and even impossible task—an endeavor best left to students in a classroom—results from a pervasive, monolithic view of monolingualism. The very word implies some kind of inveterate and entrenched condition. The "Snapshot" describing the message inscribed on a T-shirt—"monolingualism can be cured"—serves to set the stage for understanding our commonly held assumptions about what it means to be monolingual. These assumptions are then called into question by a portrayal of my colleague, Michael, who uses his native language in vividly different ways depending on the people with whom he is interacting. This portrait suggests that monolingual is not a constructive term but rather one that brands people, often disempowering them in nonproductive ways.

The section devoted to "Research Perspectives" will draw on various theories that describe language—both a person's native and second languages—as dynamic, evolving, interconnected systems that change and shape each other. These theories underscore the degree to which the word monolingual does not encompass the diverse and creative ways people use their native languages. In fact, these theories support my notion that virtually everyone is, in the broadest sense, multilingual. In addition, we will see that Cook's (1991, 1999, 2002b) notions of multicompetence help reframe our view of second language use. In particular, his notion of the L2 user—a unique, individual speaker-hearer of a target language—stands in contrast to an idealized native speaker.

In "Perspectives for the Classroom" we will see that a revised understanding of what it means to be multilingual underscores the need for creating multilingual classrooms in which all languages are valued. In particular, multilingual classrooms have important implications for understanding second language learner identities and for promoting the development of what I call multicompetent second language learners. This multilingual approach is not intended to replace the important target language activities designed to promote proficiency in the second language. Rather, this approach should be viewed as a philosophy or a new way of thinking about second language learning. In particular, this approach underscores the idea that second language learners are not monolinguals with blank slates. Instead, they are people with fully developed and operative first (and often second) languages. Moreover, they come to the classroom with varied backgrounds and unique identities that must be acknowledged and valued in the context of the foreign language learning experience. The "Concluding Propositions" reiterate the idea that multilingual classrooms can promote multicompetent second language learners who do not perceive themselves as monolingual, deficient native speakers of the target language but as emerging multicompetent L2 users.

SNAPSHOT

The Tennessee Foreign Language Teachers Association (TFLTA) sold T-shirts at the annual convention declaring "monolingualism can be cured!" I bought one and wore it to the grocery store one day where another customer in the check-out line read the logo and remarked kindly, "I don't know anybody who has that, but I hope you find a cure." It took me several seconds to react, but I thanked her. My T-shirt looked like so many that seek to raise awareness about some kind of disorder or medical condition. The nice customer's spontaneous reaction made me realize that the proclamation on the T-shirt makes it seem as though monolingualism is an illness, an ailment, or a condition that happened to a healthy person. I considered it more closely. The words *can be* are hopeful and optimistic because they suggest that the treatment for the illness is already available. If the statement had said monolingualism could be, must be, might be, or should be cured, the meaning would suggest that a cure would be difficult to find. However, the logo plainly states that treatment for the illness is already available. Finally, the word *cure* leads us to believe that a procedure of some sort can restore a person to health. To come to the point, the logo on the T-shirt implies that monolingualism is a disease or condition a healthy person does not have, but the remedy for this illness is at hand. As a foreign language teacher and member of the TFLTA, I initially wore the T-shirt with pride and felt glad to be part of the cure. However, I kept thinking about what the saying actually implied.

Several weeks later, when Michael, my colleague in the English department, said jokingly, "I speak university and redneck," I began to rethink the logo on my T-shirt. Michael did not speak a foreign language, but he certainly participated in the speech communities of various subcultures in the American south. When I visited his lively, southern, peanut farmer family Michael fell easily into their accented, friendly banter, sharing inside jokes and childhood stories. In his classroom, however, his standard American English speech was complex and sometimes difficult to understand for the uninitiated in the field of literary theory. Strictly speaking, Michael would be considered monolingual; however, his facility with different registers and dialects suggested a multilingual understanding of language. Like most people from all walks of life and with varying educational backgrounds, he knew intuitively that different settings require subtly different uses of language. A casual but polite greeting using simple declarative utterances directed at a clerk in a grocery store would be replaced by complete, coherent sentences and a careful choice of words when talking with one's superior about an important project. People spontaneously change their way of talking—pronunciation, intonation, word choice, syntax, and discourse—to suit the setting. Every situation—work, school, place of worship, and so forth—calls for an adjustment in register. These subtle changes in register are not generally considered to be changes in language;

however, this intuitive capacity to adjust one's speech to fit the setting suggests that most people have both a conscious and unconscious awareness of the many ways language can be used. In the end, I stopped wearing my T-shirt because it seemed increasingly clear that there is no illness to be cured and that the word monolingualism has little to do with what real people know and do with language.

→ YOUR VIEW 1

Talk to several people from different professions (students, teachers, business owners, etc.) and ask them to describe the differences in ways they talk to people—close friends, family members, work colleagues, and so forth. Make a list of the different registers of speech they identify and the words they use to describe each register.

RESEARCH PERSPECTIVES

The clever logo on the T-shirt announcing that "monolingualism can be cured" serves as a warning to those who might be complacent as users of only one language. It is also an appeal to foreign language teachers in the United States to stamp out a condition that is potentially detrimental to learners and to our society at large. Above all, it lays a heavy burden on the foreign language teaching profession, conferring on us the responsibility for transforming today's students into bilingual or multilingual citizens of a 21st century world. However, foreign language teachers are generally unable to live up to expectations to cure monolingualism; the problem is too pervasive and the goal seems unattainable. Although often unexpressed, teachers and students frequently leave the classroom with a sense of failure.

Rather than perpetuating the idea that the problem lies with inefficient teachers and poor students, it is essential to examine some of our fundamental assumptions about monolingualism. Specifically, we will demonstrate that the word monolingual is insufficient for explaining what real people do with their native languages. Furthermore, we will see that monolingual is not the opposite of bilingual and that people do not fall neatly into these two categories. In fact, rather than endorsing any notion of a continuum with monolingual at one end and bilingual at the other—with one being positive and the other being negative—we will reframe the issue in a nonlinear way to reflect the value of many kinds of language use. In addition, we will explore the meaning of the word *multilingual* in light of recent models that draw on dynamic systems theory to explain language development. In addition, Cook's (1991, 2002b, 2009 in press) notion of multicompetence and the L2 user serves to operationalize a dynamic understanding of second language development and use. Above all, we will show that the term monolingual is a theoretical construct and that all typically learning people have the necessary competencies to participate in multilingual, multicultural communities.

Deconstructing monolingualism

People who speak only their native language certainly exist in our 21st-century world, but they are fewer and farther between. Research indicates that multilingualism has increased significantly over the last decades and is far more common than many people realize (Herdina & Jessner, 2002). Nevertheless, it is frequently the case that many Americans living in the United States have limited contact with other language groups and are considered monolingual. However, as we saw in the snapshot of Michael, people often adapt their speech to those with whom they interact. That is, typically functioning people are aware that different groups of people use different **registers**, or ways of speaking (or writing), in their native language depending on the context. Moreover, they are likely to use different registers when speaking to children, to older people, to colleagues at work, or to intimate peers. The use of registers, therefore, is an indication that monolingualism is multidimensional and variable.

Indeed, registers in the mind of a monolingual speaker are very much like languages in the mind of a bilingual or multilingual person. In Cook's (2000b) view, "[t]here is no more separation between the two languages in the multicompetent mind than there is between different styles and genres in the monolingual; *plane* and *avion* are choices for expressing the same concept, just as say *plane* and *jet* are choices for the monolingual" (p. 16). Although Cook's notion of the multicompetent mind refers principally to the interconnected knowledge of two languages in the mind of one person, he implicitly acknowledges that registers in one's native language are similar to a multilingual person's use of several languages. Moreover, this switching of registers to adapt to a particular setting is similar to bilingual code-switching.[1] Paradis (2004) notes that "interference and switching can occur between languages as they occur between registers in a unilingual speaker" (p. 187). Therefore, whether intentional or unconscious, people switch between registers in their native language very much like bilingual people switch between their two languages.

The fact that speakers are capable of changing register or language to suit a particular setting suggests that each person has a unique language system comprised of multiple codes, or modes of expression. In other words, language can be viewed as a single, multilayered, multidimensional phenomenon in the mind of individual speakers. This idea is consistent with theories proposing that a bilingual person is not two monolinguals in one body but rather a single speaker with a distinctive linguistic system (Cook, 1991, 1992, 2002b, 2003; Grosjean, 1997, 2001; Herdina & Jessner 2002). In Grosjean's (2001) opinion, bilingual people operate along a continuum, using just the first language, or both first and second languages, or just the second language. This holistic view of language use does not differentiate between monolingualism and bilingualism. Instead, it is based on the idea that the fundamental construct of monolingual and bilingual brains is the same (Paradis, 2004).

If monolingualism and bilingualism are varying manifestations of the same sets of language phenomena, we can regard all people as occupying, or functioning in, multiple linguistic universes. Moreover, this expansive, holistic view of language implies that monolingualism is a theoretical construct that does not describe the ways real people use language. Rather, we must consider that no one is really monolingual and that all people have a multilayered, multidimensional language system. Although it may be overstated to say that all people are inherently multilingual, it is congruent with current holistic theories that take a dynamic view of language systems. Herdina and Jessner's (2002) dynamic model of multilingualism (DMM) views a multilingual speaker as a "complex psycholinguistic system comprising individual language systems" (p. 3). Their model accounts for the fact that multilingual speakers have separate language systems but describes them as subsystems that "interact with each other and influence each other within the complex and dynamic system we call multilingualism" (Herdina & Jessner, 2002, p. 150). This view of language as a complex array of subsystems sets the stage for an understanding of multilingualism, rather than monolingualism, as the foundation for second language development. In the final analysis, monolingualism is an inadequate description that does not account for the kinds of competencies a learner brings to the second language learning task.

Multilingualism reconsidered:

Recent theories that view language as a dynamic system (de Bot, 2008; de Bot, Verspoor & Lowie, 2007; Cook, 2003, 2007; Herdina & Jessner, 2002; Jarvis & Pavlenko, 2008; Pavlenko, ed., 2006) offer new ways of thinking about the terms monolingual, bilingual, and multilingual. Rather than considering them each as distinct descriptions with particular sets of attributes, they become variants of one language system. In his review of dynamic systems theory (DST), de Bot (2008) states that "DST is a part of the study of systems, in which systems are studied as a whole rather than with a focus on their parts" (p. 176). This theoretical stance supports an understanding of the languages in the mind of one person as a single system rather than as a series of individual languages. Moreover, this view underscores the interconnectedness of languages within one system, thereby making monolingual, bilingual, and multilingual descriptions of the same language system. In fact, given this holistic understanding of language, multilingual is the only term that captures the range and multiplicity of language use.

Herdina and Jessner's (2002) DMM takes a dynamic systems approach to understanding multilingualism:

> A dynamic systems approach makes clear that in this non-linear world which is holistic, everything is interconnected and surface structures can be seen as implicitly correlated to a high degree. This leads to the assumption that there must always be a subtle

order present.... Order, chaos, complexity and wholeness are all tied together and thus nowadays more and more researchers feel the futility of studying parts in isolation from the whole. (p. 84)

Among the most important characteristics of Herdina and Jessner's (2002) model of multilingualism are nonlinearity, interdependence, and complexity. These characteristics account for first and second (and third, etc.) language development, language attrition in any of the languages, and the interrelatedness of these processes. Above all, the DMM is a holistic understanding of multilingualism, viewing one, two, three, or more language systems as interconnected.

DST has been applied to many different fields, including economics, biology, and cognitive science; however, it is only recently that it has been used to describe language development. Both first and second language development (as well as additional languages) are viewed as complex, nonlinear processes (de Bot, 2008; de Bot, Verspoor & Lowie, 2007; Herdina & Jessner, 2002; Jarvis & Pavlenko, 2008). Moreover, the various languages that a person knows and uses influence and shape each other over time and with use (Cook, 2003; Herdina & Jessner, 2002; Jarvis & Pavlenko, 2008). Even a person's native language goes through transformations. As Pavlenko (2006a) notes, "monolingualism is indeed a dynamic phenomenon. Even with the confines of one language, we continuously acquire new linguistic repertoires and behave and feel differently when talking, let's say, to our parents versus our children" (p. 1).

Above all, DST expands our understanding of multilingualism by offering a holistic understanding of second language development. This understanding implicitly rejects a binary monolingual-bilingual view of second language learning in which learners progress along a linear continuum from some zero, monolingual state to a more advanced stage of bilingual functioning. Rather, a dynamic understanding of language development creates the possibility for viewing multilingualism as the default state in which it is of "little consequence whether the respective language system is available in its incipient form or as a mature one" (Herdina & Jessner, 2002, p. 4). Furthermore, rather than viewing multilingualism as some idealized condition characterized by advanced language proficiency in more than two languages, it is considered a dynamic system that accounts for the natural ebb and flow of a person's native language as well as other languages in various stages of development. This new sense of multilingualism includes registers and dialects in one's native language and any foreign languages, both incipient and highly developed. Moreover, this understanding accounts for different competencies in different languages. For example, being able to read Spanish, understand Dutch and German, but speak only one's native language represents multilingual functioning. In the end, DST offers an opportunity to reconsider our definition of multilingualism so as to include the many ways that people use their native languages and other languages to interact with all kinds of people of similar and different linguistic and cultural backgrounds.

→ **YOUR VIEW 2**

Read the following quotation taken from Philip Herdina and Ulrike Jessner's (2002) book, A Dynamic Model of Multilingualism: Perspectives of Change in Psycholinguistics. *Analyze their claim about multilingual proficiency in the context of the notion that register in one's native language constitutes a kind of multilingual functioning.*

"The development of multilingual proficiency leads to an enrichment of the individual language system but, as the whole system adapts to new environmental and psychological communicative requirements as perceived by the speaker, also changes its nature." (p. 160)

Multicompetence and the L2 user:

In recent years, Cook (1991, 2002b, 2003) has made significant contributions to our understanding of second language development and use. In particular, he has proposed a theoretical framework called **multicompetence** that accounts for an individual's knowledge of language, including both first language competence and a developing understanding of a second language. His most recent definition of *multicompetence* is "the knowledge of two languages in one mind" (in press). In addition to offering a new approach to understanding people who know and use more than one language, multicompetence serves as a way of avoiding the terms monolingual and bilingual. In addition to being fraught with subjective meaning, these two terms do not describe the ways real people use language. As we will see in Chapter 2, there are more than 30 definitions of the word bilingual and little agreement as to its meaning. Multicompetence is, therefore, an inclusive term that encompasses a dynamic understanding of multilingual language use.

Recently, Cook's notion of multicompetence has been applied to research on multilingualism. According to Jarvis and Pavlenko (2008), "the multicompetence approach allows us to theorize the interaction between multiple languages in the speaker's mind as a natural and ongoing process and to understand why multilinguals may perform differently from monolinguals in all of their languages, including the L1" (p. 17). Similarly, Herdina and Jessner (2002) cite the significance of Cook's notion of multicompetence for their DMM. They note that Cook's model of multicompetence is unitary and views language systems as a whole rather than as separate systems, whereas their model recognizes that language systems can be interpreted as separate subsystems that interact with each other. In other words, they do not agree with Cook's view of a single language system in which, for example, "the bilingual speaker of French and English does not have command of the language systems French and English but of a unitary language system we would have to call French–English" (p. 149). Instead, they consider French and English as two separate but interconnected language systems. Despite slightly varying views, there is no question that Cook's multicompetence framework offers a way for rethinking multilingual language use and language development. Implicit in the notion of multicompetence is the idea that people who know more than one language have a distinct, compound state of mind that is not equivalent to two (or more) monolingual states.

The most important contribution of Cook's multicompetence framework is his notion of the **L2 user**. He defines the *L2 user* as "any person who uses another language than his or her first language (L1), that is to say, the one learnt first as a child" (2002b, p. 1). He goes on to show that the term L2 user encompasses an extensive range of language use, including "an English school child staying with a family in Germany on an exchange, . . . a Canadian trucker with L1 English driving through French-speaking Montreal, a street trader in Singapore switching between English and two Chinese dialects" (Cook, 2002b, p. 1), and so on. The importance of this term lies in the fact that it takes the place of the word bilingual, which implicitly suggests that a person has a relatively advanced level of proficiency in his second language. Because Cook states that the term L2 user can refer to "a person who knows and uses a second language at any level" (2002b, p. 4), a person's level of proficiency in the second language is not a consideration. *Multicompetent L2 user* is, therefore, a comprehensive way of describing a person who knows and uses more than one language.

→ YOUR VIEW 3

Consider Cook's notions of multicompetence and the L2 user. List all the words that come to mind when you think about a person who is bilingual or multilingual. Then, list the terms that are associated with multicompetence and L2 user. What are the principal differences between your two lists? How do Cook's terms help reframe our understanding of second language learning?

PERSPECTIVES FOR THE CLASSROOM

The questions that should shape our thinking about language teaching in the 21st century involve the ways we want to prepare learners for life in a multilingual, multicultural world. In the preceding section we established that monolingualism is a term that does not adequately describe language use among speakers of one language. Specifically, we determined that registers within one language constitute a kind of multilingual functioning, suggesting that all second language learners, regardless of their particular background, come to the classroom with a nascent sense of what it means to be multilingual. In this section we will analyze the meaning of *native speaker* in an effort to show that this term can be detrimental in fostering a positive sense of self in relation to the target language. In particular, we will explore the ways that an idealized, native-speaker model can affect the ways learners perceive themselves in relation to the target language and culture. That is, a monolingual orientation implicitly reinforces the dichotomy between monolingual native speakers of a particular target language and nonnative speakers of all kinds—teachers, learners, and many others.

Ultimately, we will see that the foreign language classroom can be an ideal site for learners to develop unique identities that will empower them as second language learners.

To affirm the value of all languages and identities, we will examine the role of a multilingual foreign language classroom. Although many teachers stress the importance of an exclusively target-language approach, research shows that most foreign language classrooms are already sites of multilingual engagement. That is, despite their best efforts to curb the use of English in the classroom, both students and teachers use their common language for a variety of reasons. Rather than viewing this as a negative strategy, however, we will examine the ways that multilingual classrooms help students develop an awareness and appreciation of linguistic and cultural diversity. Finally, we will define the multicompetent second language learner who is empowered by a growing awareness of his unique identity between his native language and his developing second language.

Constructing multilingual identities:

Students choose to study a foreign language for a variety of reasons, both academic and personal. The very fact of choosing a particular language—Italian, Russian, Chinese, or Arabic—may reflect a student's self-image and sense of self in the world. Some students may feel very positive about the language-learning task before them, whereas others may harbor resentment or dread; each student brings unique ways of understanding his place in the world to the language-learning experience. Additionally, students' learning goals—both conscious and unconscious—are likely to vary widely as well. They may be motivated by external factors, such as wanting to satisfy a requirement or earning a good grade, or by personal goals, such as wanting to speak the target language well enough to travel. The point is that each student in a classroom has a unique identity that plays an important role in the ways he engages in the language-learning task.

One of the critical issues related to identity in the foreign language classroom involves the role of the idealized native speaker. That is, all second language learners have a perception of how a native speaker of the target language talks, and even what she looks like. Although teachers may vary with regard to cultural background or proficiency in the target language, they are also likely to hold up the native speaker as a role model for their students. Moreover, most all learning resources—textbooks and ancillary materials—reinforce this model of a standard, monolingual native speaker. Some students may try to imitate this idealized native speaker in an effort to be recognized and validated by members of the target culture, whereas others may prefer to retain an identity as an outsider. Regardless of a learner's purpose, however, it is evident that both students and teachers define good and poor language learners in terms of their semblance to native speakers. In other words, the implicit authority of the native speaker in a foreign language classroom can play a significant role in defining learners' identities as successful or inadequate.

Interestingly, Ellwood's (2008) study of students of diverse language backgrounds in an English language classroom shows that code-switching serves as a way of indicating certain things about the students' identity. When students in the study talked to each other in their shared native languages they often revealed their sense of self as good learners who were aligned with the learning tasks or as resistant learners who were not. Ellwood states that the "multilayered and emergent nature of identity means that the bodies in our classrooms are not merely learners, but are complex beings engaged in an ongoing process of constructing and enacting new selves; their code-switches make it clear that how they present themselves and how they wish to be seen by others are both of great significance" (p. 554).

The fact that a student's identity as a language learner may be shaped by his perception of an idealized native speaker is problematic. In addition to the fact that native-quality speech is unattainable for most adult learners, the very idea of a native speaker is an inadequate abstraction:

> In recent times, the identity as well as the authority of the native speaker have been put into question. The "native speaker" of linguists and language teachers is in fact an abstraction based on arbitrarily selected features of pronunciation, grammar and lexicon, as well as on stereotypical features of appearance and demeanor. . . . The native speaker is, moreover, a monolingual, monocultural abstraction: he/she is one who speaks only his/her (standardized) native tongue and lives by one (standardized) national culture. In reality, most people partake of various languages or language varieties and live by various cultures and subcultures. (Kramsch, 1998a, pp. 79–80)

Rather than endorsing a monolithic native speaker standard, Kramsch (1998a) proposes that a multilingual identity resides in a third space, between the native language and the target language. She describes "language crossing" as "living, speaking and interacting in between spaces, across multiple languages or varieties of the same language" (p. 70) and argues that by "crossing languages speakers perform cultural acts of identity" (p. 70) that allow them to display multiple cultural memberships. Similarly, Train (2002) rejects the binary notion of the first versus the second language and favors a third space "where language study is an initiation into a kind of social practice that is at the boundary of two or more cultures and languages" (p. 13).

This notion of a third space, or an identity that lies somewhere between a person's native language/culture and the target language/culture, suggests that language learning can play an important role in helping students define themselves as second language learners. That is, rather than measuring themselves against an idealized native speaker, learners can create a sense of self that is located between their native language and their developing second language— an identity that offers them a unique perspective on both languages and cultures. The idea that identity is shaped by the language-learning experience is consistent with Watson-Gegeo's (2004) theory about how language, culture, and mind interactively shape each other such that learners' first and second (and more) languages constitute multiple representations of the world. It also coincides with Norton and Toohey's (2002) proposition that language learning affects learners' identities and can expand their understanding of the ways language is used as a social practice:

> Language learning engages the identities of learners because language itself is not only a linguistic system of signs and symbols; it is also a complex social practice in which the value and meaning ascribed to an utterance are determined in part by the value and meaning ascribed to the person who speaks. Likewise, how a language learner interprets or constructs a written text requires an ongoing negotiation among historical understandings, contemporary realities, and future desires. Thus, language learners are not only learning a linguistic system, they are learning a diverse set of sociocultural practices, often best understood in the context of wider relations of power. (p. 115)

Norton and Toohey (2002) go on to say that our understanding of the relationship between foreign language learning and identity is still in its infancy and that research is needed to explore the ways foreign language study shapes a person's identity:

> The goal we see for future research on identity and language learning is to develop understandings of learners as both socially constructed and constrained but also as embodied, semiotic and emotional persons who identify themselves, resist identifications, and act on their social worlds. Learners' investments in learning languages, the ways in which their identities affect their participation in second language activities, and their access to participation in the activities of their communities, must all be matters of consideration in our future research. (p. 123)

Even though research is needed to shed light on this important dimension of language learning, it is clear that learning goals that explicitly articulate the value of exploring a privileged third space can help learners establish identities that are consistent with their unique histories and experiences. As Pavlenko (2002) notes, language learning is a "site of identity construction" (p. 286) in which "the two-way relationship between language and identity recognises that languages serve to produce, reproduce, transform and perform identities, and that linguistic, gender, racial, ethnic and class identities, in turn, affect the access to linguistic resources and interactional opportunities, and ultimately, L2 learning outcomes" (p. 298). The idea that the foreign language learning experience should value learners' unique identities is echoed in Kramsch's (1998a) concept of appropriation, "whereby learners make a foreign language and culture their own by adopting and adapting it to their own needs and interests" (p. 81). Kramsch goes on to say that "the ability to acquire another person's language and understand someone else's culture while retaining one's own is one aspect of a more general ability to mediate between several languages and cultures, called cross-cultural, intercultural, or multicultural communication" (p. 81).

To develop students' abilities to engage in multicultural communication, we must avoid designing learning goals defined in terms of native speaker standards that contribute to an identity as a deficient second language user. Instead, goals should empower learners to view themselves as standing between two (or more) cultures and two (or more) peoples. Furthermore, they should come to understand this third space as a multilingual reality in which they can move between their language and culture of origin, the target language and culture, and those of the diverse community of learners with whom they share the classroom. Indeed, as current research suggests, multilingualism "must not only be accepted as the linguistic norm, it must also be realized that it is closely linked to the concepts of personal identity, ethnicity, multiculturalism" (Herdina & Jessner, 2002, p. 1).

→ YOUR VIEW 4

Interview students studying several different languages and try to determine how their sense of self, or their identity, is connected to or shaped by their classroom foreign language learning experience. Questions might include why they chose to study the language, what they hope to achieve, how they view the target language and culture, their perceived proximity or distance from speakers of the target language, what it means to be a successful learner, whether or not they consider themselves good learners, and so forth.

The multilingual classroom:

The first step in helping students construct a multilingual identity is to accept the idea of a multilingual classroom. This proposition is no small thing given that many foreign language teachers believe that using the target language exclusively in the classroom is an essential component of good teaching practice. Research shows that many teachers—both experienced and novice teachers—use English in the classroom, but that they believe steps should be taken to curb this negative pedagogical practice (Bateman, 2008; Kramer, 2006; Turnbull & Arnett, 2002; Warford, 2007; Wilkerson, 2008). According to Train (2002) "the [foreign language] classroom is often an ideologically monolingual space in which only the target language is supposed to be used (e.g., a leave-your-English-at-the-door stance) and students will be discouraged from using their L1 (through disapproval, poor grades, and even punishment)" (p. 9). The fact is, however, that both teachers and students do not use the target language exclusively, and therefore any notion of a monolingual foreign language classroom is a myth.

An open acknowledgment that both English and the target language have a role in the foreign language classroom can serve to help students develop an awareness of their relationship to both their native language and the target language. In particular, students can see that learning a second language does not mean disregarding or even abandoning their first language. As Pavlenko (2002) states, "this monolingual bias is most evident in the unidirectional perspective which posits the necessity to abandon one's first language and culture in order to learn a second language and acculturate into the TL [target language] group." (p. 279). A multilingual approach, on the other hand, does not hold the target language in a position of special esteem, but rather recognizes the value of all languages. Moreover, a multilingual approach does not assume that learners want to acculturate to the target language group, but instead leads them to explore their linguistic, psychological, and social relationship with the target language. This approach attempts to "investigate and to theorise the role of language in construction and reproduction of social relations, and the role of social dynamics in the processes of additional language learning and use" (Pavlenko, 2002, p. 282).

Clearly, the target language and culture must remain the central focus of instruction. As we will see in Chapter 2, teachers and students can work together to design a language-use contract for the classroom that specifies why and when English is acceptable and the target language is essential. In other words, a multilingual approach does not mean that arbitrary or pervasive use of English is acceptable. Rather, it is a way of conceiving of the foreign language learning experience in such a way as to affirm the value of all the languages that students may bring to the foreign language classroom. For example, a student in a Spanish class whose parents speak Korean might have a unique perspective to offer his or her monolingual English-speaking classmates. Asking such a student to discuss her linguistic and cultural background and experiences may help others develop an awareness of what languages are valued and of who decides to speak what language where and why. In fact, recognizing the many languages students bring to the learning task can help teachers and students develop an awareness of the ways that a native standard language—such as British English or Parisian French—are related to issues of power and national elitism. These kinds of discussions can help students explore the perceived status of their own languages and cultures as well as that of the target language and culture. Ultimately, students may gain a clearer understanding of their relationship to the target language and culture.

The most important feature of a multilingual classroom is that it serves to deconstruct students' concept of the native speaker. As we discussed previously, the notion of a native speaker is a monolingual, monocultural abstraction; real people do not speak one particular standard version of English, French, German, or Spanish. When students understand that they do not have to compare themselves to a mythical native speaker, they will be able to explore what it means to construct their particular identities, taking into consideration their backgrounds and language experiences. This kind of activity allows for every student in the classroom to have a distinct profile, or an identity anchored in what Kramsch (1998a) calls a "third space" between their native language and culture and the target language and culture.

If we agree that second language learners should explore their unique identities, we will have to reassess learning goals that are not based on native-speaker standards. In particular, this means envisioning teaching materials and assessment instruments that do not focus uniquely on developing accuracy in the target language. Current approaches to foreign language teaching that seek to promote proficiency in listening, speaking, reading, and writing are implicitly founded on the idea that students must achieve certain levels of correctness. Moreover, these approaches describe progress in terms that are closely related to demonstrating an increasingly accurate command of the target language. Although it is not my purpose to outline specific learning goals suited to a multilingual approach, I hope each chapter in *Double Talk* will contribute to shifting our conception of the role of grammar and accuracy in second language learning. The essential point at this juncture is to begin to explore what it might mean to value and respect competencies beyond grammatical accuracy.

Practically speaking, teachers must arrive at an understanding of how to manage a multilingual classroom. The essential component of this approach, however, involves creating the opportunity for students to discuss their preconceived notions about monolingualism, multilingualism, and native speakers. These kinds of discussions will open up the possibility for students to understand their unique and evolving identities as second language learners. Obviously, these discussions will need to be in English. Although some teachers may not consider this kind of activity among their traditional responsibilities as foreign language teachers, there is every reason to believe that helping students develop an awareness of these issues will empower them to become life-long second language learners.

In the end, a multilingual approach to foreign language teaching implicitly recognizes that learners bring many different languages to the foreign language classroom and that all these languages play a role in the learning process of individual learners. Furthermore, this approach goes beyond traditional definitions of the native speaker and creates opportunities to recognize and respect variations of standard languages. Most especially, this approach values learner language with all of its quirks, faults, and inaccuracies. Although there is no question that input and interaction in the target language are crucial to second language development, exclusion of all other languages is counterproductive. That is, rather than prohibiting the use of any particular language, a multilingual approach values the potential contributions of all languages and affirms the identities of all learners.

→ YOUR VIEW 5

Spend 15 minutes during class time talking with students in an elementary-level foreign language class. Find out how many different languages the students have been exposed to—either formally or casually—during their lives. Make a list of all the languages on the board and then engage students in a discussion about what these languages/cultures represent to them. Ask them to reflect on which of these languages are similar and dissimilar from the target language and why. Ask them to explain which of their peers might be at an advantage in learning the target language. Finally, determine their reaction to learning how many languages are "unspoken" and hovering in their classroom.

Defining multicompetent second language learners:

As we saw earlier, Cook's (1991, 2002b) notion of multicompetence serves as a theoretical framework for describing multilingualism. The idea that two (or more) languages are not separate entities but rather are interconnected in the mind of one person offers a holistic way of examining the relationships between a person's first, second, and other languages. Various phenomena, including language development (first, second, third, or more), attrition, and maintenance, as well as cross-linguistic influences, can be seen as related occurrences within the mind of one person. Therefore, the *multicompetent mind* refers to the integration of two or more languages in the mind of one person. Cook's notion of the L2 user is a person with a multicompetent mind who uses whatever linguistic resources he has "for real-life purposes, such as reporting symptoms to a doctor, negotiating a contract, reading a poem" (Cook, 2002b, p. 2). *Multicompetent L2 user* is, therefore, a broad term that describes a person's composite knowledge and use of two or more languages.

The importance of Cook's notion of the multicompetent second language user lies in the fact that it has the potential for empowering second language learners. That is, becoming a second language user is clearly a more attainable goal than achieving native-like command of a second language. According to Cook, "ultimate attainment is a monolingual standard rather than an L2 standard" (Cook, 2002b, p. 6) and that "any use counts, however small or ineffective" (Cook, 2002b, p. 3). This view of the second language user stands in stark contrast to traditional goals that seek to promote accurate, native-like speech. As Cook (2002c) notes, for most approaches in the 20th century "the goal set for students was mostly to get as close as possible to monolingual native speakers. The situations they encountered in books were those based on monolingual native speakers; the teachers that were most acceptable were native speakers." (p. 329). These kinds of goals can disempower teachers and students alike:

> If L2 learners feel that the chief measure of L2 success is passing for native, few are going to meet it. Both teachers and students become frustrated by setting themselves what is in effect an impossible target, ugly ducklings regretting they will never become ducks without appreciating that they are really cygnets. (Cook, 2002c, p. 331)

Goals defined in terms of becoming a multicompetent second language user suggest a significant shift in our thinking about foreign language teaching and second language learning. In fact, this approach calls for an entire rethinking of what we want students to know and do with their second language. To frame this rethinking we will talk about goals that promote multicompetent second language learners—learners who will be prepared to be second language users.

Rather than outlining prescriptive goals designed to promote multicompetent second language learners, we will explore a new way of thinking about what we do as foreign language teachers. Our objective will be to advance a philosophy about foreign language teaching that will foster the development of multicompetent second language learners. In other words, it is not a question of changing everything we do in our classrooms, but rather of carefully rethinking goals and re-envisioning the characteristics of successful learners. To that end, three central principles will guide our thinking throughout *Double Talk*:

1. First, we must provide models of real people using their second languages successfully. Instead of using the native speaker as the model for second language learners, we should offer models of real language use by real multilingual people. In Cook's (2002c) words, "students need to be shown the richness of L2 use. Rather than a few L2 users stumbling through conversations with powerful native speakers, they need to encounter the language of people who use the language effectively as a second language, who, because they speak two languages, can say things that monolingual native speakers can never say" (p. 338).

2. Second, we must promote awareness about the vast array of issues related to language learning and language use. We cannot assume that students understand complex issues, such as the relationship between language and identity, definitions of monolingual or multilingual, or the idea that languages interact in the minds of multilingual people. Train (2002) argues in favor of developing critical language awareness,[2] or "creating a space for the exploration of beliefs and experiences concerning language that all students bring with them from the first moment they set foot in class" (p. 17). Making students aware of the attitudinal stances they bring involves exploring their beliefs (ideologies, biases, prejudices) toward the language, appreciating the diversity of expression among speakers of that language, questioning how the native standard language is constructed and represented, and reflecting critically on individual uses and institutionalized norms. Multicompetent learners have a growing awareness of the ways that language and power are inextricably linked, and understand that their attitudes, as well as those of their teacher and peers, shape their view of that language. Having the opportunity to explore the many questions that arise naturally from encountering a new language and culture should be part of foreign language learning.

3. Third, and perhaps most important we must give students opportunities to use English in the classroom. A monolingual, target language classroom does not offer a realistic vision of our 21st century multilingual world. Moreover, using English in the foreign language classroom allows students to discuss the complex issues related to language and culture in intellectually stimulating ways—perhaps motivating them to continue their study of the target language.

In the end, the notion of a multicompetent second language learner serves to reframe our thinking about foreign language teaching and second language learning. Above all, this notion underscores the importance of learning goals that are not based on a monolingual, native speaker standard but rather on a newly defined understanding of the second language user.

> ### → YOUR VIEW 6
>
> *The idea of a multicompetent second language learner is based on Cook's (2001) notion of the multicompetent L2 user. One of the characteristics of a multicompetent second language learner is awareness of language and language learning. Given what you have read in this chapter, list the specific things you consider important to know. How does your list contribute to your understanding of a multicompetent second language learner?*

Concluding Propositions

Proposition 1.1

> Monolingualism *is an inadequate term for describing 21st century language use.*

Most people believe they are monolingual if they can't speak another language fluently. In fact, there is often an implied sense that monolingualism is the norm and that bilingualism is reserved for a privileged few. As Wei notes, "people who are brought up in a society where monolingualism and uniculturalism are promoted as the normal way of life often think that bilingualism is only for a few 'special' people" (2000, p. 5). This unspoken understanding that monolingual people are linguistically deficient, whereas bilingual people are linguistically superior, not only dissuades people from learning a second language but also disempowers learners who perceive language learning as a daunting task. The fact is, however, that fewer and fewer of people in the United States live in linguistic and cultural isolation. Anyone with access to television and the Internet is likely to be exposed to another language. Moreover, there are increasing numbers of products sold in grocery stores and large chain stores that have notices and directions in other languages. The point is, people no longer live in linguistic isolation and they have regular encounters with other languages besides English:

> In our days of frequent border crossing, and of multilingual, multicultural foreign language classrooms, it is appropriate to rethink the monolingual native speaker norm as the target of foreign language education. As we revisit the marked and unmarked forms of language usership, I propose that we make the intercultural speaker of the unmarked form, the infinite of language use, and the monolingual monocultural speaker a slowly disappearing species or a nationalistic myth. (Kramsch, 1998b, p. 30)

In addition, research suggests that alternating between registers in one's native language is similar to alternating between languages for a bilingual person (Cook, 2002b; Pavlenko, 2006). That is, being able to adapt one's speech to a particular setting, such as talking to children, to peers at a social event, or to superiors in a work environment, reflects a kind of multilingual functioning. In other words, language use in one's native language is multidimensional and adaptable. By extension, learners come to the second language learning task with a set of competencies that cannot adequately be described as monolingual. In the end, the word monolingualism means different things to different people and is an abstract concept that does not describe what real people do with language.

Proposition 1.2

Multilingual classrooms empower second language learners.

Although most foreign language teachers endorse a target language approach to foreign language teaching, both students and teachers use English for a variety of reasons. Instead of viewing the use of English as a negative strategy, it is important to recognize the many positive effects of creating a multilingual foreign language classroom. First, it reflects real language use in the world; in settings where people speak more than one language people alternate between their languages. Second, a multilingual approach to foreign language teaching implicitly recognizes that learners bring many different languages to the foreign language classroom and that all these languages play a role in the learning process of individual learners. Furthermore, this approach goes beyond traditional definitions of the native speaker to include variations of standard languages. Finally, this approach values learner language with all of its quirks, faults, and inaccuracies. Rather than measuring a learner's developing language against a monolingual, native speaker standard, we must adapt our goals to account for successful second language use. Although there is no question that input and interaction in the target language are crucial to second language development, exclusion of all other languages is counterproductive. That is, rather than prohibiting the use of any particular language, a multilingual approach values the potential contributions of all languages.

Proposition 1.3

Multicompetent second language learners become successful second language users.

Cook's (1991, 1992, 2002b) notions of multicompetence and the L2 user serve to reframe our goals for second language learners. The idea that multicompetence describes the sum of all languages in the mind of one person offers a holistic view of language that values the roles of both the fully developed native language and the developing second language. In addition, Cook describes the L2 user as a person who uses any language at any level for any purpose. This broad, holistic understanding of language development and language use offers a new vision for articulating goals for classroom foreign language learning. In particular, it challenges us to model real multilingual language use in our classrooms and to make our students aware of their potential as second language users. The multicompetent second language learner, therefore, has ample opportunities to interact in the target language and to come to understand and appreciate his distinctive capabilities as an L2 user. As Pavlenko (2002) says, "the key to success is seen in plentiful interactional opportunities, while the desired outcome is multi-competence rather than idealized 'native-speakerness'" (p. 298). Learning goals that are articulated in terms of developing multicompetent second language learners will promote multicompetent second language users.

Suggested Readings on Multilingualism

Cook, V. (Ed.). (2002). *Portraits of the L2 user*. Clevedon, UK: Multilingual Matters.

Herdina, P., & Jessner, U. (2002). *A dynamic model of multilingualism: Perspectives of change in psycholinguistics*. Clevedon, UK: Multilingual Matters.

Jarvis, S., & Pavlenko, A. (2008). *Crosslinguistic influence in language and cognition*. New York: Routledge.

Kramsch, C. (1998). *Language and culture*. New York: Oxford University Press.

Kramsch, C. (2002). The privilege of the non-native speaker. In C. Blyth (Ed.), *AAUSC 2002: The sociolinguistics of foreign-language classrooms* (pp. 251–262). Boston: Heinle.

Train, R. W. (2002). The (non)native standard language in foreign language education: A critical perspective. In C. Blyth (Ed.), *AAUSC 2002: The sociolinguistics of foreign-language classrooms* (pp. 3–39). Boston: Heinle.

Researching Your Language Stories

1. Using YOUR VIEW 5, have students in the classroom keep a journal of the ways their sense of self in relation to the target language/culture shifts over the course of the semester.

   a. Ask each student to begin his journal with a detailed portrait of his language experiences—both native and second languages.

   b. Give students specific instructions regarding the number of times they should write in their journals. For example, you might have them write five or six entries over the course of a semester. Be sure to collect their journal entries once or twice during the semester to be sure they are following your directions.

   c. At the end of the semester collect all the journals. Read them carefully to ascertain the kinds of topics that seem to be especially pertinent. Create a list of common comments, both positive and negative.

[YOUR VIEW 5: Spend 15 minutes during class time talking with students in an elementary-level foreign language class. Find out how many different languages the students have been exposed to—either formally or casually—during their lives. Make a list of all the languages on the board and then engage students in a discussion about what these languages/cultures represent to them. Ask them to reflect on which of these

languages are similar and dissimilar from the target language and why. Ask them to explain which of their peers might be at an advantage in learning the target language. Finally, determine their reaction to learning how many languages are "unspoken" and hovering in their classroom.]

2. Use the list you devised for YOUR VIEW 6 with the topics of what a multicompetent second language learner should know about language learning. Choose four or five of the most interesting topics and transform them into questions.

   a. Interview two students, one English-speaking student with little exposure to a second language and one bilingual student for whom the target language is a third language (e.g., a Chinese–American student who is studying German). Ask each of them the questions based on your list of topics to find out what he knows about language learning.

   b. Compare the students' answers to determine the differences between what a multilingual language learner and a beginning language learner knows about language learning. Note how their perceptions are similar or different.

[YOUR VIEW 6: The idea of a multicompetent second language learner is based on Cook's (2001) notion of the multicompetent L2 user. One of the characteristics of a multicompetent second language learner is awareness of language and language learning. Given what you have read in this chapter, list the specific things you consider important to know. How does your list contribute to your understanding?]

Notes

1. We will see in Chapter 2 that code-switching is common among bilingual people of all ages.

2. The notion of critical language awareness (CLA) was first introduced by British linguist Norman Fairclough (Fairclough, N. (Ed.). (1992). *Critical language awareness* [Harlow, UK: Pearson Education Limited]; Fairclough, N.(1995). *Critical discourse analysis: The critical study of language* [Harlow, UK: Pearson Education Limited,]) and sought to consider and act on the sociopolitical nature of language use, in particular its relation to the exercise of power.

CHAPTER 2

"Regarde le dog!"

OVERVIEW

The word *bilingual* has a sophisticated, even magical meaning for many people. It signifies having membership in a community of people who can travel to another country, talk with speakers of another language, and maybe even pass as insiders among them. Being bilingual implies a person has the language, the code, the secret knowledge of another people; it is perceived as a privilege that guarantees one's status as cosmopolitan and multinational. Above all, it is considered to be a ticket away from commonplace American monolingualism. Many students in foreign language classrooms across the United States dream of becoming bilingual. They may participate enthusiastically in classroom activities and work hard to improve their language skills, but at the end of the semester, or the year, they are often disillusioned. Their goal of becoming bilingual seems increasingly remote. If they have encounters with native speakers of the target language, they are likely to feel stupid or embarrassed. In the end, the dream fades and only a few resilient students stay the course. Among those who continue their studies, not many learn the language well enough to feel at ease using it. Those who do achieve advanced-level proficiency in a second language can attest to the hours of hard work that made it possible. The dream of becoming bilingual is elusive at best.

This all-too-familiar scenario of disillusioned foreign language learners is self-defeating at a time in history when Americans more than ever need to be prepared to become successful and engaged members of our 21st century world. The foreign language classroom is the ideal setting for addressing these new challenges; however, we must articulate learning goals that are realistic and empowering rather than idealistic and fundamentally unattainable. To that end, we will go beyond the walls of the classroom and analyze the ways bilingual people communicate with those around them.

The "Snapshot" 3-year-old Emma sets the stage for understanding spontaneous bilingual utterances that reveal many layers of meaning. This real-life language story offers insight into the ways bilingualism is not "an expanded version of monolingualism" (Pavlenko, 2006, p. 1), but rather a language phenomenon that is complex and dynamic, involving two languages simultaneously. In "Research Perspectives" we will explore various definitions of bilingualism to show that there is no simple or straightforward definition of this term. In particular, we will see that code-switching, the alternation between two languages, is a typical occurrence among people who speak the same two languages and may be one of the most important indicators of a person's ability to function in two languages. Both the linguistic and the social dimensions of bilingual code-switching reveal the spontaneous yet organized features of this language phenomenon.

The analysis of bilingualism and code-switching offers important insights for the foreign language classroom. In "Perspectives for the Classroom" we will expand on the idea of the multilingual classroom presented in Chapter 1 and question the profession's long-held principles regarding the advantages of a monolingual, target language approach to foreign language teaching. Furthermore, we will consider the idea of a language-use contract designed to help teachers and students alike agree on why and when English and the target language should be used. Finally, we will propose that developing awareness about bilingualism can encourage a realistic sense of what it means to learn a second language. "Concluding Propositions" emphasizes that code-switching is a natural and normal feature of bilingual language use, and that appropriate use of English in the classroom can model real bilingual language use and foster the development of multicompetent second language learners.

SNAPSHOT

Three-year-old Emma cried out when she saw my white poodle: "Regarde le dog, Maman. Il est si cute!" (Look at the dog, Mommy. He is so cute!) Emma's mother, my friend Jeanne, seemed not to notice this mixing of French and English, saying to Emma, "Oui, il est tout petit. Tiens. Caresse-le. Doucement." (Yes, he is really little. Here. Pat him. Gently.) When Bill walked up, Emma shouted while pointing: "Daddy! See? Le petit dog!" He squatted down next to her. "A little dog, just your size. Pat her gently. Like this." The toy poodle was the center of attention for Emma, Jeanne, and Bill; their bilingual interactions were seamless and unconscious.

Although there seemed to be nothing remarkable about Emma's use of French and English together, I decided to explore what she was doing when she said these two sentences. My research led me to realize that what Emma was doing was both simple and complex. Simply speaking, she was alternating between French and English; on a more complex level, however, it wasn't clear whether she was borrowing words from English and inserting them into French, or experiencing interference from one or both languages.

To demonstrate the complexity of the phenomenon, I examined Emma's utterances carefully:

> *Regarde le dog, Maman. Il est si cute!*
> [Look at the dog, Mommy. He is so cute!]

Emma's first sentence, directed at her mother, begins with the French verb *regarder* in the imperative form followed by the masculine form of the definite article *le*. The initial sentence appears to be in French except for the word *dog*. Similarly, the second sentence—in the present indicative, with a pronoun *il* and a correctly conjugated form of *être*—is in French except for the word *cute*. These two sentences appear to be in French with English words inserted. When I asked if Emma knew the words *dog* or *cute* in French, her mother stated unequivocally that *chien* and *mignon* were certainly in her repertoire.

> *Daddy! See? Le petit dog!*
> [Daddy! See? The little dog!]

In these short utterances, directed at her father, Emma uses the English verb *see* rather than *regarde* as she had done when speaking to her mother. *Regarder* means "to look at," whereas *see* corresponds to the French word *voir*. Emma's use of *regarde* is natural and idiomatic in French. Speaking to her American father, however, Emma uses the word *see* and points at the dog. In her final utterance—an exclamation—she uses the French adjective *petit* and repeats the English word *dog*.

Although initially Emma's utterances appeared to be French with embedded English words, further reflection brought to light what Emma did not say. When talking to her mother she did not choose the French verb *voir* (which would have been awkward), she did not put the English definite article *the* in front of the French noun *chien*, and she did not use an English subject *he* with a French verb *est*. That is, she did not say "Vois, Maman. The chien. He est si cute!" Although a monolingual speaker of either English or French might consider these three short sentences acceptable, a bilingual speaker of French and English would consider them unacceptable, even ungrammatical. Ultimately, it became clear that Emma had spontaneously uttered several short sentences that conform to an unspoken set of rules about what is and is not acceptable when switching between French and English. The sight of my little white poodle had triggered a complex but entirely natural language phenomenon.

→ **YOUR VIEW 1**

Do you know bilingual people who alternate between two languages, or code-switch, when they talk to each other? What kinds of words or utterances do they say in each of their languages? In your view, why do they code-switch? What roles does the code-switching play in their interactions?

RESEARCH PERSPECTIVES

What does it mean to be bilingual? Does a person need to have native-like proficiency in two languages? Is Emma bilingual even though she has limited proficiency in English, has a developing proficiency in French, and alternates between her two languages? Are her parents bilingual even though her mother is more proficient in her native French and her father is more proficient in his native English? These questions have no simple answers because no one really knows what it means to be bilingual. In this section we will explore several definitions of bilingualism to show that there is no simple way to describe what people do with two languages. Specifically, we will see that the word bilingual encompasses a wide variety of cross-linguistic phenomena, including the alternation between two languages, or code-switching (henceforth CS). Our discussion of the linguistic dimensions of CS will reveal that it is not a careless language behavior but rather a predictable, rule-governed occurrence. Moreover, we will see that CS can be used in interpersonal interactions to indicate intimacy or distance. Ultimately, we will see that bilingualism is a multifaceted and dynamic phenomenon and that bilingual people use their two languages in complex and creative ways.

Bilingualism reconsidered

If asked, most people would define bilingualism as being fluent in two languages. When pressed to clarify what they mean by *fluent*, however, the issue becomes problematic because the words *fluent* and *bilingual* mean different things to different people. To show how difficult it is to say who is and who is not bilingual, Wei lists 37 different varieties of bilinguals in his introduction to *The Bilingualism Reader* (2000, pp. 6–7). Figure 2.1 includes some of the more common definitions of bilingual people.

This abbreviated version of Wei's (2000b) list illustrates that there is no single definition of the term *bilingual*. Moreover, these definitions offer no indication of how much a person needs to know about two languages to be described as bilingual. In fact, linguists have long debated how competent a person has to be in order to be considered bilingual, and the literature on the subject remains inconclusive. In response to this ongoing discussion, Auer (1988/2000) proposes that bilingualism is something a person can do with language and not something a person knows about language:

Common definitions of bilingualism

→ Balanced bilingual: someone whose mastery of two languages is roughly equivalent

→ Compound bilingual: someone whose two languages are learned at the same time and often in the same context

→ Co-ordinate bilingual: someone whose two languages are learned in distinctively separate contexts

→ Dominant bilingual: someone with greater proficiency in one of his or her languages and who uses it significantly more that the other language

→ Receptive bilingual: someone who understands a second language, in either its spoken or written form, or both, but who does not necessarily speak or write it

→ Early bilingual: someone who has acquired two languages in early childhood

→ Late bilingual: someone who has become bilingual later than childhood

→ Secondary bilingual: someone whose second language has been added to a first via instruction

[Adapted from Wei, 2000, pp. 6–7]

FIGURE 2.1

> The impasse reached can only be overcome if bilingualism is no longer regarded as something inside the speaker's head, but as a displayed feature in participants' everyday behavior. You cannot be bilingual in your head, you have to use two or more languages "on stage," in interaction, where you show others that you are able to do so. (Auer, 1988/2000, p. 167)

This definition of bilingualism shifts the focus away from any prescribed notion of what a person knows about two languages to what a person can do when using her two languages.

Much research has been devoted to the ways bilingual people interact. Although there is no real understanding of the underlying processes that govern comprehension and production of two languages, the data come mostly from documenting spontaneous conversations between bilingual people (Grosjean, 2000). Of particular interest is bilingual CS, or the alternating use of two languages. As de Bot (2002) notes, "the study of code-switching provides us with a unique window on the ways languages can interact in language processing, and the way the various languages are used together can help us understand the cognition of bilingualism" (p. 288). Researchers are mainly interested in studying "how languages are selected for production and how languages are kept apart in situations in which switching is not an option" (de Bot, 2002, p. 299). CS is, therefore, a focus of research and also a key feature of bilingual functioning.

Grosjean's (1988, 1997/2000) bilingual model of lexical access (BIMOLA) is one of the more important models for explaining bilingual language use. This model is based on two main assumptions:

> First I assume that bilinguals have two language networks (features, phonemes, words, etc.) that are both independent and interconnected. They are independent in the sense that they allow a bilingual to speak just one language, but [they] are also interconnected in that the mono-lingual speech of bilinguals often shows the active interference of the other language and in that bilinguals can code-switch and borrow quite readily when they speak to other bilinguals. . . . The second assumption is that, in the monolingual language mode, one language network is strongly activated and the other is activated very weakly . . . , whereas in the bilingual language mode, both language networks are activated, but one more than the other. (Grosjean, 1997/2000, p. 466)

Grosjean uses the term *language mode* to refer to a bilingual person's speech as ranging from the monolingual language mode to the bilingual language mode. In other words, he views them as operating along a continuum, using just the first language, or both first and second languages, or just the second language.

This idea of a bilingual language mode continuum supports the notion that a bilingual person is not two monolinguals in one body but rather a single speak-er-hearer with a unique and complete linguistic system (Grosjean, 1997/2000, 2001). As we saw in Chapter 1, Cook's (1991, 2002a) multicompetence frame-work, which has guided much of the research on bilingualism, accounts for a per-son's knowledge of language that includes both first language competence and a developing second language. This framework is based on the theory that people who know more than one language have a distinct compound state of mind that is not equivalent to two monolingual states (Jarvis & Pavlenko, 2008). Furthermore, this idea is consistent with other current theories proposing that a bilingual person has one dynamic linguistic system comprised of several subsys-tems (de Bot, 2008; Grosjean, 1997/2000, 2001; Herdina & Jessner, 2002).

These holistic theories that view a bilingual person's languages as interact-ing dynamically seek to account for a variety of linguistic phenomena, such as CS, transfer, borrowing, and interference. However, there is little consensus about the distinctions between these terms. Herdina and Jessner (2002) use the term *cross-linguistic interaction*, noting that this concept "can be taken to include not only transfer and interference . . . but also CS and borrowing phenomena and is thus reserved as an umbrella term for all the existing transfer phenomena" (p. 29). According to their dynamic model of multilingualism (DMM), "transfer phenomena should be viewed as a coherent set of phenomena" (p. 19). In fact, they do not ac-cept the distinction between CS and transfer, stating that "in DMM we assume that the traditional distinction between code-switching in research on bilingualism and transfer in SLA [second language acquisition] research is historically understandable but methodologically unfounded, impeding research on transfer in multiple language systems" (p. 19). Similarly, Odlin (2003) uses the terms *language transfer* and *cross-linguistic influence* interchangeably. In his view, "language transfer affects all linguistic subsystems including pragmatics and rhetoric, semantics, syntax, morphology, phonology, phonetics, and orthography" (Odlin, 2003, p. 437). Like Odlin, Jarvis and Pavlenko (2008) use the term *cross-linguistic influence*, defining it as "the influence of a person's knowledge of one language on that person's knowledge or use of another language" (p. 1). Although there may be little agreement about what to call various cross-linguistic phenomena in bilingual language use, there is general consensus that bilingualism is characterized by a variety of cross-linguistic phenomena.

Pavlenko (2006a) defines the term *bilingual* as referring to "speakers who use two languages in their daily lives" (p. 2); however, this simple definition implies a myriad of complexities. Factors such as linguistic similarities between a bilingual person's two languages, cognitive and developmental characteristics of the speaker, age of acquisition, length of exposure to the languages, and level of proficiency in the two languages play significant roles in the many different kinds of cross-linguistic interaction in bilingual speech. Bilingualism must be defined, therefore, in terms that account for cross-linguistic phenomena. What is certain is that CS is normal for bilinguals (Wei, 2000b), and it may even be a measure of a person's bilingual ability (Poplack, 1979/2000). Ultimately, then, any definition of bilingualism must take into consideration how, when, why, and where bilingual people alternate between their two languages.

→ YOUR VIEW 2

How would you answer if someone asked you "What does it mean to be bilingual?" Do you consider yourself bilingual? Explain your answer.

Code-switching and cross-linguistic interaction

CS is something that bilingual people of all ages do. Emma's alternation between French and English, as described above, is common in children who are learning to speak two languages. It has been documented in children as young as two years old (Meisel, 1994), and research indicates that acquisition of two languages simultaneously does not put a child at risk for delayed linguistic or cognitive development (Genesee, 1989/2000, 2001, 2002). In fact, CS in bilingual children may be indicative of sophisticated linguistic competence:

> Child bilingual code-mixing, like adult code-switching, is not random but is systematic and constrained in accordance with the grammatical principles of the target languages. Thus, contrary to lay opinion, and even that of some scientists, the language that bilingual children

acquire is not deviant. The linguistic competence that underlies their performance in both of their languages reveals the same underlying linguistic competence as that of monolinguals in most significant respects. Moreover, the systematic on-line coordination of two languages during code-mixing that most bilingual children engage in reveals a kind of linguistic competence that exceeds that which is demonstrated by monolinguals.[1] (Genesee, 2002, p. 192)

The idea that CS is a skilled form of language behavior rather than some kind of language deficiency was recognized in an early study by Blom and Gumperz (1972). Since then, many studies have explored the multifaceted dimensions of CS in adults as well as in children. In general, these studies can be divided into two main areas: linguistic studies that describe the lexical and grammatical dimensions of CS and ethnographic studies that describe the interpersonal and social settings in which CS occurs. Studies of CS as a linguistic phenomenon focus on the grammatical structure of a speaker's utterances, exploring the words or phrases that occur in each language. To the untrained ear, it might seem that CS occurs in a random fashion or when the speaker lacks competence in one language. Most linguists, however, agree that CS is rule-governed and may even be a type of skilled language performance. In his volume on bilingualism, Wei (2000b) makes a strong case for understanding CS as an indicator of language proficiency rather than deficiency:

> There is a widespread impression that bilingual speakers code-switch because they cannot express themselves adequately in one language. This may be true to some extent when a bilingual is momentarily lost for words in one of his or her languages. However, code-switching is an extremely common practice among bilinguals and takes many different forms. . . . It has been demonstrated that code-switching involves skilled manipulation of overlapping sections of two (or more) grammars, and that there is virtually no instance of ungrammatical combination of the two languages in code-switching, regardless of the bilingual ability of the speaker. (Wei, 2000b, pp. 16–17)

Given this understanding of CS, we can say that Emma's bilingual sentences are examples of rule-governed, and maybe even skilled, language production typical of a bilingual child.

At the age of 3, Emma spontaneously said "Regarde le dog, Maman. Il est si cute!" She clearly had two languages at her disposal. She did not, however, speak French and English equally well. Most of her time was spent with Jeanne, her French mother, and with French-speaking children in her preschool; French was clearly her dominant language. In fact, the features of Emma's CS is probably affected by the fact that French is her dominant language. According to Myers-Scotton's matrix language frame model (1993b), one language in bilingual speech production is more dominant and activated than the other; the dominant one is called the **matrix language** and the secondary one is the **embedded language**.

Myers-Scotton's model predicts that the grammar of the matrix language governs the morphology and the syntax in CS.[2] For example, in Emma's simple sentence, "Regarde le dog," both word use and word order are consistent with French grammar. If she had said "Regarde *à* le dog," the sentence would not have been consistent with French grammar; the French verb *regarder* does not require the preposition *à* (unlike the English verb *to look*, which can be followed by the preposition *at*), making this sentence impossible according to French syntax. For Emma, therefore, her matrix language (French) governs the morphology and syntax of her CS.

Although CS occurs at various levels of speech, including morpheme, word, clause, sentence, and discourse level (Petersen, 1988, p. 480), 80 percent of CS involves single words (Genesee, 2001). Studies of CS show that words, such as nouns, adjectives, verbs, adverbs, and prepositions from the embedded language may appear in the matrix language. They also show that CS can occur with discourse markers, such as *well* or *OK*, from the embedded language. The clearest indication of the degree to which CS is rule governed comes, however, from studies of ways grammatical morphemes are used. For example, grammatical morphemes, such as *the, my, a*, from the matrix language may co-occur with lexical morphemes of either the matrix language or the embedded language. In the case of Emma, the grammatical morpheme *le* comes from French (her matrix language), and could have been used either with *chien* or *dog*. On the other hand, grammatical morphemes of the embedded language may co-occur only with words of the embedded language. The grammatical morpheme *the* from Emma's embedded language (English) could co-occur with an English word but not with a French word. That is, she could have said "the dog" but not "the chien."[3] Table 2.1 shows acceptable and unacceptable CS when French is the matrix language and English is the embedded language, and vice versa.

This detailed deconstruction of Emma's simple little utterance may seem excessive, but it serves to show how her spontaneous reaction to seeing the dog was expressed in two languages working together in a predictable, coherent, grammatical, permissible, and acceptable way. In other words, Emma was engaged in rule-governed CS—a natural behavior frequently observed in interactions among bilingual people of all ages.

TABLE 2.1 Acceptable and Unacceptable Code-Switching (CS) for Matrix and Embedded Languages

	Acceptable CS	Unacceptable CS
French = matrix English = embedded	*le* dog *un* dog *mon* dog	the *chien* a *chien* my *chien*
English = matrix French = embedded	the *chien* a *chien* my *chien*	*le* dog *un* dog *mon* dog

It is important to reiterate that CS, or transfer, is not a negative term in current research on bilingualism. Jarvis and Pavlenko (2008) note that transfer is no longer considered "the result of ignorance or sloppy thinking" (p. 10) but rather a rich and complex language phenomenon. Their theoretical and empirical work on cross-linguistic influence reveals that it occurs across 10 dimensions (area of language knowledge/use, directionality, cognitive level, type of knowledge, intentionality, mode, channel, form, manifestation, outcome),[4] allowing them to distinguish more than 5,000 types of transfer. This research, as well as that of others (Cook, 2003; Grosjean, 2001; Herdina & Jessner, 2002; Odlin, 2002; Paradis, 2004; Pavlenko, 2006), confirms that all kinds of cross-linguistic interaction are manifestations of highly sophisticated language phenomena that have yet to be fully explored.

For many people the term **borrowing** refers to the conscious introduction of words from one language to another. The existence of the French word *le weekend* is an example of borrowing. Sometimes single words are modified—syntactically, morphologically, or phonologically—and incorporated into the matrix language. For example, an English speaker who knows some French might say "I have beaucoups ["boo-cooze"] of things to do today." This kind of borrowing, or language play, is frequently observed among multilingual people.[5] Like CS, borrowing is considered to be one of many cross-linguistic phenomena. According to Herdina and Jessner (2002) "there is no fundamental difference between CS and borrowing phenomena and . . . they must therefore be interpreted as variants of the same feature which we may term transfer in agreement with traditional terminology" (p. 24).

Interference is another term that is used to describe structures in the new language that mirror structures in the native language. A German learner of English might say, "I go not," because the equivalent sentence in German is "ich gehe nicht" (R. Ellis, 2003, p. 58). A French learner of English might say, "I am living here since four years," because in French the use of the word *depuis* with the present tense indicates an ongoing state; "j'habite ici depuis quatre ans" should be translated as "I have been living here *for* four years" and not "*since* four years." Errors that are caused by interference may be cultural, semantic, lexical, grammatical, and/or phonological (Mackey, 1962/2000, p. 43). These errors were traditionally referred to as **negative transfer** because they resulted in inaccuracies—both oral and written—in the second language and reflected a person's underlying knowledge of the language. The German speaker cited above might not know, for example, that "I go not" is incorrect in English. Paradis (2004, p. 188) makes another distinction with regard to interference, distinguishing between *static interference* in which a person's underlying grammatical competence in one language includes structures from another language rendering the first one deviant, and *dynamic interference*, which results from performance errors or the inadvertent inclusion of structures from one language into another and could be corrected by the speaker. It is essential to note that interference is rarely described in negative terms in current research. According to Jarvis and Pavlenko (2008) "recent findings have firmly moved us away from the positive/negative transfer dichotomy toward a more complex view that incorporates preferences and avoidance" (pp. 212–213). In addition, Odlin (2003) reminds us that the kind of target language that a bilingual person hears may result in interference that is not necessarily related to structures in a person's native language:

> Many discussions of transfer . . . use data based simply on comparisons of an interlanguage structure with something in the native language. In such cases, claims that transfer has—or has not—taken place may be indeterminate, as when, for example, Spanish learners of English use double negators: for example, "I didn't see nothing." Since the native language translation equivalent has two negators ("*No* vi *nada*"), a claim about cross-linguistic influence is plausible. However, there remains the possibility that "I didn't see nothing" reflects the influence of a non-standard variety of the target language, and it may also be that natural principles of language acquisition are at work. In such a case it would clearly help to look at what kind of target language input learners hear and also to compare how often speakers of another language use double negation. Without those methodological improvements, claims that Spanish is or is not involved remain inconclusive. (pp. 448–450)

The purpose of this discussion is to show that CS, transfer, borrowing, and interference are variations of the same language phenomenon (Herdina & Jessner, 2002, p. 24). In addition, this discussion illustrates that Emma spontaneously engaged in predictable, rule-governed CS. What we see in Emma's utterances are words from her embedded language (English) inserted into her matrix language (French). These transfer phenomena are highly complex and indicative of sophisticated bilingual functioning. In fact, Auer's (1998/2000) study of children of Italian heritage living in Germany provides evidence that CS and transfer often go in different and predictable directions, with CS going from the second language (embedded language) to the first language (matrix language) and transfer going from the first language (matrix language) to the second language (embedded language).

→ YOUR VIEW 3

Listen to a conversation between two people who are bilingual in the same languages. Note incidences of CS and analyze which levels of their speech are most affected by CS—phonemes, morphemes, lexical items, syntax, or entire sentences. Does the CS occur within sentences, or between sentences? Are you able to determine the matrix and embedded languages for each of the speakers? How?

Code-switching and interpersonal interaction

In addition to the linguistic dimensions of CS, or the lexical and grammatical constraints that operate when a bilingual speaker switches between two languages, there are subtle interpersonal and social dimensions of this language phenomenon. Myers-Scotton (1993a) explores bilingual and multilingual practices among people in several African countries and illustrates what can be gained by CS. In describing people who speak English, Swahili, and a variety of indigenous languages, she notes that CS does not reflect a deficiency in one of the speakers' languages, but rather is a complex, intentional phenomenon that is motivated, either consciously or subconsciously, by a desire to achieve a variety of purposes. To explain her theory about how CS may operate to achieve some kind of social purpose, Myers-Scotton (1993a) describes her markedness model:

> The argument . . . is that all speakers have a "markedness metric," an innate, internalized model which enables them to recognize that all code choices are more or less "unmarked" or "marked." "Unmarked" is used to mean that the choice of a particular linguistic variety is *expected* as the medium for a talk exchange, given the norms of the society regarding the salience of specific situational factors present (e.g., the speaker and addressee, the topic, the setting). "Marked" choices are at the other end of a continuum; they are not usual, and in some sense they are *dis-identifications* with what is expected. (p. 151)

In analyzing instances of CS among bilingual and multilingual people, Myers-Scotton noted that "speakers and addressees know (as part of their communicative competence) that choice of one linguistic variety rather than another expresses social import" (1993a, p. 151). She further noted that when CS was marked, it indicated that a speaker was attempting to communicate something more subtle, or perhaps enhance his or her own position: "In making a marked choice, the speaker is saying in effect, 'Put aside any presumptions you have based on societal norms for these circumstances. I want your view of me, or of our relationship, to be otherwise'" (1993a, p. 131). In other words, the very act of CS sends a message of its own; it can be an intentional strategy to negotiate a change in the expected social distance between speakers, either increasing or decreasing it.

Myers-Scotton's markedness model is particularly helpful in analyzing the ways CS is used, sometimes intentionally, to prescribe social distance or gain power. Interactions between Emma's parents can illustrate the ways that CS is used to signal a change in emotional state. When Jeanne and Bill talk casually to each other they alternate regularly between French and English. Jeanne is a native speaker of French and Bill is a native speaker of English; both of them speak French and English fluently. They have been together for more than 15 years and have always interacted in both languages simultaneously. In fact, their exchanges seem like "total communication" in that they use words and expressions from both languages to convey meaning creatively and succinctly. They make plays on words and laugh uproariously. For effect, they intentionally pronounce French words with an American accent, or English words with a French accent. Sometimes French is the dominant language, and English words and phrases slip in naturally. At other times, English is their lingua franca and French sneaks in. Regardless of which language is dominant in their exchanges, alternations between French and English are generally free flowing and spontaneous. However, when one or the other is angry, there is a change in language use that creates a tangible chill. Jeanne's French words come faster, peppered with colloquial expressions, in syntactically complex sentences. There is a formality in the noticeable absence of English words; she may even use the plural *vous* to refer to Bill as a representative of all Americans after he has made a questionable remark about politics in public: "Vous êtes tous des ignorants!" (A colloquial translation of this sentence would be something like "You're all a bunch of ignorant fools!") Bill's English responses often take on an exaggerated accent of his childhood southern English and he may make obscure references to American cultural icons that Jeanne would not understand. During their spats, the use of French or English is a calculated choice, designed to create distance rather than intimacy. The change in how they use their two languages leaves a perceptible tension in the air. After their disagreements, however, warmth and good nature return quickly, and their mutually established code choice is evident again.

Using Myers-Scotton's markedness metric, we can describe the CS in Jeanne and Bill's ordinary exchanges as unmarked. Both French and English may serve as the unmarked code, depending on the situation and the context. When their conversations center on subjects that have an American context, such as Bill's work, family, and travel, English is the unmarked code; when they talk about subjects that have a French context, such as shopping, Jeanne's work, or the children's friends, French is the unmarked choice. Without full, conscious awareness, Jeanne and Bill have developed mutually understood habits of communicating in which CS is used in an unmarked way. As Myers-Scotton notes, people in a community establish conventions of interaction in which "speakers have some sense of 'script' or 'schema' for how interactions are to be conducted in an unmarked way" (1993a, p. 152). By contrast, the CS in the angry interactions between Jeanne and Bill would be described as marked—that is, it is unexpected and perhaps even used for shock value. By switching to the marked language, Jeanne or Bill is suggesting that the understood norm for interacting has changed and there is a shift in the power of their relationship.

Research shows that bilingual (or multilingual) people may also switch languages when expressing strong emotions. Dewaele (2006) notes that multilingual people are not always adept at assessing the degree of emotional intensity in a second language and often have a preferred language for anger: "L1 seems to be the obvious choice for many multilinguals as it usually has the strongest emotional connotations due to early and prolonged socialization in that language" (p. 126). He notes, however, that extended exposure to sociocultural and sociopragmatic norms in the other language can contribute to a person's ability to express anger in that language (p. 149). Other intense emotions, such as grief and elation, are likely to be expressed in a preferred language as well.

In addition to Myers-Scotton's markedness model, the notion of a social network, often used by social anthropologists, is helpful in understanding when and why a person may engage in CS. Wei, Milroy, and Pong, 1992 define this theory as follows:

> A social network may be seen as a boundless web of ties which reaches out through a whole society, linking people to one another, however remotely. But for practical reasons social networks are generally "anchored" to individuals, and interest focuses on relatively "strong" first-order network ties, i.e., those persons with whom ego directly and indirectly interacts. This principle of "anchorage" effectively limits the field of network studies, generally to something between 20 and 50 individuals (p. 190).

We can imagine that a person's social network influences her language mode. That is, she would engage in CS quite differently with people with whom she has first-order network ties, such as family and friends, than with others who are more remote. In a similar vein, Grosjean (2001) notes that a bilingual speaker may or may not engage in CS depending on specific circumstances: the language proficiency of the speakers, their relationship, and their socioeconomic status; the setting in which the interaction occurs; the topic of the conversation; and whether the speakers are communicating information, telling a story, or trying to create social distance or intimacy. Emma's American father offers a good example of a bilingual speaker whose CS varies according to the setting in which he finds himself. Bill's interactions at work, at Emma's school, and at home reveal at least three different kinds of language use. For Bill, a dominant bilingual (he is more proficient in English) and a late bilingual (he acquired French after puberty), French is the language of his workplace. He works with French people in an art dealership, has mastered much of the language required for dealings in the import/export art business, feels at ease in French, and rarely engages in CS. His use of French in this setting is an indication of his full and equal membership in this professional community. When Bill is in Emma's French preschool setting talking to her teachers, however, he doesn't know the French words for the apron Emma will need for her finger painting or how to clearly describe her behavior since the birth of her baby brother. He knows that Emma's teachers understand some English, so he feels comfortable inserting an occasional English word into his French to make his meaning clear. We might describe this language behavior as intentional survival CS because it is conscious and serves to make up for communicative gaps. At home, where Bill and Jeanne are equal bilinguals, he feels no communication constraints and engages freely in mutually agreed-on, grammatical CS that is largely spontaneous and unconscious. In summary, Bill's language behavior in French falls on a continuum from no evidence of CS (at work) to conscious and limited CS (at Emma's school) to spontaneous and pervasive CS (at home with Jeanne). This range of bilingual behavior is natural, represents real bilingual functioning, and should be included in any definition of what it means to be bilingual.

→ YOUR VIEW 4

Read the following quotation taken from Carol Myers-Scotton's (1998/2000) article, "Code-Switching As Indexical of Social Negotiations." Analyze her views regarding the relationship between code choice and individual rights and obligations.

"While conveying referential information is often the overt purpose of conversation, talk is also always a negotiation of rights and obligations between speaker and addressee. Referential content—what the conversation is about—obviously contributes to the social relationships of participants, but with context kept constant, different relational outcomes may result. This is because the particular linguistic variety used in an exchange carries social meaning. This model assumes that all linguistic code choices are indexical of a set of rights and obligations holding between participants in the conversational exchange." (pp. 137–138)

PERSPECTIVES FOR THE CLASSROOM

Being bilingual is much more than simply knowing two languages. Rather, bilingualism refers to a wide range of language knowledge and use. In particular, bilingualism is characterized by cross-linguistic phenomena that reflect a bilingual speaker's linguistic skill as well communicative intent. Above all, bilingualism is not a description reserved for people who are equally proficient in two languages. To demystify what it means to be bilingual, foreign language teachers must first confront their biases against bilingual language use in the classroom. Specifically, we must recognize that English has an important role to play in the foreign language classroom. Furthermore, to avoid random and disruptive language mixing, we will explore the idea of a language-use contract that recognizes the rights and responsibilities of both teachers and learners. Finally, we will propose that developing learners' awareness of what it means to be bilingual promotes multicompetent second language learners.

Confronting our biases against English in the foreign language classroom

For more than 25 years, good foreign language teaching has been defined by the quality and quantity of target language in the classroom. In fact, teachers' successes are often measured by the degree to which they can keep classroom activities in the target language. Krashen's (1981) hypothesis that comprehensible input in the target language is essential to second language acquisition encouraged teachers to focus on using as much target language as possible to model authentic, correct, native-like use of the foreign language.[6] Later, theorists argued that interaction is as important as input for second language acquisition (Gass, 1997; Long, 1981, 1996; Pica, 1987, 1994; Pica, Young, & Doughty, 1987). In addition, those who adopt a sociocultural perspective with regard to second language teaching and learning stress the importance of input and interaction in the target language, although they acknowledge the role of the native language in second language development (Lantolf, 2002; Lantolf & Thorne, 2006). In general, most people endorse approaches to foreign language teaching that stress the importance of target language input and interaction. The idea that it is important to immerse students in the target language to the greatest extent possible is certainly sound and serves to inform teaching practice in important ways. However, this idea may also constrain any frank discussion about the role of the native language in the foreign language classroom. Our target-language-only approach is motivated by sound research, but it may also hinder our thinking.

If foreign language teachers in the United States want to promote bilingual functioning they will need to confront long-held views about the role of English in the classroom. In particular, they will need to recognize that a target-language-only approach does not help students become bilingual because it involves a primarily monolingual encounter with the second language. As we saw in Chapter 1, students cannot learn what it means to be bilingual (or multilingual) if they are immersed in a monolingual classroom environment. Most foreign language teachers have not thought about this contradiction because they are largely unaware of what it means to be bilingual. Moreover, most foreign language methods texts review theories and research about second language learning and teaching without addressing the subject of bilingualism.[7] Simply put, foreign language teachers have not been trained to analyze what bilingual people do and are therefore unable to see how their teaching can be informed by studies in bilingualism.

One of the principal reasons foreign language teachers adhere to a target-language approach lies in their belief that using English will have a negative effect on students' second language development. Cook (2001, 2002b) challenges the assumption that students should avoid using their native language so they can learn to think and speak in the second language:

> The usually unstated belief is that students would fare better if they kept to the second language, i.e., a coordinate relationship in which the languages in the mind are kept in separate compartments. The L2 user perspective suggests, however, that in general teachers should recognise the classroom as an L2 user situation. In particular, they should develop the systematic use of the L1 in the classroom alongside the L2 as a reflection of the realities of the classroom situation, as an aid to learning and as a model for the world outside. (p. 332)

Furthermore, Cook (1999, 2001, 2002c) challenges the foreign language profession to reconsider the role of the first language in the second language learning process. He argues convincingly that we should confront our bias against the first language and recognize the value of CS in the foreign language classroom, in particular with task-based approaches:

> Code-switching is a normal feature of L2 use when the participants share two languages. . . . Through the L1, they may explain the task to each other, negotiate roles they are going to take, or check their understanding or production of language against their peers. These purposes for the L1 clearly fit well with the overall rationale for the task-based learning approach, even if they have so far been discouraged or ignored. (Cook, 2001, p. 418)

Jarvis and Pavlenko (2008) agree with Cook, noting that "this assumption is incompatible with the findings of CLI (cross-linguistic influence) research that show very clearly that a dominant L1 cannot be simply 'turned off' for fifty minutes a day, rather it continues to mediate linguistic and cognitive activities in the classroom" (p. 217). Given this understanding, using both English and the target language is a potentially productive classroom practice.

Although research is needed to fully assess the implications for a foreign language teaching approach that allows for CS, there is some indication that CS can serve a positive role. In a study by Nichols and Colón (2000), a teacher in a high school Spanish for Spanish speakers program used CS as a teaching strategy and accepted students' use of both Spanish and English in the classroom. During observations, "code-switching was clearly used as a resource to help students as well as to demonstrate that dual language proficiency is a resource within a public academic setting. By modeling this carefully constructed use of code-switching, the teacher taught a lesson that students would carry with them into more challenging academic settings" (pp. 507–508). Similarly, Liebscher and Dailey-O'Cain's (2004) study indicates that in a content course for advanced second language learners who were given permission to code-switch, the learners "did not merely fall back on the L1 when they encountered a deficiency in their L2 learning; they also made frequent use of language alternation to indicate changes in their orientation toward the interaction and toward each other" (p. 519).

Although it would be counterproductive to endorse a teaching approach that promotes the use of CS for its own sake, allowing students to engage in CS may lead to a heightened awareness about the language itself as well as about how language functions in communication.[8] Belz (2002) believes that allowing students to code-switch leads to language play within or across languages as well as encourages meta-linguistic awareness. Her study of students reading a bilingual text (English and German) shows how students are encouraged to rely on their multilingual competence, thereby occupying "third places from which they could both play with and reflect on multiple linguistic identities" (p. 234). This third place is neither a monolingual nor a bilingual identity, but rather a third one—a privileged identity between the two languages—that learners create through formal classroom study. Belz also states that "L1 and/or multiple language use [in the classroom] may provide insight into the ways in which multicompetent language users inhabit and relate to a pluralistic, multilingual world" (p. 216).

In addition to confronting their preconceived notions about English in the foreign language classroom, teachers will have to change their views about what it means to be a good second language learner. In other words, the capacity to speak and write with grammatical accuracy cannot be the only measures of success. Gomes de Matos (2002) outlines his ideas about learners' rights, stating that there has to be a move away from criterion-focused (i.e., proficiency-based) assessments to ones that value nonnative language use. In this same vein, Cook (2002c) believes that "the standards against which L2 users are measured should be L2 user standards, not L1 native speaker standards. Success should be measured by the ability to use the second language effectively" (p. 335). Moreover, Cook (2002c) suggests de-emphasizing the spoken language and articulating goals that focus on other competencies.

Finally, as we saw in Chapter 1, multilingual classrooms that do not hold up idealized native-speaker standards offer real models of bilingual language use. Moreover, these kinds of classrooms can promote the development of positive second language learner identities. Ultimately, confronting our bias against the use of English in the foreign language classroom is an important step toward promoting bilingualism. It may even transform our teaching and our students:

> The L2 user perspective reminds us that teaching is concerned with changing students' minds, hopefully for the better. (Cook, 2002c, p. 334)

> Language teaching transforms people into something they would not otherwise be. The L2 user concept reinstates language teaching as a profound influence on the students; it justifies language teaching educationally and restores it to the humanistic "civilising" tradition, where it has barely figured for many years. (Cook, 2002c, p. 341)

→ YOUR VIEW 5

Devise a questionnaire to determine how students feel when they speak English as opposed to how they feel when they speak the target language in the classroom.

Designing a language-use contract

The idea of a teaching approach that endorses, and even encourages, the use of English in the foreign language classroom may sound acceptable in theory; however, its practical application seems elusive because there is no established understanding of when English should be used, how much it should be used, or what constitutes productive use of it. Teachers might argue that if CS, and by extension English, were allowed in the classroom, the resulting chaos would obscure pedagogical goals. A possible worst-case scenario might be that teachers would resort to translating anything students did not seem to understand and students would feel free to use English all the time. To avoid these kinds of legitimate fears, we need to develop clear parameters for using English in the foreign language classroom so that both teachers and students understand and agree on a productive multilingual approach.

To that end, teachers and students should work together to articulate a set of guidelines about how, when, and why first and second languages, as well as CS, are used. In fact, a set of guidelines, or a language-use contract, should play a central role in the course goals and requirements. All members of a classroom community should participate in determining code choice for what teachers say, including presentation of material (culture, grammar, literary texts, etc.) and classroom management activities (collecting and returning work, taking roll, assigning homework, etc.), as well as for what students say during classroom activities, such as small group work, peer editing, and so forth. Although teachers may be concerned that students will choose to use the first language or engage in sloppy language mixing, there is every reason to believe that giving students a role in determining which language is used when and why will promote conscious reflection about code choice and productive language use.

In devising a set of guidelines, or a language-use contract, it is important to bear several important considerations in mind:

1. The language-use contract should address issues related to learners' rights and responsibilities. To that end, students should be guided to consider the rights and responsibilities they would like to have in the class (Gomes de Matos, 2002). In addition, students should explore the idea that, as L2 users, they have "the right to be themselves . . . to use language differently from monolinguals . . . and to have different knowledge of the second language from that of monolingual native speakers" (Cook, 2002c, p. 335).

2. The language-use contract should outline a markedness framework. That is, teachers and students should work together to determine which language (English or the target language) should be unmarked (ordinary) and which one should be marked (unusual) for different kinds of classroom activities. Levine (2004) proposes a multilingual model that allows students at all levels of study to "have a critical stake in what goes on in the classroom in terms of the agreed-upon norms of code choice and use" (p. 113). This model "intentionally puts learners in the driver's seat in the construction of code choice norms, granting them an indispensable role in managing classroom discourse, and compelling them to reflect critically on the ways language is or can be used" (p. 125). A notable feature of this model is that the first and second languages can be unmarked or marked code choices depending on the agreement that students and teachers make. In addition, the contract should specify when and why CS would be appropriate.

3. The language-use contract should specify why certain code choices are preferable. For example, students should understand why exclusive use

of the target language is important for developing a sensitivity to the sounds and rhythms of a language. Similarly, they should understand and appreciate the value of exclusive use of the target language for certain kinds of communicative activities that are designed to promote acquisition through use.

4. In designing a language-use contract, teachers and students should discuss value assumptions about code choice. That is, neither English nor the target language should be viewed as negative, nor be used to express a power differential. This discussion should help both teachers and students articulate what is good and desirable as opposed to what is bad and to be avoided.

5. Finally, the language-use contract should include agreed-on sanctions should any member of the class refuse to abide by it. As Wei, Milroy, and Pong (1992/2000) note, "close-knit social networks seem to have a particular capacity to maintain and even enforce local conventions and norms, including linguistic norms" (p. 191). This idea is founded on an understanding of the classroom as a social network built around shared space and time together.

→ YOUR VIEW 6

Develop a language-use contract that would suit your teaching setting. This contract should reflect both student and teacher input and take into account the various kinds of activities that are typical in your classroom.

Code-switching and the multicompetent second language learner

In Chapter 1 we proposed that a multicompetent learner has a growing awareness of issues related to language learning and language use. In this chapter we will build on that notion and suggest that awareness about bilingualism dispels inaccurate preconceptions and empowers multicompetent learners. The first step in understanding bilingualism is to think critically about what it means to be a native speaker. Above all, learners must recognize that native speakers are born into a particular language community and grow up hearing and speaking that language. A person from one language community cannot become a native speaker of another language (except children who grow up in bilingual families). As Cook notes, "someone who did not learn a language in childhood cannot be a native speaker of the language. Later-learnt languages can never be native languages by definition" (1999, p. 187). Although Koike and Liskin-Gasparro (2002) point out that a native-speaker norm provides an important point of reference for language learning, it is essential for second language learners to understand that teachers do not expect them to become native speakers. Moreover, students should know that most people never achieve full mastery of another language. In fact, "few L2 users can pass for native speakers; their grammar, their accent, their vocabulary give away that they are non-native speakers, even after many years of learning the language or many decades of living in a country" (Cook, 2002b, p. 5) Therefore, learners should understand that they cannot and should not be measured against native speakers of a particular language.

In addition to developing an awareness about the notion of what it means to be a native speaker, multicompetent second language learners must also understand what it means to be bilingual. According to Jarvis and Pavlenko (2008), teachers need to gain a better understanding of cross-linguistic influence phenomena and should be prepared to teach students certain fundamental principles about what it means to be bilingual. Rather than thinking it means being able to use two languages equally well, students should learn that bilingualism refers to many kinds of dual-language functioning. Becoming bilingual might best be described using a continuum, with "incipient bilingual" on one end and "balanced bilingual" on the other, as shown in Figure 2.2. When students understand that becoming bilingual is a dynamic process and not a fixed state, they begin to consider themselves as being somewhere on the bilingual continuum. Instead of feeling burdened by a growing sense that they cannot possibly achieve native-speaker proficiency, students can be empowered by their nascent bilingual functioning.

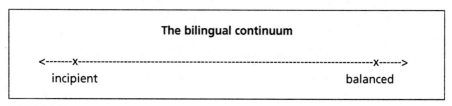

FIGURE 2.2

Understanding the terms native speaker and bilingual sets the stage for exploring the idea that CS is a natural language phenomenon that characterizes bilingual functioning. A critical aspect of any discussion of CS involves understanding that it is a language behavior that is both social and linguistic. With regard to the social dimension, learners can explore their perceptions of the status of the language they are studying—or whether they consider the target language to have higher or lower status than their native languages. This subject becomes particularly interesting for students who are heritage learners[9] of the target language and who may have mixed feelings about the language and culture they are studying in the classroom. Issues of language status in the classroom may be further compounded by the teacher's opinions. For example, teachers may unconsciously communicate their personal views regarding which language is better, more beautiful, or used by people who are considered economically or politically dominant or weak. In other words, a teacher's ideas about the status of the target language may be implicitly communicated to the students. Teachers and students can work together to explore how CS by a teacher can send an implied message, reprimand, or somehow reinforce the teacher's authority. They can analyze how a teacher's CS might occur with other kinds of behavior, such as changes in voice tone or pitch or the use of gestures or facial expressions (Martin-Jones, 1995). Students can also analyze their own use of CS in the classroom to determine if they use it as an exclusion strategy to create in-groups or to make fun of the target language by mimicking or deliberately mispronouncing words and phrases. Or perhaps CS is an indication that the demands of the target language task are too great and they need to resort to English. Ultimately, the ways that students engage in CS may reveal their sense of which language has higher status and what they are trying to achieve socially in the classroom setting. A discussion about the social role of CS might be ongoing as the climate in the classroom changes and evolves.

In addition to developing an awareness of the social implications of CS, teachers and students can analyze its linguistic dimensions. Using examples of bilingual CS they can decide which language is the matrix (base) and which is the embedded language (inserted) at any given point. They may construct sentences that demonstrate how the matrix language is dominant and generally supplies the grammar words (definite and indefinite articles, possessive adjectives, demonstrative adjectives, etc.), whereas the embedded language generally supplies the content words (nouns, verbs, adjectives, etc.).[10] Although the rules for CS are generally considered to be determined by the matrix language,[11] the foreign language classroom is, to some extent, a nonnatural environment, and therefore the matrix and embedded languages may vary. That is, if the second language proficiency of the students is quite low, the matrix language may be English. On the other hand, if students are proficient enough to use the target language for much of the classroom conversation, the target language might function as the matrix language. Or, English and the target language may alternate between being the matrix and the embedded languages. Simon (2001) points out that it may be difficult to determine what the matrix and embedded languages are in the foreign language classroom because code choice may be controlled by both teachers and learners at different times and be associated with the kinds of tasks and activities of the classroom. Nevertheless, she argues for an acknowledgment of the role of CS and its potential positive contributions to the classroom learning process.

Even though analyzing definitions of native speaker and bilingual, as well as exploring the ways teachers and students may use CS in the classroom, may seem to detract from the real business of foreign language teaching, it may ultimately support the development of multicompetence. Understanding when CS occurs, who controls it (teachers or students), and how it manifests itself linguistically can promote a conscious, purposeful, and productive code choice among both teachers and students. Finally, multicompetent second language learners understand the importance of being immersed in as much target language as possible. However, they also recognize that CS reflects the natural practices of bilingual people in diglossic communities around the world.[12]

Concluding Propositions

Proposition 2.1

Code-switching is a normal and natural occurrence among people who speak more than one language.

The portrait of Emma and her family underscores how CS is a normal and natural occurrence among bilingual people. Rather than being unusual or exceptional, this family is, linguistically speaking, quite ordinary. Like people across the world who live near communities in which other languages are spoken, their daily lives include interactions that require them to weave two or more languages together into a tapestry of communication. Whereas some CS may be deliberate, other instances of CS are entirely spontaneous. In either case, CS can serve to express nuances of linguistic and social meaning. This view challenges the notion that CS reflects communicative deficiency in one or more languages. In fact, there is increasing understanding of CS as a creative and highly proficient language practice.

Proposition 2.2

Code-switching can play a constructive role in the foreign language classroom.

The time has come for the foreign language profession to confront its bias against first language use. The monolingual foreign language classroom does not reflect language use in the real world, and it offers students a skewed vision of authentic, cross-linguistic communication. For the past several decades, foreign language teachers have subscribed to the notion that spontaneous language acquisition is better than conscious language learning. In other words, real language must be acquired naturally, much the same way that a child acquires her native language. In an effort to maximize real, natural language acquisition, teachers have made every effort to create a classroom environment that duplicates an immersion setting. Students have been flooded with target language input and encouraged to interact with teachers and peers to stimulate natural acquisition of the target language. In so doing, all other languages have been implicitly taboo.

There is little research to support the notion that exclusive use of the second language is the best way to learn it. According to Atkinson (1993) there is no research to suggest that using the target language 100 percent of the time in the classroom is the best approach. No one would argue that target language input, both oral and written, is essential for developing second language proficiency. However, most teachers would also agree that using only the target language is both unrealistic and even impossible. In addition to the fact that strict adherence to the target language does not offer students a realistic view of how bilingual or multilingual people actually interact, it also limits our teaching to simple subjects that students can handle with limited proficiency. As Chavez (2002) so aptly notes, this approach creates a language program in which real "communication takes a backseat to the strictures of language policy" (p. 194). The consequence of this approach is that the message is sacrificed in favor of simplistic content. Moreover, criticism from other disciplines charging that foreign language programs focus on skill development and not on rigorous academic content is borne out. Although an approach that endorses the use of both English and the target language may defy current practice that firmly endorses the importance of a monolingual, target-language approach in the classroom, it implicitly supports the development of real bilingual functioning.

Proposition 2.3

Multicompetent second language learners are aware of what it means to be bilingual.

Research on bilingual children suggests that they are capable of acquiring more than one language at the same time[13] and that multilingual functioning is the norm for many children in the world. Although no one would claim that adults acquire languages in the same way as children, there is every reason to believe that all typically learning people are capable of some kind of bilingual functioning. However, pedagogical goals that are based on developing native-like target language functioning for all students are doomed from the outset. Rather, goals should be described in terms of real bilingual language use: People gesture, imitate, use intuitive interpretation, and include words from their own languages to communicate a message. These kinds of skills, and especially code-switching, represent bilingual functioning.

Teaching about code-switching promotes an understanding of both its social and linguistic dimensions. However, rather than allow arbitrary CS in the classroom—which is likely to result in some kind of language-mixing chaos—an intentional plan for code choice can promote a deep understanding of how language works in communication. In an effort to address the problems inherent in trying to carry out all tasks in the foreign language classroom entirely in the target language, Atkinson argues that "classroom methodology ought to allow learners to maintain a firm sense of their own non-target language/culture identity while developing knowledge of and empathy towards the target culture itself. A careful, principled balance of the two languages is . . . one of the bases of such a methodology" (1993, p. 4). Learning about CS and recognizing the subtle dimensions of code choice can promote multicompetent second language learners who recognize the kind of real language use they are likely to encounter outside the classroom.

Suggested Readings on Bilingualism and Code-Switching

Appel, R., & Muysken, P. (1987). *Language contact and bilingualism*. London: Arnold.
Genesee, F. (2001). Bilingual first language acquisition: Exploring the limits of the language faculty. *Annual Review of Applied Linguistics 21*, 153–168.
Hamers, J. F., & Blanc, M. H. A. (2000). *Bilinguality and bilingualism*. (2nd ed.). Cambridge: Cambridge UP.
Jacobson, R. (Ed.). (2001). *Codeswitching worldwide II*. New York: Mouton de Gruyter.
Meisel, J. (1994). Code-switching in young bilingual children: The acquisition of grammatical constraints. *Studies in Second Language Acquisition 16*, 413–439.
Milroy, L., & Muysken, P. (Eds.). (1995). *One speaker, two languages: Cross-disciplinary perspectives on codeswitching*. Cambridge: Cambridge UP.
Myers-Scotton, C. (1993a). *Social motivations for codeswitching*. New York: Oxford UP.
Pavlenko, A. (Ed.). (2006). *Bilingual minds: Emotional experience, expression and representation*. Clevedon, UK: Multilingual Matters.
Toribio, J. A. (2001). On the emergence of bilingual code-switching competence. *Bilingualism: Language and Cognition 4*, 203–231.
Wei, L. (Ed.). (2000a). *The bilingualism reader*. New York: Routledge.

Researching Your Language Stories

1. Use the questionnaire developed for *YOUR VIEW 5*.
   a. Give the questionnaire to several students in a class. Compare their answers and determine whether or not their feelings and perceptions change with increased proficiency in the target language.
   b. Give the questionnaire to several students at several different levels of language study. Compare their answers and try to determine what experiences influence their perceptions of these terms.

[YOUR VIEW 5: Devise a questionnaire to determine how students feel when they speak English vs. the target language in the classroom.]

2. Use the language-use contract developed in *YOUR VIEW 6*.
   a. At the end of the semester assess students' attitudes about the benefits and drawbacks of the language-use contract. Determine the ways in which this approach changed their learning experience.
   b. Identify one or two students whose L1 is not English. Analyze their experience with the language-use contract. Assess the role that their L1 played in their

learning experiences. Determine if the language-use contract helped or hindered their learning of the target language.

[YOUR VIEW 6: Develop a language-use contract that would suit your teaching setting. This contract should reflect both student and teacher input and take into account the various kinds of activities that are typical in a classroom setting.]

Notes

1. Genesse (2002, p. 172) uses the term *code-mixing* to describe child bilingual usage and *code-switching* to refer to adults. Myers-Scotton, on the other hand, prefers not to use the term code-mixing because it implies "unpricipled chaos" (2000, p. 143).
2. According to Myers-Scotton's matrix language frame model, the grammar of the matrix language sets the morphosyntactic frame for code-switching. Her book *Duelling languages* (1993b) and her 1995 article entitled "A lexically based model of code-switching" provide further information about structural constraints in code-switching.
3. This analysis of grammatical morphemes and constraints in the matrix and embedded languages is taken from Petersen (1988) and Myers-Scotton and Jake (1995/2000).
4. See Chapter 1 of Jarvis and Pavlenko's (2008) book *Crosslinguistic influence in language and cognition* for a detailed description of these 10 dimensions.
5. Bongartz and Schneider (2003) describe both form-based and meaning-based language play in their study of two children learning German in Germany.
6. Krashen's (1981) monitor model includes five hypotheses: (1) Language acquisition is a subconscious process and is distinct from language learning, which is a conscious process; (2) the acquisition of grammatical structures follows a predictable order; (3) learning functions only as a monitor, or editor; (4) comprehensible input is essential to language acquisition; and (5) language acquisition can only occur when affective conditions (motivation, attitude, etc.) are optimal. These hypotheses are discussed in greater detail in Chapter 5.
7. The methods texts most commonly used in courses for foreign language teachers include *Teaching language in context* by Hadley (2001), *Making communicative language teaching happen* by Lee and VanPatten (2003), and *Teacher's handbook: Contextualized language instruction* by Shrum and Glisan (2005).
8. Giauque and Ely (1990) review the use of code-switching in teaching content courses in bilingual programs and propose that the same approach can be used in teaching foreign language. They describe an approach to teaching beginning French in which students are urged to use code-switching in the classroom. They cite student-generated sentences such as "Je am having difficulté," and state that students increase their use of French and decrease their use of English over time. They note that students expressed resistance to the approach, saying they felt irritated or silly while doing it. Belz (2002) notes that the goal of this approach is to use code-switching in the early stages of language learning based on the assumption that students will naturally move toward increased use of L2.
9. A *heritage learner* is defined as a student who is formally studying the language of his/her family of origin.

10. Myers-Scotton's (1995) matrix language frame (MLF) model states that of the two or more languages involved in CS, the matrix language (ML) plays the more dominant role over the embedded language (EL). According to her model, the ML supplies the system morphemes, whereas the EL supplies content morphemes. In addition, this model views intrasentential CS as a complement phrase (CP) containing at least one constituent with morphemes from two languages; the grammatical phrase of the CP comes from the ML.

11. See Myers-Scotton (1993a) and Muysken (1995) for a more detailed discussion.

12. The term *bilingual* refers to a speaker, whereas the term *diglossic* refers to the setting.

13. See Genesee (2001) for additional information regarding bilingual child language.

CHAPTER 3

"I lost my words!"

OVERVIEW

Most people in the United States have the opportunity to study a foreign language in a school setting. Typically they study a particular language for two or three years in high school, and, if they choose to go on to college or university, they may study it for one or two more years. For many of these students learning a foreign language in a classroom is a relatively brief experience, one that may leave little lasting impression. In fact, most students cannot recall much of what they learned about the target language. They may offer reasons to explain why they remember so few details, such as being poor language learners or having a bad teacher. In the end, however, they are mostly indifferent and think of their language learning experience as generally unremarkable. Even students who enjoy learning a foreign language and who experience some measure of success find that their competence and skills fade away when the course of study is over.

The fact that most students forget what they learned in their foreign language classrooms could be interpreted to mean that we, foreign language teachers, are not doing our jobs well. In fact, however, we recognize the problem and try to manage it by teaching the same things over and over again. Grammatical structures students encounter in the first year of language study are often reviewed and recycled in the second and third years in an attempt to reinforce and inscribe them indelibly in their memories. Yet, despite our enthusiasm and good intentions, our students forget much of what we teach them. Rather than suggest we have failed as foreign language teachers we often blame the system: We are asked to do too much in too little time, and students do not have sufficient exposure to the target language to develop a level of proficiency that can stand the test of time. These arguments may be true, but compounding the issue is the very real experience of language loss.

In Chapter 2 we reviewed theories that describe the dynamic nature of bilingualism, emphasizing the cross-linguistic interaction between a person's two languages. This dynamic understanding of bilingualism (or multilingualism) implies that first and second languages are not static, but rather influence each other and change over time (Herdina & Jessner, 2002). Moreover, language development and language loss are both involved in this dynamic process (de Bot, 2008). That is, language loss is considered to be a natural feature of second language development. Although there is relatively little research on second language loss per se, recent interest in dynamic models of multilingualism is shedding light on this commonplace language phenomenon (de Bot, 2008).

The "Snapshot" in this chapter tells a very personal story of how I learned Danish as a child and forgot it when I lost contact with the language. This story serves as a real-life example of the kind of language loss many multilingual people experience when a language falls into disuse. To inform our understanding of language loss, we will review various theories in "Research Perspectives" that describe how young children acquire their first language as well as how adults learn a second language. These theories, as well as others that hypothesize how language is represented in the brain, help explain the role that memory may play in first and second language acquisition and loss. In "Perspectives for the Classroom" we will explore the ways that these theories of memory and second language development challenge us to envision teaching strategies for the foreign language classroom that openly acknowledge second language loss. In particular, I will propose a model for understanding second language loss and suggest that assessing individual learners' language experiences is essential to developing an approach that includes attention to language maintenance. The "Concluding Propositions" reiterate the notion that language loss is a natural occurrence and that multicompetent second language learners are aware of the relationships among language development, language loss, and language maintenance.

SNAPSHOT

When I was nine we moved from France to Denmark. Very soon after arriving, I went off to public school with the other children on our street in a suburban Copenhagen neighborhood. My first days in the third grade were both scary and magic. I practiced saying the Danish names for oceans and seas in geography class, and I chanted the multiplication tables with increasing confidence. Within days the jangle of sounds made words, and after three months I was just another child in the classroom. I have very few memories of how Danish melted into my brain; my primary interests were riding my bicycle to school with friends; having my lunch box filled with open-faced sandwiches of meats, cheeses, cucumber, and chocolate on dark bread; and doing well in my *skriftlig dansk*[1] class. I did not set out to learn Danish systematically; the process occurred naturally and subconsciously. It simply happened to me. At the end of the school year my teacher wrote that I was no longer distinguishable from my classmates. I lived in Denmark for three years, spoke Danish like a native speaker, and told myself I was Danish like my friends.

15 years later, I decided to go back for a visit. My excitement about the trip was tempered with real fear about not being able to talk to my Danish hosts. Danish words seemed to have slipped away, and as I prepared for my trip, I played language games with myself. For example, I tried to remember how to say *cheese* in Danish, and when nothing came to mind, I put myself back in time, to the lunchroom in my school and imagined I had brought some cheese for lunch. A full sentence came out: "Jeg har taget noget *ost* med til at spise i skole i dag" (I have taken some cheese to eat in school today). *Cheese* is *ost*. I found the word. Recreating a familiar context from my childhood experience elicited not only the word I was looking for, but also a grammatical sentence—with a subject, a verb in the past tense, an object, an adverbial phrase, and a prepositional phrase. When I asked myself how to say *bed* in Danish, the word emerged only when I imagined that I was telling someone "I am going to bed": "jeg går i *seng*." Magic! The word for *bed* is *seng*. As shown in Figure 3.1, once I found a word in this way, I could transform the sentence into the present, past, or future tenses, even use the conditional; I could add conjunctions, such as *and, or, but*; I could negate the sentence; I could make it a command.

These experiences of finding words and phrases felt spontaneous and subconscious. Words like *cheese* or *bed* only surfaced as part of a phrase or a whole sentence. Danish words did not seem to live alone in some storehouse in my brain; they were embedded in utterances that were grammatical. It was as though I was unlocking grammar through words. This language game worked best for words that fit into categories, such as clothing, food, colors, numbers, and days of the week. It also worked with expletives! The memory game did not always work, however, and many words that would have been in my vocabulary as an 11 or 12-year-old child were gone: *bathtub, living room, vacation, jump, run*, and so on. My grammar seemed intact, but many words had completely disappeared.

Danish word play

Jeg går i seng nu.	I am going to bed now.
Jeg går ikke i seng nu.	I am not going to bed now.
Jeg gik i seng . . .	I went to bed . . .
men jeg kunne ikke sove.	but I couldn't sleep.
Jeg vil gå i seng.	I will go to bed.
Jeg vil gerne gå i seng.	I want to go to bed.
Jeg er gået i seng.	I have gone to bed.
Gå i seng nu!	Go to bed now!
Gå ikke i seng nu!	Don't go to bed now!

FIGURE 3.1

Nothing had prepared me for the experience on my first day back in Denmark. I listened to my hosts as they greeted me when I got off the train. Were these all my bags? Good trip? I answered *ja* or *nej* ("yes" or "no"). I realized that I understood everything they said. It felt as though words were falling into a grammatical framework that lived in my head, and they were coming in at an amazing rate. I talked hesitantly at first, then with more confidence. By the time I went to bed that evening, my brain was humming and overactive. I could not sleep, so I talked to myself in Danish, reciting experiences from childhood, imagining conversations for the next day. My old words were coming back. Even better, I felt new, adult words nudging in next to my long-ago child words. Before three days had passed, my Danish was running smoothly, like a well-oiled machine. The process seemed beyond my control; my brain was doing something quite independent of me. The neat Danish houses lined up along the streets of my old neighborhood, the open-faced sandwiches washed down with strong beer, the easy conversations with old friends had all revived an area of my consciousness that had been out of my reach. Now, more than three decades later, I still speak Danish and intentionally keep it alive in my head.

For a long time, I thought my story of rediscovering Danish was beyond belief—a sort of paranormal and unique experience. However, I have met many multilingual people since then who have had similar experiences and who have reclaimed their ability to understand or speak a language they felt they had lost. These kinds of stories raise critical questions about the nature of second language acquisition and loss. How and why did I acquire Danish? Where did this language live in my brain? Why did I lose it so quickly? And, finally, how did I recover it?

→ YOUR VIEW 1

Find a bilingual or multilingual person who has lost contact with a language he or she spoke fluently. Ask the following questions and compose a brief description of this person's language experiences: What is the person's native language? At what age did the person learn a second (third, fourth) language? At what age did the person lose contact with one of the languages? How does the person describe what he or she has forgotten about that language (e.g., vocabulary, grammar, idiomatic expressions, songs.)?

RESEARCH PERSPECTIVES

Many multilingual people have had an experience like the one described earlier. Regardless of whether a second or third language is acquired during childhood in a natural setting or as an adult in a classroom environment, people forget certain features of a language when they lose contact with it. To explore what it means to lose a language we will consider how language is acquired and what is known about language and brain functioning. Before beginning this discussion, however, it is important to clarify what the terms *learning* and *acquisition* have come to signify. Krashen (1981) makes a distinction between learning and acquisition, stating that the former is conscious and rule governed whereas the latter is subconscious and spontaneous. He further proposes that learning is an explicit process and functions as an editor or monitor, whereas acquisition is an implicit process and represents real language similar to first-language acquisition in children. Since Krashen first distinguished between these two processes, learning has generally been associated with the classroom and acquisition has been used to describe what takes place in a natural, immersion setting. To avoid contributing to a sense that these two terms represent different, and even mutually exclusive, processes, we will use the term *second language development* to refer to adults. The term development is more neutral than learning and acquisition and also implies change without necessarily suggesting gain or increase in language proficiency. The term acquisition will be used to refer to young children acquiring their first or second (or third) language.

Children and language acquisition

Parents, educators, and language specialists have always been fascinated with how children acquire language. Theories and research on this subject fill libraries, yet concrete answers remain elusive. Most people readily acknowledge, however, that acquiring language—a first, second, or even third language—is nearly effortless for children. Although hypotheses abound, there are four principal theories about the nature of first language acquisition: sensitive period, nativist, sociocultural, and cognitive-functional theories.

The fact that children have an exceptional ability to acquire language when they are young gave rise to theories about a **sensitive period** for language acquisition. Nearly half a century ago, Lenneberg (1967) proposed the **critical period hypothesis**, which states that linguistic development must occur between birth and around age 12, a period after which human beings have great difficulty acquiring language. Studies of children who have been deprived of language in their early lives support Lenneberg's critical period hypothesis in that, after a certain age, they seem to lose their ability to acquire their native language with relatively little effort.[2] There is, however, no agreement as to what marks the beginning or end of this critical period.

The term *sensitive period* has been adopted by some specialists in child language acquisition to refer to a developmental period that is not necessarily sharply set off temporally but is characterized by a greater receptivity. Hyltenstam and Abrahamsson offer the following distinction between the terms *critical period* and *sensitive period*:

> The concept of *critical period* is typically associated with those types of behavioral developments that have sudden onsets and offsets, result in all-or-nothing events, depend on instinct, are unlearned and irreversible, and for which environmental influences such as motivation do not play any role. . . . Most importantly, in the *critical period* formulation, maturation is thought to take place and come to an end

within an early phase of the life span, abruptly set off from the rest at a specific age (puberty or earlier). However, it is not always the case that periods of special adaptability in any area of temporally scheduled development are sharply set off from what comes before or follows them. This type of pattern has been referred to as a *sensitive period.* . . . As in critical period formulation, the special adaptation is thought to occur during an early phase, but in this weaker formulation, the sensitivity does not disappear at a fixed point; instead it is thought to fade away over a longer period of time, perhaps covering later childhood, puberty and adolescence. (Hyltenstam & Abrahamsson, 2003, p. 556)

The terms critical period and sensitive period are often used interchangeably. Although the latter term is less rigid, both terms are based on the notion of cerebral plasticity, or the brain's ability to make new and varied connections before it reaches full maturity around the age of puberty. Because the age and rate of language acquisition is highly individual, and because children may continue to acquire various dimensions of language (i.e., pragmatics and notions of extended discourse), the term sensitive period refers to a less restricted and more individual period of time in childhood during which language is acquired spontaneously and for which environmental influences have a limited role.

Many psychologists and linguists believe that the capacity for language is innate and seems to be "a genetically determined part of the human nervous system" (Beatty, 2001, p. 371). These **nativist theories**—or theories that language is an inborn and uniquely human capacity—are generally based on sensitive period theories. That is, they endorse the notion that children acquire language spontaneously during a window of developmental time without being taught, in the same way that they are not taught to crawl or walk. Chomsky, one of the most well-known linguists of our time, proposed that children are born with the fundamental principles of language in place and that they have something analogous to a language organ in the brain, or a **language acquisition device** (LAD), that helps them understand the grammatical principles of the language spoken by the community of people into which they are born. Chomsky further proposed that although all languages have specific grammatical rules, they share a common structural basis, or a **universal grammar** (UG) (Chomsky, 1957, 1965, 1975). According to this theory, a child in a Spanish-speaking community, for example, would be born with innate principles of language (UG), and her LAD would function to set the parameters and rules for Spanish.

One of the most convincing arguments for Chomsky's theories of the LAD and UG is that children acquire their first language in an astonishingly short period of time. In his view, the fragments and incomplete utterances that children hear between the ages of 1 and 3 cannot possibly account for the vast number of unique, rule-governed phrases and sentences they generate spontaneously. This view, referred to as the "poverty of the stimulus" argument (Chomsky, 1980), suggests that a child does not learn exclusively from what she hears, but rather deduces the underlying grammar of her language and is spontaneously creative. If a child learns to say "I want milk," she will quickly figure out that she can substitute any object for *milk*. Although it may not be grammatical at first, such as "I want cookie," in time she will discover how to use articles, "I want *a* cookie," and demonstratives, "I want *that* cookie," and so forth.[3]

Unlike nativist theories, **sociocultural theories** of language acquisition insist on the importance of interaction between the child and others in the community rather than on innate capabilities. These theories support the notion that children do not acquire their first language solely because of individual, internal, cognitive factors, but rather as a result of social interaction. The discovery of the work of Russian psychologist Vygotsky[4] during the latter part of the 20th century has shaped much current thinking in psychology, education, and second language acquisition. Vygotsky (1962) proposes that children are born with a need to make sense of their surroundings and when their caregivers talk to them, they attach meaning to objects and events. As children focus their attention on caregiver talk they learn words and phrases and form concepts that shape their developing mental functions. In his view, language does not convey thoughts that already exist in the child's mind, but rather it generates and shapes thoughts.

One of the principal tenets of sociocultural theory is that learning occurs when a child is interacting cooperatively with people in her environment who are more experienced, such as caregivers and teachers. In these interactions there are generally some functions and activities that a child can do independently and others she can only do with help from another person. Vygotsky (1978)[5] used the term *zone of proximal development* (ZPD) to describe the distance between what a child can do with help from more capable peers or adults (potential development) and what she can do alone (actual development). Once a function or activity is learned, it becomes part of the child's independent developmental attainment. Language learning, like all higher mental functions, occurs during this kind of social interaction.

Cognitive-functional theories have emerged to account for phenomena that are recognized by both nativist and sociocultural theories. These theories, also called usage based (Tomasello, 2003) or constructivist theories (N. C. Ellis, 2003), endorse the notion that language acquisition in children is integrated with other cognitive and social skills. Tomasello (2003) is a particularly outspoken critic of Chomskyan notions of UG, arguing that that the biological adaptation that distinguishes human beings from other animals is the capacity to understand the intentional and mental states of others. He believes that intention-reading and pattern-finding skills are biologically inherited cognitive and social capabilities that are uniquely human. That is, children acquire their first language (and other cognitive skills) while learning to interpret the intentions of those around them and by identifying the patterns in what they hear and see. This theory of first language acquisition is anchored in the interaction between innate cognitive abilities and social interactions.

Unlike Chomsky, Tomasello maintains that the emergence of grammar is a cultural-historical affair and not a biological affair: "There was no biological adaptation for grammar" (Tomasello, 2003, p. 40). In Tomasello's view, children have to hear language to learn it, and language structure (or grammar) emerges from language use. Moreover, he contends that whole utterances, not isolated words and morphemes, are the essential form of communicative intention. For example, a very young child (between 1 and 2 years old) might say "takaba" to mean "take a bath." This one-unit utterance is not a grammatical sentence but a word (or holophrastic expression) that has a particular meaning in a particular context. That is, *takaba* is an entire semantic-pragmatic communicative event that would direct the attention of a caregiver to a specific object and experience. Tomasello would argue that over time the child would extend "takaba" to "takawalk," "takaride," "takabite," and so on. Also, other words, such as subjects (Ellie, *I, Mommy*), or adverbials (*now, later, tomorrow*), would be added to the utterance to eventually form a grammaticized linguistic construction, such as "Ellie takaba now."

These theories that describe how children acquire their first language are often used to inform discussions of how children acquire a second language. Questions related to age and rate of acquisition are particularly salient for those who study children acquiring a second language. Some research indicates that in a natural learning setting older children (approximately between the ages of 8 and 12) acquire a second language faster and achieve better control of the language than younger children (Herschensohn, 2000; Krashen, Long, & Scarcella, 1982; Snow & Hoefnagel-Höhle, 1982). Conversely, other theories predict that second language acquisition becomes increasingly difficult during the period between birth and age 15 and that ultimate attainment in a second language varies among individuals, with social and psychological factors becoming increasingly important with age (Hyltenstam & Abrahamsson, 2003).[6] Other variables related to second language acquisition in children include how the language was acquired (naturalistic vs. instructed context) and the length of exposure to the language (Bialystok, 1999; Genesee, 1989/2001; Mesiel, 1989/2000).

In addition, there is some sense that not all features of language may be equally sensitive to age of acquisition. For example, pronunciation & intonation seem clearly susceptible to a sensitive period, whereas learning words is less associated with age. Paradis's (2004) work in neurolinguistics and bilingualism points to several features of language that are more closely related to age of acquisition than others:

> The critical period refers to the period during which individuals must be exposed to language interaction if they are to acquire linguistic competence. This period has an upper limit that varies with respect to which component of the implicit language system is acquired, namely, in chronological order, prosody, phonology, morphology, and syntax, (including syntactic features of the lexicon). But the vocabulary, i.e., the sound-meaning pairing of words, is conscious and hence subserved by declarative memory; consequently, it is not susceptible to the critical periods that apply to the various components of implicit competence. (Paradis, 2004, p. 59)

Ultimately, these four theories—sensitive period, nativist, sociocultural, and cognitive-functional—offer insights into how children acquire both their first and second (or more) languages.

→ YOUR VIEW 2

What advice would you give to a person who wants to raise a child in a multilingual family or community? Which of the four theories (sensitive period, nativist, sociocultural, and cognitive-functional) would you draw on to describe how children acquire a second language? What theoretical considerations would be helpful in optimizing the experience?

Second language development in adults

It is generally acknowledged that after the sensitive period for language learning—commonly considered to be after puberty—people rely on a variety of cognitive and social strategies to learn a second language. By and large the process is no longer spontaneous, but rather conscious and deliberate. In other words, adults (meaning people beyond the age of puberty) do not learn a second language in the same way that children learn their first language. Beyond this simple truth, adult second language development cannot be explained in clear-cut terms; it is a multifaceted process that varies radically from one person to the next.

A number of conditions affect the way adults learn a second language. The first and most important consideration is the setting: naturalistic versus instructed. Adults who learn a second language informally through interaction with native speakers in a natural setting—possibly in the target culture—often develop language competencies that match the social demands of the setting. For example, a work setting would require different language abilities than an intimate relationship. Even in a naturalistic setting, however, the learning process for adults is mostly conscious and deliberate. In an instructed setting, the learning is generally guided systematically through the use of prepared materials; the goals outlined by a classroom teacher, along with a textbook or other resources, determine the order of presentation and the activities designed to reinforce learning.

In addition to the setting, there are a number of other external and internal considerations that can affect second language development (R. Ellis, 1994, pp. 24–35). Among external considerations, we can include age, gender, social class, and ethnic membership. Each of these personal factors, or combinations of them, can have an impact on the rate of learning and the ultimate level of proficiency a learner attains. The learning environment itself can also have important consequences; a relaxed classroom atmosphere may be more likely to foster productive learning experiences than a tense or hostile one. Moreover, the kind and amount of input and interaction that learners have in the classroom setting may affect learning outcomes. With regard to internal factors, a learner's aptitude, attitude, learning strategies, and intrinsic motivation are important considerations. In addition, the influence of a learner's native language, or other languages, on the newly developing language may influence it in unique and individual ways. Ultimately, the factors that influence second language development are varied and infinite.

The research on adult second language learning is extensive. The field of applied linguistics has grown and changed dramatically over the past 50 years, giving rise to a wide variety of theoretical approaches that seek to gain insight into this important language phenomenon. Among these theories, there are two overarching theoretical perspectives: (1) formal linguistic perspectives based on cognitive theories regarding the underlying grammars of natural languages, including phonological, morphological, and syntactical dimensions, and (2) sociocultural theories founded on interactions and pragmatic perspectives and the notion "that the human mind is always and everywhere mediated primarily by linguistically based communication" (Lantolf, 2002, p. 104). All of the various theories included within these two large theoretical perspectives seek to explain the internal and external influences on second language development. In the end, research and experience tell us that adults can and do learn second languages. Unlike typically developing children who achieve mastery of their first language, however, adult second language learners exhibit great variability in proficiency. Some adults achieve native-like proficiency, whereas others experience challenges that result in limited proficiency. These issues, among others, remain vital subjects of research interest in an effort to explain the elusive nature of adult second language development.

Understanding the language brain

Recent research in neurolinguistics offers new ways of understanding first and second language development. These studies attempt to show how first and second (and third) languages are processed and represented in the brain. When talking about the language brain contemporary neurologists still refer to the parts of the brain named after two 19th-century physicians, Pierre Paul Broca and Carl Wernicke. **Broca's area** is located in the left frontal lobe and is responsible for articulated language; **Wernicke's area** is located in the left temporal lobe and accounts for comprehension of sounds and words. Broca's and Wernicke's areas are linked by a band of fibers called the arcuate fasciculus. Behavioral research and new technologies[7] have confirmed the important role of these two areas of the brain in language functioning and have added to our understanding of the neuroanatomy of the brain. In simple terms, the brain is comprised of neuronal groups organized into systems that are responsible for specific functions. Language involves hearing, processing, comprehending, and articulation, and occurs through the cooperation of many separate neurofunctional systems (Fabbro, 1999, p. 70). This vastly complex set of systems that comprise language can be described as exhibiting a hierarchical structure, with each level having its own set of neurological systems. The phonological, morphological, syntactic, and semantic levels all operate simultaneously during speech perception and production (Beatty, 2001, pp. 366–370). For most people the neural mechanisms that control language are contained in the left cerebral hemisphere; however, the distribution of cerebral dominance is different for some left-handed people, with about 15 percent of them having language in the right hemisphere and another 15 percent of them exhibiting mixed dominance in both hemispheres (Beatty, 2001, p. 372).

Much of our understanding about language functioning in the brain comes from studies on people who have suffered some kind of brain illness or trauma. For example, patients with trauma to Broca's area, or Broca's aphasia, often lose the ability to speak grammatically. Their speech (and writing) is characterized by strings of disconnected content words in telegraphic style, with very few function words, such as articles or pronouns. They can generally understand simple sentences linked by conjunctions (such as *and, or, but*) but may have trouble with complex sentences, such as those with dependent clauses. In addition, they may retain the use of certain types of language linked to routines, such as days of the week, numbers, and songs, perhaps because they were learned repeatedly and became automatized (Beatty, 2001; Berko-Gleason, 1982). Patients with trauma to Wernicke's area, by contrast, speak rapidly and effortlessly, but their speech is nearly devoid of meaning (Beatty 2001). That is, they retain a capacity for grammatically correct speech, but words appear to be meaningless fillers. A third kind of aphasia, conduction aphasia, occurs when there is damage to the arcuate fasciculus, or the band of association fibers that link Broca's area to Wernicke's area. Patients with this disorder make many errors of word usage and often search laboriously for the right word (Beatty, 2001).

The importance of these brain injury studies lies in their contributions to our understanding of how the language brain works. The loss of ability to name items (anomia) occurs with most injuries to the language areas of the left cerebral hemisphere, however naming errors do not occur randomly. Evidence shows that content words are more vulnerable to loss than function words, and nouns more than verbs. In addition, certain classes of words may be affected differently. For example, words with concrete referents, such as *chair* or *apple*, seem more resistant than abstract words, such as *principle* or *judgment*. There is also evidence that emotion-laden words, such as prayers or curse words, as well as color words, letters, and numbers, may remain intact (Obler, 1982, p. 62). Although much about the language brain remains shrouded in mystery, it is clear that different language skills are associated with different areas of the brain.

Studies of the bilingual brain offer further insight into the issues of language development and loss. In particular, linguists have tried to determine whether a bilingual person's two languages represent separate or common knowledge areas of the brain. Studies have explored the differences between people who have learned their second language early in life (early bilinguals) and those who have learned a second language after maturity (late bilinguals). New brain imaging technologies[8] provide evidence that in the frontal-lobe language-sensitive regions (Broca's area) second languages acquired in adulthood are spatially separated from native languages (Hernandez et al., 2001; Kim et al., 1997). When acquired during the early stages of development, however, native and second languages tend to be represented in common frontal cortical areas. Research on high-proficiency bilingual adults also shows that neuroanatomical representations of both languages overlap (Rodriguez-Fornells et al., 2002). Studies further indicate that age of language acquisition does not seem to affect the temporal-lobe language-sensitive areas (Wernicke's area) but may be a factor in determining the functional organization of Broca's area (Kim et al., 1997). In fact, acquiring a second language early in life may be a factor in determining the functional organization of Broca's area, and adjacent cortical areas may be required for adult second language learning (Kim et al., 1997).

The most interesting findings in bilingual brain imaging involve evidence that grammar (syntactic processing) and words (semantic processing) are organized in separate areas of the brain (Fabbro, 1999; Ullman, 2004, 2005). Research indicates that the ability to recognize and produce grammatical language is sensitive to age of acquisition (Hernandez et al., 2001; Wartenburger et al., 2003) and that early bilinguals are generally better at grammatical processing than late bilinguals, regardless of proficiency.[9] Some studies even suggest that the parallel learning of two languages since birth may be crucial in setting the neural substrate for grammar (Wartenburger et al., 2003). Unlike grammatical processing, there is evidence that the two languages of a bilingual person access a common semantic system regardless of age of acquisition (Illes et al., 1999; Wartenburger et al., 2003).[10] In other words, it appears that bilingual people of all ages and proficiencies do not have two mental dictionaries, but rather one common conceptual, semantic system that is not language specific. It is worth noting that one common semantic system may not be the same as one common conceptual system. That is, there may be one conceptual system for both languages, but perhaps two corresponding language-specific semantic systems (Paradis 2004, p. 173).[11] Nevertheless, there is evidence that early and late bilinguals with high proficiency in their second language perform equally well on semantic judgment tests for both languages, suggesting that proficiency level may have a greater effect than age of acquisition on cerebral representation of second language semantic processing (Wartenburger et al., 2003). In addition, although studies of late bilinguals indicate that second language processing requires more cortical resources than first language processing, there appears to be overlap in the bilingual lexicon (Viorica, Spivey, & Hirsch, 2003).

It is important to recognize that brain imaging technologies are still relatively new and the findings can be difficult to interpret. Paradis (2004) notes that we need to be circumspect when talking about bilingual brain imaging research because the ways that data are interpreted can be problematic in this early stage of using these technologies. He argues that there is no real evidence that the languages of bilinguals are each represented in a different locus in the brain; rather, both language systems seem to be represented as distinct microanatomical subsystems located in the same gross anatomical areas. He also notes that research suggesting increased participation of the right hemisphere in bilinguals is especially difficult to interpret because it could result from something other than the language system, such as heavier reliance on pragmatic cues. Despite these valid cautionary notes, there is substantial evidence that the brain processes grammar and words differently.

In addition to brain injury research and nonpathological neuroanatomical studies of the brain, theories and research on memory shed light on the complex phenomena involved in first and second language processing. Memory is a broad term that refers to many different things, such as spatial memory, motor skill memory, and verbal memory. Generally speaking, however, memory is divided into two fundamental categories: **short-term memory** and **long-term memory**.

Short-term memory, also known as working memory, processes and stores a limited amount of information for short periods of time, usually a few seconds. It may be envisioned as the memory of the present. Long-term memory, on the other hand, seems to have no limit to its capacity. Because everything that is remembered is stored in long-term memory, it may be envisioned as the memory of the past (Beatty, 2001, pp. 403–406).

Within long-term memory, a distinction is made between **declarative memory** and **procedural memory**. Declarative memory (also referred to as explicit memory) includes learned knowledge that can be consciously retrieved and verbalized. There are two types of declarative memory: semantic memory and episodic memory. Semantic memory includes facts, concepts, and general knowledge; it is said to be related to the meaning of things. Episodic memory includes events and personal history; it is experiential knowledge of the self. Unlike declarative memory, procedural memory (also called nondeclarative memory or implicit memory) refers to a type of learning or knowledge that is not available for conscious recall. It depends on the repeated execution of a task and generates automatic behavior. Knowing how to speak your native language, or ride a bike, is part of procedural memory. In simpler terms, we can say that declarative memory involves knowing what, and procedural memory involves knowing how (Beatty, 2001; Fabbro, 1999; Paradis, 2004). Studies of word retrieval support the notion that single-word processing is supported by declarative memory, whereas syntax is supported by procedural memory, and each involves different cerebral structures in different anatomical locations (Wartenburger et al., 2003, p. 159). Table 3.1 offers an overview of the commonly held distinctions between declarative and procedural long-term memory systems.

TABLE 3.1   Declarative and Procedural Long-term Memory

Declarative (explicit)	(a) semantic: facts, concepts (b) episodic: events, experience	available for conscious recall	knowing what (words)
Procedural (nondeclarative) (implicit)		not available for conscious recall	knowing how (grammar)

There is general agreement that both declarative and procedural memory systems are involved in native language processing; as shown in Table 3.1 words and grammar in one's native language may involve different kinds of memory systems. Given research on these two types of memory systems, words and grammar may not be equally vulnerable to loss. A person's unconscious knowledge of the rules that govern how words are ordered and linked together to make meaning (i.e., grammar) is stored in procedural memory. This knowledge, acquired in childhood, is particularly resistant to loss. Words, on the other hand, are stored in declarative memory and may be more susceptible to attrition. That is, words and meaning-bearing phrases appear to fade when they are no longer reinforced by use. For the purpose of this discussion, the term *word* is used in its broadest sense to refer to content words (nouns, verbs, adjectives, etc.) and clusters of words that refer to a single concept. Ultimately, this understanding of language and memory suggests that when grammar is acquired early in life it is stored in procedural memory and can remain nearly intact throughout a lifetime; by contrast, words acquired at any age are stored in declarative memory and can fade or be forgotten due to lack of exposure to the language.

→ YOUR VIEW 3

Read the following quotation taken from Kees de Bot, Wander Lowie, and Marjolijn Verspoor's 2005 book Second Language Acquisition: An Advanced Resource Book. *Analyze their view that implicit (procedural) and explicit (declarative) systems are separate but that explicit knowledge may become implicit knowledge over time. Do you agree with this view? In other words, do you think that the grammar of a second language learned later in life (stored and processed in declarative [explicit] memory) can eventually become part of procedural (implicit) memory like the grammar of one's native language?*

"With learning a skill, we gradually rely more and more on the implicit knowledge and the explicit knowledge set can then be left to fade. It is a common finding among language learners that they have acquired a set of rules and applied them explicitly and consciously for a while, with the implicit knowledge system gradually taking over. In the end the explicit knowledge and the rules so laboriously learned are no longer needed, and learners may behave as if they are still applying the explicit rule knowledge, while in fact they use the implicit knowledge in which access to such rule systems probably play no role at all." (p. 63)

PERSPECTIVES FOR THE CLASSROOM

The language story in this chapter describes a real and personal experience of language acquisition and loss; it also captures the dynamic experience of recovery. As a child I acquired Danish naturalistically and subsequently lost it when I moved away from Denmark. In my endeavor to recover Danish I used the resources of one language (English) to stimulate my memories of a second language (Danish). The most surprising part of the experience, however, was the distinction between my memory of Danish words and grammar; I had forgotten many common words but had retained my grasp of grammar. By putting myself back into typical situations—such as going to school or going to bed—I generated grammatical sentences that contained many of my lost words. This conscious memory exercise triggered an experience of language recovery that underscored both the distinction between words and grammar and the dynamic inter-relatedness between words and grammar. My experience with Danish—probably typical of language acquisition and loss among people who acquire a second language in childhood—may not be representative of the kinds of experiences most adults have after learning a second language in a classroom setting. Nevertheless, this story highlights the fact that grammar and words seem to rely on different memory systems and that loss can vary for these two features of language.

The subject of language loss is rarely discussed among language teachers. In fact, it is seldom included in materials designed to prepare foreign language teachers for classroom teaching. Moreover, there is relatively little research on language loss despite the fact that it is a common phenomenon. To begin to address this issue I will review a model of second language acquisition and propose a model of second language loss that can serve as the basis for thinking about language loss for both traditional and multilingual second language learners. Finally, I will conclude with the idea that an awareness of the role of memory in language development fosters an understanding of the experience of language loss. Above all, we will see that multicompetent second language learners have a growing understanding of the dynamic relationship between language loss and recovery.

A model of second language development and loss

Language loss is a real and observable experience. Students are generally aware of how quickly they seem to lose their language skills after completing a course of study, and most teachers have heard former students say the equivalent of "I took two years of Spanish and I can't remember anything!" All too often teachers and students think of these experiences of second language attrition as failures. In fact, we generally avoid talking about the issue of language loss in the classroom and focus our energies on activities that promote second language development. Obviously we should continue to concentrate on language development; however, it is important to confront issues related to second language loss and maintenance as well. In particular, we need to develop a model for understanding language loss that can help learners develop and maintain their second language skills.

Ullman's (2004, 2005) declarative/procedural model offers a particularly useful approach for discussing the role of memory in second language development and can serve as a basis for understanding both second language loss and maintenance. The central premise of Ullman's model is that the distinction between words and grammar may be linked to declarative and procedural memory systems. This model predicts that for late second language learners—meaning those who are past the sensitive period for language acquisition—both lexical and grammatical processing in the second language are supported by declarative memory systems. That is, "adult second language learners rely particularly heavily on declarative memory, depending on this system not only for storing idiosyncratic lexical knowledge, but also for memorizing complex forms and 'rules'" (Ullman, 2005, p. 157). Ullman's theoretical model is supported by Fabbro (1999), who states that "the frontal lobe structures organize the syntactic components of a language only if it is learnt before the critical age. Afterwards, other brain structures account for the organization of the grammatical aspects of the second language, probably through explicit learning" (p. 101). Likewise, Paradis (2004) states that "we have ample clinical, neuropsychological and neuroimaging evidence that implicit linguistic competence and metalinguistic knowledge are each subserved by separate, neurofunctional mechanisms" (p. 12). Ullman (2005) cites additional studies supporting his notion that learning a second language late in life has a negative effect on the acquisition of grammar but not on the acquisition of lexical items. Table 3.2 summarizes Ullman's theory that children rely on both procedural and declarative memory systems to process their first (or second) languages, whereas adults rely nearly exclusively on declarative memory systems to process the second language.[12]

TABLE 3.2 Procedural and Declarative Memory Systems for L1 and L2[13]

	Procedural memory (implicit knowledge)	Declarative memory (explicit knowledge)
Child L1/L2 acquisition	grammatical processing (forms and rules) (grammar)	semantic processing (lexical knowledge) (words)
Adult L2 development		grammatical processing (grammar) semantic processing (lexical knowledge) (words)

Although Ullman's declarative/procedural model accounts principally for second language acquisition, it offers important insights into second language loss. First, as we saw in the previous section, knowledge stored in procedural memory is generally more resistant to loss than knowledge stored in declarative memory. Because neither second language grammar nor words rely on procedural memory, this kind of memory may play a limited role in second language development. Second, certain types of explicit knowledge supported by declarative memory are more resistant than others. Research indicates that length of time away from the second language does not affect attrition of lexical aspects, whereas it does affect attrition of grammar (de Bot & Hulsen, 2002). Specifically, second language words appear to be more resistant to loss than second language grammar. Third, evidence from people with brain damage to the language areas of the left cerebral hemisphere indicates that words with concrete referents, such as *house* or *book*, seem to be more resistant than abstract words; these kinds of words seem to create a richer semantic representation than abstract words that vary according to the context in which they are used (Saffran & Sholl, 1999). In summary, these findings suggest that, for adult second language learners, words—especially concrete words—may be more resistant to loss than grammar.

As we saw earlier, my memory of Danish grammar remained relatively intact, whereas words seemed inaccessible. This experience is consistent with languages learned in childhood. More precisely, the grammatical system of Danish was probably supported by procedural memory and was, therefore, more resistant to loss; Danish words were most likely supported by declarative memory and were more vulnerable. By contrast, a second language learned in adulthood will have different patterns of loss. In particular, loss of words and grammar for adult second language learners may be the inverse of what is apparent for a language (first or second language) learned in childhood.

In other words, although declarative memory is generally more vulnerable than procedural memory, and although both words and grammar learned later in life are supported by declarative memory systems, words and grammar are not equally vulnerable to loss. Table 3.3 illustrates different patterns of loss for words and grammar acquired during childhood and for words and grammar learned in adulthood.

TABLE 3.3 Model of L1 and L2 Loss

	Child L1/L2	Adult L2
Words	vulnerable to loss	resistant to loss
Grammar	resistant to loss	vulnerable to loss

This understanding of memory and language can serve as an important model for developing approaches to foreign language teaching that address language maintenance. Specifically, this model of second language loss predicts that words are more resistant to loss than grammar for adult second language learners. By extension, this model suggests that activities designed to promote language maintenance should concentrate principally on learning and using words. (In Chapter 4 we will focus on approaches to teaching second language that emphasize the importance of words and their role in the development of grammatical language.)

Current research indicating that "language is seen as a dynamic system, and language development, both acquisition and attrition, as a dynamic process" (de Bot, 2008, p. 166) underscores the fact that, like language development, language loss is a natural process. This constructive, developmental view challenges us to explore the connections between language development and language maintenance. Although this kind of thinking is still in its infancy, Ullman postulates that "because the functional and biological characteristics of the two memory systems are reasonably well understood, one should be able to predict how to manipulate them in order to improve the rate and ultimate proficiency levels of L2 learning. For example, one should be able to exploit the functional characteristics of declarative memory, such as promoting learning in rich semantic contexts" (Ullman, 2005, p. 160). This idea that foreign language teachers can exploit declarative memory by creating learning environments that are meaningful and context-rich suggests that strategies for promoting language maintenance are within our grasp.

→ YOUR VIEW 4

Find a person who studied one or two years of a second language several years ago. Interview the person to determine which features of the language he or she still remembers and those that seem to have faded away. Determine how you might create a profile of language loss for this person.

Accounting for diverse learners

Although second language learners vary widely (length and kind of exposure to the target language, attitude, motivation, general learning strategies, etc.), the typical foreign language classroom in the United States today is likely to include three kinds of students: (1) late second language learners who are beyond the sensitive period for language acquisition and who are encountering the target language for the first time, (2) multilingual learners who are encountering the target language for the first time but have some knowledge of other languages, and (3) **heritage learners** who have some knowledge of the target language from exposure to it through their family or community. Late language learners and other multilingual learners with no previous exposure to the target language may have somewhat predictable patterns of learning and loss. That is, grammar may be difficult to learn and highly vulnerable to loss, whereas words and short meaning-bearing phrases may be easier to learn and more resistant to loss. Among these diverse learners in a classroom, however, heritage learners may present the most complex challenge.[14] For example, a Chinese-American student whose parents and grandparents spoke Chinese in the home but who grew up speaking English with American peers will come to the Chinese language classroom with many different kinds of language memories. Likewise, a student with Spanish-speaking parents will have varying levels of proficiency in understanding, speaking, reading, and writing. Some heritage learners may have had full use of the target language at a young age and subsequently lost contact with it, whereas others may hear it spoken regularly in their families or communities but have little functional ability. Each of these learners will have had different language experiences and will come to the foreign language classroom with varying areas of proficiency and deficiency (Lacorte & Canabal, 2002).

To maximize the learning experiences of students with different language backgrounds, it is essential to determine when and how they acquired the target language, the level of competence they may have achieved, and the period of disuse. In addition, it is important to assess what kinds of knowledge are available for conscious recall (stored in declarative memory). For example, teachers can ask students to name objects and concepts in the target language to get a sense of what kinds of words they know. Although it may be relatively simple to ascertain what kinds of words students recognize and can use, assessing their knowledge of the grammatical system (stored in procedural memory) may be more challenging. Teachers can devise assessment tools to determine how well a student understands certain subtle features of the target language, such as the ability to identify major time frames (past, present, future) from oral input. Teachers may also want to evaluate a student's ability to read the target language. Above all, both teachers and students can benefit from an exploratory analysis of which features of language have been retained and which have been lost or do not exist.

Taking the time to construct detailed language profiles of all learners can be beneficial for supporting second language development as well as for promoting recovery of various features of the target language that a student may have forgotten. Understanding the wide range of language experiences among the learners in a classroom can help teachers and students alike develop an awareness and appreciation of diverse learners. This awareness can, in turn, promote successful second language users who are conscious of the ways their own individual language profiles play a role in their second language development and loss.

→ YOUR VIEW 5

Find a person who is a heritage learner in a foreign language class. Interview the person to determine what kind of contact he or she has had with the target language and over what period of time, and whether (and, if so, under what circumstances) he or she has lost touch with the language. Ask the person what features of the language he or she uses comfortably and which aspects of the language he or she controls less now than in the past, or perhaps not at all. Determine how you might create a profile of language acquisition and loss for this person.

Language maintenance and multicompetent second language learners

Learning a second language is not a linear process but rather a dynamic one that involves both progress and regression. As learners become familiar with new structures, previously learned ones may temporarily fade; language development involves a natural receding and resurgence of competencies. As Jessner (2003) notes, "neither language acquisition nor language attrition can adequately be understood if they are discussed as processes in isolation. . . . The two processes have to be seen as an integrated part of an evolving dynamic system, in other words language attrition is a function of language acquisition" (p. 242). Although there is relatively little research on how language attrition occurs (de Bot & Hulsen, 2002), this dynamic understanding of growth and decline sets the stage for exploring second language maintenance.

In Chapter 1 I argue that multicompetent second language learners have a growing awareness of issues related to second language learning and use. In the context of the current chapter, this awareness should be extended to include theories that account for the role of memory systems in second language development and loss. To that end, we must consider three important principles:

1. Multicompetent second language learners are aware of the role of memory in second language learning. Using Ullman's (2004, 2005), declarative/procedural model learners can explore the distinction between procedural and declarative memory systems in native and second language functioning. Furthermore, they can examine the idea that adult second language learners rely on declarative memory systems to process both words and grammar. This theory can shed light on the reasons that learning grammar in a classroom setting is not likely to result in the kind of automatic and natural access they have to native language grammar.

2. Multicompetent second language learners are aware that words are more re-sistant to loss than grammar. Using the model of language loss, learners can predict which features of the target language are most likely to be vulnerable to loss. They can examine the idea that words—especially concrete words—may create more robust memory traces than grammar. Furthermore, they can investigate the notion that learning words in semantically rich contexts is par-ticularly important. To illustrate this point, teachers and students can think about what happens when they learn verb conjugations. For example, learn-ing to conjugate the irregular French verb *faire* ("to make" or "to do") might not promote an understanding of what this verb means and how it is used in context. Instead, the conjugation (*je fais, tu fais, il/elle fait, nous faisons, vous faites, ils/elles font*) would probably become fixed in declarative memory in the same way as a song or days of the week. If, on the other hand, *faire* was learned in meaningful contexts with common expressions, such as *faire du ski* ("to go skiing") or *faire du jogging* ("to go jogging"), a learner would be more likely to internalize what it means and develop robust memory traces of this meaning. Although knowing a verb's conjugations can be useful, it may be counterproductive to learn it principally as a grammatical structure or paradigm. It is interesting to note that syntactical aspects of a word may be lost without the word itself being lost. For example, the *-ed* past tense mor-pheme in the word *jumped* may be lost, while the word *jump* may remain in memory. This idea underscores the importance of focusing on the meaning of words in context rather than on grammatical morphemes. Furthermore, because concrete words are more resistant to loss than abstract words, learn-ers should be encouraged to learn words—both concrete and abstract—in vivid, meaningful contexts to anchor them in memory.

3. Multicompetent second language learners are aware that the productive skills—speaking and writing—are more vulnerable to attrition than the re-ceptive skills—reading and oral comprehension (Oxford, 1982; Williamson, 1982). De Bot and Hulsen (2002) cite research indicating that receptive skills are not subject to attrition even after several years of disuse. In fact, they state that "listening and reading proficiency even increased significant-ly over time" (p. 259). It is important for learners to know that the ability to read in a second language remains nearly intact throughout life, whereas the ability to speak fades very quickly.

These three principles underscore the importance of learning about language development and loss as well as of developing strategies for language mainte-nance. Multicompetent learners have a growing awareness about language learning that enables them to reflect on the role of memory systems in second language development and loss, as well as to think about the kinds of learning activities that are likely to promote language maintenance. They are conscious that activities such as conjugating a verb, learning a grammar rule, or learning words in isolation are unlikely to support language maintenance. By the same token, they are aware that semantically rich input in meaningful contexts and activities that require them to use language to express personal meaning may contribute to memory traces that are less likely to fade. Finally, multicompetent learners recognize that focusing principally on developing oral proficiency may not promote language maintenance. By contrast, attention to developing literacy skills may have a significant effect on a person's ability to retain and use the second language throughout life.

→ YOUR VIEW 6

Drawing on what you have learned in this chapter, list the kinds of teaching strategies that might support second language maintenance.

Concluding Propositions

Proposition 3.1

Second language loss is a normal and natural occurrence.

Capturing the process of language loss would be as difficult as capturing the process of language development. The same variables that give rise to the wide variation in adult second language development are certainly at play in second language loss. As Jessner notes, "the question of what exactly is lost and when attrition starts is difficult to answer" (2003, p. 238). In fact, the term *loss* might not be suitable for describing this phenomenon. Rather, we might say that certain features of a second language erode over time and become unavailable.[15] Regardless of whether we describe the phenomenon as loss or attrition, the experience is certainly real and an integral part of second language development.

Many variables are at play in any consideration of language loss. Clearly, length of study, level of proficiency, attitude, and motivation are among the most important factors. We can also consider the degree to which different language skills (reading, writing, listening, speaking) are affected. Or, we can take into account linguistic features of the second language, such as phonology, morphology, the lexicon, and syntax. All of these variables are highly individual and preclude any fixed definition of second language attrition. Ultimately, however, second language loss is not a sign of failure on the part of a learner or a teacher; rather, it is a normal human occurrence.

Proposition 3.2

Words are more resistant to loss than grammar in second language learning.

For years after learning a second language in a classroom setting, people are able to recognize words. Although they may not be able to understand them when they hear them, they are able to recall the meanings of many words when they see them in writing. Grammar, on the other hand, is quite different. A person may be able to recite grammar rules that were learned in paradigms—such as verb conjugations or rules for forming the past tense—but using the rules spontaneously may prove to be a challenge. Understanding the role of declarative and procedural long-term memory systems in how people process their native and second languages can help to explain the difference between learning grammar and learning words, and can ultimately mitigate experiences of language loss.

In addition, there is clear evidence that learning a second language affects brain functioning. Research on brain activity of adult second language learners reveals that after 14 weeks of study learners can distinguish between target language words and pseudo words (McLaughlin, Osterhout, & Kim, 2004). These findings documenting changes in brain functioning, even after limited exposure to a second language, suggest that second language learning generates memory traces of conceptual learning. It stands to reason, therefore, that learners have memory traces from the second language that remain part of overall language functioning. Teaching strategies that capitalize on these memory traces will help learners at all levels of study maintain some level of functional ability in the second language.

Proposition 3.3

Multicompetent second language learners are aware of the relationship between language development and language loss.

In the final analysis, how we frame the issue of language loss—how we conceive of it and talk about it—may have an effect on the experience of loss. Rather than denying or overlooking the issue of second language attrition, foreign language teachers should acknowledge this natural dimension of second language learning. Moreover, instead of being a negative, or the flipside of language acquisition, attrition should be viewed as a cognitive phenomenon that is normal, natural, and worthy of consideration. Ultimately, students who are given opportunities to use their first language in the classroom to discuss the dynamic relationship between language learning and attrition become multicompetent learners who aspire to maintain their knowledge and use of a second language. As Jessner (2003) notes, "maintenance work in multilinguals . . . involves metalinguistic and monitoring processes in order to reduce interference as a processing phenomenon and to ensure a certain speed of recall of information among other aspects" (Jessner, 2003, p. 241). In other words, talking about language attrition can raise learners' awareness of the kinds of strategies they can use to promote language maintenance. Ultimately, this awareness fosters the development of multicompetent learners who recognize the role of memory in second language development, appreciate the diversity of language experiences, and are conscious of the value of learning activities that focus on building rich semantic knowledge.

Suggested Readings on Second-Language Acquisition and Loss

de Bot, K., Lowie, W., & Verspoor, M. (2005). *Second language acquisition: An advanced resource book.* New York: Routledge.

Ellis, R. (1994). *The study of second language acquisition.* New York: Oxford.

Fabbro, F. (1999). *The neurolinguistics of bilingualism: An introduction.* East Sussex, UK: Psychology Press, Ltd.

Lambert, R. D., & Freed, B. F. (Eds.). (1982). *The loss of language skills.* Rowley, MA: Newbury House.

Paradis, M. (2004). *A neurolinguistic theory of bilingualism.* Philadelphia: John Benjamins.

Sharwood Smith, M. A. (1989). Crosslinguistic influence in language loss. In K. Hyltenstam & L. K. Obler (Eds.), *Bilingualism across the lifespan* (pp. 185–201). Cambridge: Cambridge UP.

Weltens, B., & Grendel, M. (1993). Attrition of vocabulary knowledge. In Schreuder & B. Weltens (Eds.), *The bilingual lexicon* (pp. 135–156). Philadelphia: John Benjamins.

Researching Your Language Stories

1. Using the information you collected from *YOUR VIEW 4*, devise a questionnaire to assess the language attrition experiences of people who have studied a second language for two years or less.
   a. Give the questionnaire to at least five people. Compare their answers and determine whether or not there are patterns of language attrition.

[YOUR VIEW 4: Find a person who studied one or two years of a second language several years ago. Interview the person to determine which features of the language he or she still remembers and those that seem to have faded away. Determine how you might create a profile of language loss for this person.]

2. Using the information you collected from *YOUR VIEW 5*, devise a questionnaire to assess the language attrition experiences of heritage and multilingual learners.
   a. Give the questionnaire to at least five heritage learners of the same language e.g., Spanish) at the beginning of a course of study. Compare their answers and determine whether or not there are patterns of language attrition.
   b. Devise a follow-up questionnaire for these heritage learners after completing a course of study to determine which features of the target language were recovered and which features were new.

[YOUR VIEW 5: Find a person who is a heritage learner in a foreign language class. Interview the person to determine what kind of contact he or she had with the target language, how long he or she was exposed, and the circumstances under which he or she lost touch with the language. Ask the person what features of the language he or she still remembers and those that seem to have faded away. Determine how you might create a profile of language acquisition and loss for this person.]

Notes

1. *Skriftlig dansk* literally means "written Danish," or an elementary school equivalent of language arts.
2. The most infamous case of language deprivation is Genie, a 13-year-old girl discovered in California in 1970, who had been denied normal human interaction from a very early age. Various psycholinguists studied Genie's language development over a period of years and determined that she was able to learn words, but never mastered syntax. Information about this case can be found in a NOVA film entitled *Secret of the wild child* (PBS, airdate March 4, 1997), as well as on various Internet sites.
3. Pinker, whose work is inspired by that of his mentor, Chomsky, offers many insightful examples of creative child language in his book *The language instinct* (London: Penguin, 1994).
4. Because of the political situation in Russia during his life, Vygotsky (1896–1934) did not publish much of his work. His theories about the social origin of human mental functioning are currently enjoying much popularity in the Western world.
5. Theories about the ZPD are discussed in Vygotsky's work *Mind in society: The development of higher psychological processes*, translated and published in 1978 by Harvard University Press.
6. In discussing second language acquisition in children, Hyltenstam and Abrahamsson (2003, p. 574) state: "Although the cases of delayed L1 acquisition are very rare, they nevertheless give us a clear indication of how an already established L1 positively affects the acquisition of an L2."
7. Five new technologies are particularly useful in studying the language brain: (1) Dichotic listening tests examine what people hear and remember when different kinds of messages (words, water flowing, bird song, melodies) are sent to the right ear (processed by the left brain hemisphere) and the left ear (processed by the right brain hemisphere); (2) an electroencephalogram (EEG) records electrical activity of the brain during cognitive and language tasks; (3) positron emission tomography (PET) involves injecting slightly radioactive substances into the bloodstream to analyze how they are used by the brain as sources of energy during sensory-motor or cognitive tasks (the parts of the brain that are most activated during the tasks take up more of the radioactive substance); (4) functional magnetic resonance imaging (fMRI) records hemodynamic changes in blood oxygenation during cognitive tasks and is particularly sensitive to activation of cerebral structures during language tasks; (5) synthetic brain imaging (SBI) uses computer models to show activation of neurons (this technology is still in the exploratory stages; however, it has the potential to provide credible models for different types of cognitive functioning, including language).
8. Functional magnetic resonance imaging (fMRI) records hemodynamic changes in blood oxygenation during cognitive tasks and is particularly sensitive to activation of cerebral structures during language tasks.
9. Wartenburger et al. (2003) used brain imaging to study the effect of age of acquisition and proficiency level on neural correlates of grammatical and semantic judgments in bilinguals (Italian/German) who learned the second language at different ages and had different levels of proficiency. Their results suggest that age of acquisition "might have a greater impact on the cerebral correlates of grammatical processing than on semantic processing" (p. 167).
10. See also Kroll and Sunderman (2003) for an overview of research on the development of bilingual lexical and conceptual representations.

11. Paradis (2004) makes an important point about research on bilingualism when he argues that studies involving word retrieval cannot be generalized to language because words by themselves are not language.

12. An e-mail exchange with Michel Paradis confirmed my understanding that implicit memory is not involved in instructed L2, especially at the early stages of learning. Research is needed to explore the degree to which more proficient L2 learners demonstrate an increase in automatic execution that is similar to implicit memory processing.

13. Ullman (2005) makes a distinction between the terms explicit / implicit and declarative / procedural memory. For our purposes they are used interchangeably.

14. *Teaching heritage language learners* (Webb & Miller, 2000) includes several stories of students engaged in formal study of a language with which they have lost touch.

15. Hamers and Blanc (2000) give three reasons for language attrition: environmental attrition due to reduced use of a language, old-age attrition due to the aging process, and brain disease or injury.

CHAPTER 4

"I speak in nouns!"

OVERVIEW

Many people who learn a second language formally in a classroom or informally in a natural setting do not achieve advanced proficiency. As we saw in Chapter 3, various external and internal considerations can have an effect on second language development, and people differ widely in the features of language that they master as well as in ultimate attainment. Although foreign language teachers hope their students will develop at least functional competency in the target language, the hard fact is that most students abandon their study of the language after two or three years and subsequently forget much of what they learned. Interestingly, however, when people are faced with having to use the target language—even years later—they often manage to piece together words and short phrases in order to communicate. In fact, they may become increasingly adept at communicating, albeit in short, nongrammatical utterances. This kind of talk—what we might call tourist talk—is not generally recognized as real language because it is characterized by gaps in knowledge as well as by systematic and repeated errors.[1] It is, nevertheless, a mode of communication for many people in the world who have limited contact with people of another language group.

Learning goals for our students should be articulated in terms that encourage them to think of foreign language learning as a lifelong endeavor. To work toward this goal it is important to provide students with models of the target language that are recognizably native-like (Koike & Liskin-Gasparro, 2002) rather than models that exhibit limited proficiency. It would be equally important, however, for students to recognize that there is a wide range of ways people use second languages to achieve different purposes. In other words, attaining native-like proficiency in a second language is not the only way to measure success; people can experience success even when they have incomplete knowledge of the second language. In an effort to recognize the value of second language use characterized by limited proficiency, we will continue the discussion from Chapter 3 in which we outlined the differences between the ways words and grammar may be processed in the brain and, by extension, their role in adult second language development.

This chapter begins with a "Snapshot" of Sarah, an adult who studied French in college and visited France for the first time 25 years later. An examination of her use of French during daily interactions with native speakers illustrates that any definition of bilingual (or multilingual) functioning should be broadened to include the ability to use words and short utterances in the second language. Although sentence-length, grammatically accurate use of a second language clearly reflects bilingual ability, Sarah's less-than-proficient use of French demonstrates a kind of bilingual functioning that is based on her understanding of the nature of language combined with a capacity for learning new French words. In "Research Perspectives," an analysis of the role words may have played in the evolution of language, as well as a review of theories about how they are represented in the brain, helps explain why Sarah, like many adults, can learn and use words in a second language with relatively little difficulty. The idea that words may be the essential building blocks of language informs our understanding of their role in second language development. Moreover, this idea suggests that lexical knowledge may be more important than grammar in adult second language learning. In "Perspectives for the Classroom" we will explore the ways the research outlined in this chapter lays the foundation for a lexical approach to foreign language teaching that emphasizes the importance of words and short utterances. Building on perspectives outlined in the preceding chapters, we will broaden our definition of multicompetent second language learners to include awareness of the role of words and utterances in second language development. The "Concluding Propositions" underscore the idea that people can learn new words throughout their lifetime and that words and short utterances are the foundations of grammatical language.

SNAPSHOT

Several years ago I spent the summer in France with my friend Sarah. After four short weeks she felt comfortable in the noisy outdoor market, where she had become acquainted with many of the merchants. She knew which ones offered the best deals on fruits and vegetables, and she patronized them regularly. Going from stand to stand, she greeted them and made her purchases with confidence:

Bonjour madame. Olives, oui, bon, merci; pêches, quatre; les tomates s'il vous plaît. Merci madame. Combien?

[Hello madam. Olives, yes, good, thanks; peaches, four; tomatoes please. Thank you madam. How much?]

She took particular pleasure in going to the jewelry stand because the sales-woman seemed to enjoy talking to her. When Sarah wanted to buy necklaces for her three daughters, her French appeared hesitant, but spontaneous and assured:

Bonjour, ah. . . . Comment ça va? Um . . . je voudrais un bijou pour ma . . . um . . . ma fille dans Etats-Unis. Croix de Camargue, l'argent, une cœur petit (indicating neck). (Not satisfied with what the merchant shows her . . .) *Um . . . ah . . . autre chose. Exemple plus petit, s'il vous plaît.* (Merchant brings another necklace.) *Ah oui! Si parfait. Je voudrais trois pour ma . . . mon . . . trois filles . . . MES trois filles.* (Engages in small talk about the necklace.) *Ah . . . um . . . um . . . allez-vous à St. Tropez . . . à demain . . . demain?* (Merchant answers affirmatively.) *Où est chez nous?* (Merchant answers that she lives in St. Tropez.) *Allez-vous en vacances cet été? En août?* (Merchant answers in detail. Sarah listens to the merchant's long, chatty answer, nods to indicate she understands, and then returns to the purchase of the necklaces.) *Merci beaucoup. Très joli.* (Merchant asks about the ages of Sarah's daughters.) *Um . . . trois âges . . . vingt-six, um . . . vingt-trois, et dix-sept. Ma bébé est ici avec moi!* (Sarah beams triumphantly saying this final sentence. Then, she prepares to leave.) *Je vous voir dimanche . . . non, mardi?* (Merchant answers affirmatively.) *Au revoir. Merci beaucoup mon amie.*

[Hello, ah . . . how are you? Um . . . I would like a little jewel for my . . . um . . . my daughter in United States. Cross of Camargue, silver, a heart little (indicating neck). (Not satisfied with what the merchant shows her . . .) Um . . . ah . . . other thing. Example smaller, please. (Merchant brings another necklace.) Ah yes! So perfect. I would like three for my . . . my (incorrect singular masculine form) . . . three daughters . . . MY (correct plural form) three daughters. (Engages in small talk about the necklace.) Ah . . . um . . . um are you going to St. Tropez . . . until tomorrow . . . tomorrow? (Merchant answers affirmatively.) Where is our home? (Merchant answers that she lives in St. Tropez.) Are you going on vacation this summer? In August? (Merchant answers in detail. Sarah listens to the merchant's long, chatty answer, nods to indicate she understands, then returns to the purchase of the necklaces.) Thank you very much. Very pretty. (Merchant asks about the ages of Sarah's daughters.) Um . . . three ages . . . twenty-six . . . um twenty-three, and seventeen. My baby is here with me! I to see you Sunday . . . no, Tuesday? (Merchant answers affirmatively.) Good bye. Thank you very much my friend.]

I listened carefully to Sarah's interactions with the merchants. Two years of college French 25 years previously seemed to serve her well in the *marché*—she could engage in a naming activity that included a few polite interjections and many gestures. She used memorized phrases, such as "je voudrais" (I would like) and "s'il vous plaît" (please), and she corrected herself when she sensed she had made a mistake. Her speech was hesitant, filled with repetitions and reformulations, and was creatively interwoven with nonverbal cues. She used intonation to ask a question or negate something; she indicated confusion when she didn't understand; she listened carefully and reacted appropriately to what she did understand. Many of her utterances followed English grammar rules, such as "j'aime tomates" (I like tomatoes) rather than correct French syntax with the definite article, "j'aime *les* tomatoes." When she used a verb, it was generally in a simple, active, declarative, present-tense utterance. It was clear that when I (her French-teacher friend) accompanied her to the *marché*, she was a little self-conscious and monitored her speech more closely. For example, after tasting a sample of a ripe tomato offered to her, she exclaimed to the merchant "Tomates bons!" When I modeled the sentence correctly—"Les tomates sont *bonnes*"—Sarah responded dejectedly, but with humor, "Oh, tomatoes are females, huh?" Later, describing her French to me, Sarah said jokingly, "I speak in nouns!" Although I knew she made regular, tentative efforts to improve her proficiency, she generally accepted her limited French without shame.

→ YOUR VIEW 1

Find a person with limited ability in a second language gained principally through classroom exposure. Ask him or her to imagine being left alone at a market in the target culture. Ask the person to describe his or her feelings about the situation (fear, insecurity, confidence, etc.). Ask what resources (linguistic and any others) he or she might draw on for ordinary daily activities, such as buying food in a market, reserving a hotel room, asking about train or bus schedules, ordering a meal in a restaurant, and so forth.

RESEARCH PERSPECTIVES

Does Sarah speak French? Most of the rules that make language orderly and ensure communication are missing. Moreover, she is limited to the here-and-now concrete present by her language constraints. Sarah's claim that she speaks in nouns is generally true; her utterances in French have more nouns than other kinds of words because she mostly engages in a point-and-name kind of communication. Although she does use some other words—verbs, adjectives, pronouns, and formulaic expressions—her speech is generally characterized by a series of utterances comprised of no more than three or four words. By most pedagogical standards Sarah's limited mastery of French would be described as that of a novice speaker. Despite her low level of proficiency in French, however, she communicates successfully in several contexts. Foreign language teachers might acknowledge that many of their students—both current and former students—would speak like Sarah if put in that kind of situation; they would not be likely to claim, however, that this limited ability exemplifies the kind of second language functioning they would seek to foster. Nevertheless, this tourist language may represent a natural ability among adult second language learners that is normal, valid, and worthy of closer attention. As we saw in Chapter 3, adults who lose contact with a second language learned after the sensitive period may retain words but not grammar. To further explore this limited second language use among nonproficient adults, we will examine the nature of words, how they may have evolved in the history of human language, and how they are processed and stored in the brain.

What is a word?

We use thousands of words every day to describe events (buying tomatoes) and nonevents (enjoying eating tomatoes) without thinking about them. Yet, as Bickerton aptly notes, it is nearly impossible to define the word *word*:

> Were someone asked what a sentence was, the reply would almost certainly include something about words—that a sentence consisted of words strung together, or something of that sort. But when you think of words, what are they exactly? The word *word* seems to have some sort of intermediate existence between, on the one hand, very concrete terms like *table* and *chair* and, on the other, very abstract ones like *chore* and *nothing*. . . . Any word may appear in a variety of guises: as sound-waves between a mouth and an ear; as marks on a page; and—in some sense yet to be defined—as things we have in our brains. (Calvin & Bickerton, 2000, p. 13)

> A word is the combination of a mental representation of something, which may or may not exist in the real world, with a mental representation of a set of symbols (phonetic, orthographic, manual, etc.). What you utter are not words, but only the phonological representations of words. What you write are not words, only the orthographic representations of words. What you sign, if you know one of the sign languages of the deaf, are not words but only signed representations of words. (Calvin & Bickerton, 2000, p. 24)

Although any single definition remains elusive, most people would agree that words are arbitrary, symbolic signs with meanings that have been established by historical and cultural convention. For example, the words *dog*, *chien*, and *hund* are different signifiers (English, French, and Danish) that refer to a four-legged animal—three unrelated and arbitrary terms referring to the same animal. In brief, words serve to identify things and concepts.

To complicate things, however, different words play different roles. To identify these roles, linguists have organized words into categories. One such category is **open class words**, which includes nouns, verbs, adjectives, and adverbs; this class can be considered limitless in that new words are added continually. Another category is **closed class words**, which includes pronouns, prepositions, and conjunctions and other grammatical words; new words are rarely added to this class of words. Open and closed class words are also referred to as *content morphemes* and *function morphemes* to indicate the difference between words with a lexical (dictionary) meaning and words with grammatical meaning. There is no agreement regarding the distinction between content and function morphemes (Muysken, 1995),[2] in part because discourse markers (e.g., *because, so, well*) do not fit into either category. Nevertheless, the two terms serve to illustrate the naming function and grammatical function of words.

In addition to being described as simply having naming or grammatical functions, words are often defined in broader, more conceptual terms. For example, the expression "I would like a" may not be a string of individual words in the mind of the speaker, but rather a whole unit that represents a single communicative intention. Tomasello (2003) refers to multiple-word utterances as **holophrases** and believes that they can function as a single word-concept referring to one object or one event. Similarly, the term **lemma** can refer to a conceptual notion that goes beyond the boundary of a word:

> A lemma can be defined as a carrier of lexical-conceptual structure and an associated predicate-argument structure and concomitant morphological realization patterns. . . . They [lemmas] are not concrete; that is, they are not lexical items with subcategorization features. Rather, they support such items. In order for this to be so, what is their nature? Each one includes the specific bundling of semantic and pragmatic features that encodes the lexical-conceptual structures that represent the speaker's communicative intentions. (Myers-Scotton & Jake, 1995/2000, pp. 286–287)

In addition, the term **chunk** is used to refer to words or morphemes that are combined into a single unit as a result of frequent repetition (Bybee, 2002, p. 130). Similarly, the word **collocation** denotes sequences of words that often occur together (Gitsaki, 1999), such as *last night* or *make a decision*. These broader definitions may be more helpful in describing Sarah's speech as presented earlier. Rather than thinking of her language as speaking in nouns, we can say that she strings together an ever-growing number of open class (content) words interspersed with formulaic expressions, such as où est (where is) and s'il vous plaît (please). More specifically, we might describe her speech as short utterances containing a series of words, often occurring in intonation units or holophrases, and some occasional function words.

Although Sarah experiences success in the market, there is no question that her speech impedes her ability to engage in any kind of complex interactions. Bickerton (Calvin & Bickerton, 2000, p. 30) refers to this kind of language as "protolanguage"[3]—or language that is characterized by a few words (mostly nouns) strung together with little conformity to customary word order. Protolanguage, nearly devoid of grammatical words (articles, prepositions, conjunctions, etc.), is fraught with ambiguities and may make little sense when taken out of the context in which it occurred. Even though Sarah's speech appears to be a simple kind of naming activity and could be referred to as protolanguage, it typifies much adult second language use and contains the rudiments of bilingual functioning.

→ YOUR VIEW 2

Ask several people—teachers, students, and people outside the academic sphere—how they would define the word word. Identify two or three of the most common definitions and explain why they may be incomplete.

The evolution of words and grammar

The events that led to the emergence of language are mostly speculative. Because there is no such thing as a behavioral fossil record, there is little understanding of when or why our ancestors first began to use language. Some scholars believe that the evidence of a protolanguage is still present in chimps and children. Studies on language and cognition in chimpanzees (Gill, 1997; Savage-Rumbaugh, Shanker, & Taylor, 1998; Smillie, 1995; Tomasello & Call, 1997) demonstrate their ability to learn sign language and suggest that gesturing and signing may be the rudiments of modern human language. Research on child language development, with its characteristic progression from single-word utterances to increasingly complex grammatical language, supports the argument that child language contains basic elements of early human language (Halliday, 2004; Matthiesen, 2004). Smillie and Tomasello express similar views regarding the notion that language development in children (ontogenesis) is analogous to language development in the human species over evolutionary time (phylogenesis):

> Early developmental features of humans may give us some clues to immature traits that existed in earlier forms. In the case of language, where it is difficult to reconstruct the behavioral sequences of ancestral species, we may get a clue to paleolinguistic origins by a close examination of the earliest stages of language development in contemporary infants, although it must be added that such evidence can only be suggestive. The infant's first words are to a large extent referential in nature, indicating an interest in objects, events, situations that have relevance for social others. While infants do also develop, at an early stage of language acquisition, words that subserve social coordination functions such as greetings and requests, consistent with the pattern of animal communication . . . , they also show a strong propensity to name objects, particularly items capable of being manipulated. It is notable that the first linguistic expressions of the child reflect to a significant degree an orientation that would have been important in the lives of early tool users working together in a cooperative enterprise. (Smillie, 1995, p. 269)

> The actual events that led to the emergence of language historically are gone and can never be observed. But some of the processes that were at work in this evolutionary event are still at work in the ontogeny of language in young children. Much can be gained by looking at the processes in detail and by comparing them to those that might have occurred when language began. (Tomasello, 2002, p. 325)

When learning to communicate with people around them, young children, like chimps, use signals that refer mainly to content words standing for objects, actions, and qualities that occur in the external world (Aitchison, 1995). Unlike chimps, however, children progress from gesturing and naming concrete objects in their immediate surroundings to engaging in complex communicative interactions by age 4. The idea that this development may be an accelerated version of how human language evolved over millions of years becomes even more speculative when we try to account for the leap from words to grammatical language. Several theories attempt to explain what might have happened in the history of early humans to have made it necessary to connect words together in a predictable, rule-governed way. One such theory suggests that grammar may have developed as a social practice when early humans began to live in communities that depended on mutuality. One-word interactions may not have been sufficient when they no longer competed for food, and rule-governed language that could take temporal and spatial relations into account became necessary (Hildebrand-Nihlson, 1995).[4] In this kind of setting members of a community might share goods, engage in bartering, negotiate, plan events, and tell stories. Moreover, as Pinker (1994) suggests, social interactions of this nature are mediated by argument and persuasion and would have brought about dramatic advances in both cognitive and linguistic skills. Ultimately, this theory is founded on the idea that the social demands of early hominid communities would have required elaborate references to time and space that words alone did not permit.

Another theory about the development of grammatical language relates to the number of words that became part of the collection of words that speakers in a community used to communicate with each other. Li (2002) postulates that when the lexicon reached a critical mass it would have forced language use into simple word order with grammatical markers. That is, individuals would have spontaneously developed ways to sequence the increasing numbers of words into larger communicative units. He further suggests that grammar may have evolved over generations, beginning with a few word-order principles and grammatical markers and evolving into the kind of complex rules we see in contemporary language grammars. Similarly, Bybee (2002) hypothesizes that language may have evolved "from a set of relatively short utterances consisting of first one, then two units, to much longer utterances with apparent hierarchical structure via the concatenation of preformed chunks" (p. 131). These chunks may then have become increasingly elaborate and strung together in longer grammatical utterances.

In a slightly different vein, Liska (1995) proposes a theory for the development of grammar that she attributes to the evolution of sign capabilities among early hominids. She notes that there is general agreement that words are arbitrary symbols arranged according to a set of rules, generally called *syntax*. She further argues that syntax is also an arbitrary symbolic system and that a particular word order can be a symbol. In her view, syntax does not only reflect the order of events in reality, but is also a symbol that stands for a relationship among symbols. This argument suggests that language evolved as an increasingly symbolic behavior, developing from a set of concrete word-symbols to an increasingly complex arrangement of syntactic symbols.

Even though we know relatively little about how language came into being, both biological and cultural/historical theories offer insights. Pinker espouses a biological view, stating that "though we know few details about how the language instinct evolved, there is no reason to doubt that the principal explanation is the same as for any other complex instinct or organ, Darwin's theory of natural selection" (1994, p. 333). That is, evolution and natural selection account for the development of language just as for other complex biological traits in humans.[5] Bichakjian (1995), on the other hand, claims that "the facts will indeed suggest that languages can be seen as implements, which, like all other human implements, have evolved in time and can be found in space in various degrees of development" (p. 34).[6] Similarly, Tomasello (2003) argues that there was no biological adaptation for grammar:

> The human use of symbols is primary, with the most likely evolutionary scenario being that the human species evolved skills enabling the use of linguistic symbols phylogenetically. But the emergence of grammar is a cultural-historical affair—probably originating quite recently in human evolution—involving no additional genetic events concerning language per se (except possibly some vocal-auditory information-processing skills that contribute indirectly to grammaticalization processes). (p. 9)

Tomasello proposes that language, or grammar, emerged because of the evolutionary adaptation for understanding others as "intentional agents like the self" (2003, p. 40) and the subsequent desire to manipulate those intentional states. Burling (2005) shares the view that language and intelligence evolved as a means for dealing with other members of the community; however, he takes this argument a step further, proposing that language evolved by sexual selection rather than natural selection. In his view, natural selection produces "efficient survival machines" (p. 197), whereas sexual selection "leads to some of the most flamboyant products of evolution" (p. 197). Like the colorful feathers of the peacock, male hominids with particularly good and showy language skills (such as the ability to persuade, entertain, or speak or sing poetically) might have had better success in attracting females than those who used language simply for utilitarian purposes. This theory is particularly interesting because it suggests that language ability varied, and that highly effective speakers coexisted with lackluster speakers, with the former gaining gradual evolutionary advantage:

> This has to mean that, during the period when the ability to use increasingly complex language was evolving, individuals must have varied from one another in their inherited capacity for language. To attribute individual differences in language ability to genetic differences badly violates the egalitarian assumptions that linguists usually hold about language, but the capacity for language surely did evolve, and it could not have done so without a variable genetic base upon which selection could work. Heritable differences in linguistic ability must have contributed to varied reproductive success. (Burling, 2005, p. 185)

Burling notes that this argument may not be particularly popular because it suggests that variability in language ability persists among current humans. That is, if such things as the size of vocabulary that individuals were able to control or the complexity of grammatical detail they were able to manage varied and played a part in sexual selection, there is every reason to believe that these kinds of language advantages still play a role. Linguists today may shy away from these kinds of discussions because there are few, if any, credible criteria for describing good versus poor language skills. Most standardized tests implicitly privilege one language or one dialect over another and do not assess the rich complexity of language that might be used by less privileged members of any particular society.

Although disagreement persists about whether language is an innate capacity unique to humans or that it is a tool that became progressively more complex through natural or sexual selection, there is general agreement that it grew from a simple to a more complex symbolic system and that words preceded syntax. Burling sums up the issue as follows:

> It is well to remember, however, just what syntax is used for. It is needed to serve the lexicon. We use syntax to arrange our words in efficient and unambiguous ways and it would serve no purpose at all without words. For most ordinary speakers, if not for linguists, meaning is what language is all about, and while syntax certainly contributes to meaning, words do more. Because syntax needs words, while even single lonely words that have no syntax can easily convey meanings, words must have come first in the course of human evolution. (Burling, 2005, p. 19)

Over the course of centuries words and phrases were compressed and abbreviated causing a grammaticalization of language. Function words would have been invented (perhaps formed from content words) to serve various purposes, such as connecting two concepts, showing relationships of space and time, and indicating causation (Burling, 2005, pp. 174–175), and language would have gradually evolved from words into the grammatically complex system we know today.

Words and the brain

As language evolved over time, it surely changed human physiology. The larynx, vocal cords, tongue, and lips are under full neocortical control, making humans unique in the animal world and an evolutionary novelty:

> Even the seat of human language in the brain is special. The vocal calls of primates are controlled not by their cerebral cortex but by phylogenetically older neural structures in the brain stem and limbic system, structures that are heavily involved in emotion. Human vocalizations other than language, like sobbing, laughing, moaning, and shouting in pain, are also controlled subcortically. Subcortical structures even control the swearing that follows the arrival of a hammer on a thumb, that emerges as an involuntary tic in Tourette's syndrome, and that can survive as Broca's aphasics' only speech.

> Genuine language . . . is seated in the cerebral cortex, primarily the left perisylvian region. (Pinker, 1994, p. 334)

One of the many interesting features of human language is that words appear to represent multiple kinds of brain functioning. According to Pulvermüller, the "processing of words with strong associations to actions and that of words with strong visual associations appears to activate distinct sets of brain areas" (2002, p. 5). Research further suggests that nouns, generally associated with the names of objects, act as attentional cues and may activate the parts of the brain related to sensory and associative processing; verbs, on the other hand, are associated with manipulation tasks and actions performed by agents, and may activate the motor areas of the brain (Cangelosi & Domenico, 2004; Saffran & Sholl, 1999). There is even some indication that nouns may have evolved in the brain before verbs (Cangelosi & Domenico, 2004).[7] In general, it appears that semantic information is distributed over a number of brain areas and that certain kinds of information are localized in different areas of the cerebral cortex (Saffran & Sholl, 1999). Moreover, evidence suggests that there is considerable variation among individuals with regard to the localization of vocabulary and that several cortical areas are activated depending on the properties inherent in the word[8] (Bickerton, Calvin 2000 & Honjo, 1999).

Although there are individual differences in the way people acquire object concepts related to words (some people have direct experience with an object, whereas others may hear or read about it), there is some indication that the brain organizes words by semantic category. For example, fruits and dairy products might be organized in two distinct categories. In addition, it appears that words are organized based on how the objects they represent are perceived. For example, living things, such as fruits and animals, are thought to be perceived with the senses—shape, color, touch, or smell. On the other hand, inanimate objects, such as tools, are thought to be perceived visually for their functional or associative properties. Moreover, there is both behavioral and anatomical evidence that right hemisphere mechanisms seem to provide more support for concrete than for abstract words (Saffran & Sholl, 1999).

With regard to bilingual word processing, one of the central questions involves whether or not a person's first and second language words share one representational system or have two separate lexicons. Research on proficient early bilinguals suggests that there is one conceptual store, or one mental lexicon, and that lexical items are retrieved based on the information necessary to express the intended meaning (de Bot, 1992/2000). Studies also show that a bilingual person recognizes known words automatically and does not immediately distinguish what language the words are because the words are associated with their mental representations in a single conceptual store (Paradis, 2004). Proficient bilinguals, despite the age at which they acquired the second language, also appear to activate information about words in both languages regardless of the language they intend to use (Sunderman & Kroll, 2006). Brain imaging studies confirm that proficient bilinguals show little difference in brain activation for each language during object naming tasks (Hernandez et al., 2001). According to Paradis's direct access hypothesis, "a word in either language is perceived as a word, that is, a sound with corresponding meaning, irrespective of which language it belongs to" (2004, p. 203). There is also evidence that concrete words share more conceptual representations across languages than abstract words (de Groot, 1993; Kroll & Tokowicz, 2001). In all probability, abstract words have only partial meaning overlap because cultural contexts determine their meaning. Some researchers, on the other hand, argue that the notion of a single lexicon is simplistic and that bilinguals probably have two language networks that are both independent and interconnected (Grosjean, 1997/2000).

With regard to late second language learners with low proficiency, there is little consensus concerning whether or not words in the first and the second languages share a common representational system. Some researchers believe that the lexicons for first and second languages are distinct, represented by different processing systems, and are independently and separately accessed (Forster & Jiang, 2001). There is some sense, however, that second language learners go through a developmental shift as they increase proficiency (Kroll, 1993; Kroll & Tokowicz, 2001) and that patterns of cross-language influence change over time (Jarvis & Pavlenko, 2008; Sunderman & Kroll, 2006). In the early stages of language learning the meaning of second language words may not be accessed directly but rather through the first language (Hulstijn, 2001). In other words, the first language may act as a go-between until learners are able to conceptually mediate the second language directly. This idea that second language words are mapped onto first language words implicitly suggests that the adult learners rely on their existing conceptual system in the first language to learn words in a second language:

> Adults already possess a well-established conceptual and lexical system, and most L2 words have a correspondent concept and translation in the adult learner's first language (L1). Thus, there is little need for them to learn new concepts or meanings while learning L2 words, at least in the early stages of L2 acquisition. The lack of contextualized input and the presence of an existing conceptual and L1 system make adult L2 vocabulary acquisition fundamentally different from vocabulary acquisition in the L1. When children learn new words in their L1, they learn words and concepts at the same time. As a result, word form and meaning are often inseparable. Thus, when children or adults see a word in their L1, its meaning becomes available automatically. When people speak in their L1, the retrieval of lexical forms is usually spontaneous and effortless. In contrast, adult L2 vocabulary acquisition is accompanied by little conceptual or semantic development. Instead, the existing L1 linguistic and conceptual systems are actively involved in the L2 learning process. (Jiang, 2004, p. 417)

No one fully understands how adults learn and retrieve words in a second language; however, it is likely that first and second language words are both linked and independent. Although the similarities between two languages (e.g., French and English share more in common than Chinese and English), the learner's level of proficiency, and individual learning strategies may have an effect on word learning, both languages are likely to work in concert. Although it appears that the connection between second language words and their corresponding concepts strengthens with proficiency and that dependency on the first language decreases, there is evidence that both languages remain active in some way. Sunderman and Kroll cite evidence that attaining proficiency in a second language does not imply that "the individual has acquired the ability to switch off the influence of the L1" (2006, p. 388). Rather, the first language appears to play some role in both comprehension and production of words in a second language at all levels of proficiency.

What seems quite clear is that the brain is more sensitive to certain features of language during childhood. Native speakers of a language acquire the rhythm, intonation, sounds, and grammar of a language during the sensitive period for language acquisition. Words, on the other hand, can be learned at any age. According to Paradis (2004), the vocabulary, or the sound–meaning pairing of words, is conscious and subserved by declarative memory, which is not susceptible to the sensitive period.[9]

Given these theories about the evolution of language and how words are represented in the brain, it is possible to imagine that the sensitive period for learning grammar served as an important mechanism for determining community or tribal boundaries among early humans. If adult speakers of another language group sounded like outsiders, they could be recognized and would not be able to pass as insiders. On the other hand, because learning words is not sensitive to age it is also possible to imagine that under friendly circumstances an outsider would have been able to learn a sufficient number of words and utterances of another language to engage in bartering and other kinds of superficial exchanges. This scenario suggests that the brain may be naturally adapted for identifying foreigners and is not equipped to master a second language well enough to allow an outsider to sound like an insider. By extension, this notion suggests that many adults may have difficulty acquiring the syntax of a second language and that their functional ability—in particular their ability to speak—may remain limited to what we might describe as protolanguage.

→ YOUR VIEW 3

Read the following quotation from Judith F. Kroll and Gretchen Sunderman's 2003 article, "Cognitive Processes in Second Language Learners and Bilinguals: The Development of Lexical and Conceptual Representations." In this article they review research supporting the idea that in proficient bilinguals lexical and semantic information in the first language is activated during both comprehension and production in the second language. Analyze their view that skilled bilinguals and beginning bilinguals differ in their ability to control cross-linguistic word use. Do you think that using the first language in the classroom would help or hinder the development of cross-linguistic control?

"While evidence from psycholinguistic literature overwhelmingly suggests that words [from both the L1 and L2] are active simultaneously in the proficient bilingual, we know that it is not the case that skilled bilinguals often produce words in the "wrong" language. Therefore, . . . a regulatory mechanism must control cross-language competition in skilled bilinguals. However, we do know that beginning bilinguals in the second language classroom often produce words in the wrong language. The critical question then becomes how learners begin to modulate the cross-linguistic activation that is present in the system in a manner similar to proficient bilinguals, and why some learners are more successful at it than others.

There are many questions in second language pedagogy that could be answered by psycholinguistic research. For example, do certain learners struggle in communicative classrooms that use only the L2 because they fail to inhibit the L1 as easily as others? Is it the case that inhibition of cross-linguistic interference is a critical component of second language acquisition?" (pp. 123–124)

PERSPECTIVES FOR THE CLASSROOM

The preceding descriptions of how language may have evolved suggest that early humans, like modern children, used words before gradually developing grammatical language. Whether or not we agree that ontogeny recapitulates phylogeny with regard to language development, it is clear that children progress in stages from words and short utterances to complex syntax. If this sequence of development is true for children we might wonder if it is also characteristic of second language development in adults. In other words, do adult second language learners go through similar kinds of developmental phases as children learning their first language? Using the example of Sarah's interactions in the market, it is readily apparent that her French did not resemble child language; on the contrary, she relied fully on adult communicative strategies to make her purchases. The first indication that Sarah functioned as an adult language user was the way she processed the information she heard. For example, when a merchant gestured to a display of vegetables and said, "Les courgettes sont très bonnes aujourd'hui" (The zucchini squash are very good today), Sarah understood everything except the focal word *courgette*. She understood the merchant's intention clearly— namely, that something on the stand was very good and he wanted her to buy it. Making her confusion evident, she pointed to the leeks. "Ça?" (This?) When the merchant said, "Ça, c'est des poireaux" (Those are leeks), she knew the word *poireaux* was not in his initial utterance. Moreover, the merchant knew Sarah's French was limited and worked collaboratively to make his meaning clear by pointing directly at the zucchini and saying "les courgettes."[10] She was grateful ("ah! merci!") and ended up buying several zucchini. This guessing game may resemble childlike word learning; however, at the outset a young child does not have enough experience to know whether a word refers to an object, an action, or a quality. For example, if a child hears "dog" when a woman walks by with a small white poodle on a leash, the child could imagine that *dog* means a small, furry, four-legged thing, or the little wagging tail, or the whole phenomenon of a person walking a dog. As the child becomes increasingly aware of the nature of how language is used to describe the world and more and more capable of understanding the communicative intentions of her caregivers, she becomes progressively more skilled at identifying the object of a reference. According to Tomasello (2003) child language development is characterized by a growing awareness of both the pragmatic context of an utterance and the intention of the speaker. Adults do not need to go through this process because the sophisticated cognitive problem-solving capacities and the linguistic knowledge they bring to the second language learning task are very different from those of a child learning her native language. As Perdue notes, "the adult's knowledge of how information is organised in coherent discourse is immediately useful" (2002, p. 142). Moreover, adults have well-developed pragmatic routines, such as how to be polite or how to apologize, that can be very important when interacting with people of another language and culture. Therefore, despite the fact that Sarah uses words and short utterances like a child, she is clearly relying on adult native language competence to function in a second language.

Although we cannot compare Sarah's experiences using and learning French to what a child does acquiring her first language, the prevalence of words and short utterances is evident. In fact, Sarah's interactions with French-speaking people seem to help her learn new words and phrases and string then together in increasingly idiomatic ways. Furthermore, she does not appear to be attentive to the grammatical structure of her utterances. Rather, grammar words (e.g., articles, pronouns, conjunctions) and grammatical morphemes (e.g., tense and mood markers, masculine and feminine adjectival forms) are lexicalized and embedded in the multiword utterances that are part of her real-life interactions. In this section we will explore the ways that Sarah's untutored, somewhat spontaneous process of word learning represents a natural capacity for adult language learners. This ability to learn words and short utterances sets the stage for exploring an approach to foreign language teaching that focuses on the primacy of words. In the end I will propose that multicompetence includes an awareness of the role of words in second language development.

Words, grammar, and adult second language learners

As we saw in Chapter 3, there are age-related and neurological reasons to explain why adults find it difficult to learn grammar in a second language. Both behavioral and brain imaging studies provide evidence that there is a sensitive period for acquiring syntax in a second language; what is more, syntactic processing may be more sensitive to age of acquisition than semantic processing (Fabbro, 1999; Hernandez et al., 2001; Paradis, 2004; Patkowski, 1982; Ullman, 2004, 2005; Wartenburger et al., 2003). In a discussion of why the brain has difficulty with syntax later in life, Hyltenstam and Abrahamsson (2003, p. 562) cite substantial research showing that the areas of the brain that sequence phonemes, syllables, and words are highly functional early in life but become increasingly inefficient with age; a person's age, on the other hand, has less effect on semantics and pragmatics. Indeed, they find it remarkable that adults actually do experience success in learning the grammar of a second language:

> Given that maturation has [a] strong influence on second language acquisition, it should come as no surprise that nativelike proficiency in a second language is unattainable. More surprising . . . are the miraculous levels of proficiency that second language learners (at all ages) in fact *can* reach, despite the constraints that are imposed by our biological scheduling. (Hyltenstam & Abrahamsson, 2003, p. 578)

Some linguists discount the idea that innate predispositions for language acquisition wither at some point after the onset of puberty. For example, Krashen (1982b) believes that adults can acquire a second language in adulthood, arguing that Chomsky's (1965) language acquisition device (LAD) does not shut off or degenerate after a certain age. He believes the LAD, triggered by comprehensible input, can account for adult second language acquisition if affective factors, such as anxiety and low motivation, do not prohibit its functioning. Following this same line of thinking, Herschensohn argues that, regardless of age, adults can learn grammar in a second language:

> The biological engine that spontaneously operates in child language invention runs low on fuel in the teen years; it must be primed with instruction and maintained with organized input to allow it to acquire a fairly complete grammar. There is a critical age after which adults cannot acquire language involuntarily or completely, but that does not mean that they are incapable of acquiring an L2 grammar altogether. In fact, quite to the contrary, it is clearly possible to acquire an L2 after the Critical Period, and to acquire it well. This is the important point for linguists to explain, not the so-called failure of L2A [second language acquisition], quite easily attributable to non-linguistic factors. Unlike sensitive period phenomena that have strict temporal limits after which further reorganization is impossible, language acquisition allows temporal extension once the original learning (L1A) has been established. It is never too late to learn another language, it is simply more difficult, given post-pubescent disincentives such as lack of motivation, acculturation, and free time. (pp. 52–53)

Clearly, some adults can overcome disincentives related to motivation and attitude and learn a second language. Nevertheless, the neurological evidence that processing grammar and processing words are based on two different systems suggests that it is by and large easier for adults to learn words than to learn grammar.

Although it may take less effort to learn words than grammar, words by themselves do not constitute language; to communicate even simply, adult second language learners need to be able to sequence words in meaningful ways. Returning for a moment to Sarah's interactions in the market, it is evident that she was learning new words and utterances with relative ease. Even more interesting, however, was that using these new words and utterances seemed to elicit grammatical language. In fact, learning words and grammar appeared to be part of a single process. For example, after she learned the word *courgette* (zucchini) and had heard the merchant tell her "les courgettes sont très bonnes" (the zucchini are very good), she spontaneously said, "Je voudrais les courgettes, s'il vous plaît . . . les courgettes sont bonnes" (I would like the zucchini, please . . . the zucchini are good) during a subsequent trip to the market. This utterance contained four memorized chunks: *je voudrais / les courgettes / s'il vous plaît / les courgettes sont bonnes*. Rather than relying on grammar rules governing tense or word order, she was putting together a series of familiar words and utterances that appeared to become increasingly refined, accurate, and complex with use. This example supports Tomasello's (2003) usage-based theory positing that language structure emerges from language use and that "learning words and learning grammar are really all a part of the same developmental process" (p. 42). He views linguistic competence "not in terms of possession of a formal mastery of semantically empty rules, but rather in terms of the mastery of a structured inventory of meaningful linguistic constructions" (2003, p. 99). Although Tomasello was referring to first language acquisition, this theory is entirely plausible with regard to second language learning. Not only does it capitalize on adult second language learners' natural capacity to learn words, but also advances an understanding of grammatical language that emerges from word use rather than from learning rules.

This view of language learning is supported by Savage-Rumbaugh and Rumbaugh (1993), whose studies of apes learning language led them to conclude that human language is founded on the notion that syntax is a skill that arises naturally from the need to process sequences of words. Even though apes and children learning their first language are unlike adults learning a second language, it is logical to imagine that when learners want to express complex ideas that require several words, they learn the ways that groups of words are related to other words and how to avoid repetition and redundancy. Syntax serves a communicative purpose and solves these problems. Similarly, Herschensohn proposes a theory of constructionism in which second language grammar acquisition can be accounted for through a "systematic integration of morpholexical constructions that provide the scaffolding for the L2 syntax" (2000, p. 223).[11] That is to say, constructions made up of words carrying both lexical and grammatical meaning are joined together in organized ways that supply a structure for the second language. Sarah's use of words and phrases exemplify this understanding of how grammar can emerge spontaneously from language use.

→ **YOUR VIEW 4**

Interview several teachers who teach elementary-, intermediate-, and advanced-level foreign language students to determine how they feel about teaching grammar. Do they think learning grammar is difficult for their students? If so, why? How do they assess their students' feelings about learning grammar? To what degree do they consider teaching grammar to be a central part of their responsibility?

A lexical approach to second language learning

For many teachers and learners, learning a second language in a classroom is primarily about learning grammar. Moreover, most methodological approaches concentrate on teaching students how to decode and construct grammatically accurate sentences.[12] N. C. Ellis suggests that a focus on grammar can be short-sighted because grammatical language is not necessarily idiomatic or accept-able, whereas learning words and word sequences may serve a critical role in developing correct usage of a second language. To illustrate his point he gives an example of a grammatically correct but awkward sentence in English: "Your marrying me is desired by me" (2001, p. 45); a more appropriate idiomatic sen-tence would be "I want to marry you." Ellis offers this example as support for the importance of learning words and groups of words that occur together: "Speaking natively is speaking idiomatically, using frequent and familiar collo-cations, and learners thus have to acquire these familiar word sequences" (N.C. Ellis, 2001, p. 45). Given this notion, as well as the idea that words can elicit grammatical language, it stands to reason that foreign language teachers should adopt an approach in which learning words takes precedence over learning grammar.

The idea of a lexical approach to foreign language teaching is certainly not new. Richards and Rodgers (2001) list the lexical approach among several "alternative approaches and methods" (p. v) and note both its potential value and its limitations:

> The status of lexis in language teaching has been considerably enhanced by developments in lexical and linguistic theory, by work in corpus analysis, and by recognition of the role of multiword units in language learning and communication. . . . It remains to be convinc-ingly demonstrated how a lexically based theory of language and lan-guage learning can be applied at the levels of design and procedure in language teaching, suggesting that it is still an idea in search of an approach and a methodology. (p. 138)

Although Richards and Rodgers's argument regarding the limitations of a purely lexical approach may be valid, there is no question that foreign language teachers (and the profession in general) need to develop an awareness of the role of words and collocations in the acquisition of grammar. As Gitsaki notes, the excessive focus on syntax in second language acquisition research has obscured the degree to which the "acquisition of collocations plays a major role in the acquisition of grammar" (1999, p. xviii).

Adopting a lexical approach poses challenges in part because learners in a foreign language classroom do not have constant and ready access to large quantities of the target language. Even though most teachers make efforts to simulate real-life situations, the classroom remains a formal, mostly structured learning environment. Nevertheless, **input** and **interaction**—two fundamental principles of current classroom teaching practice—can maximize learners' opportunities to learn and use words and phrases. Clearly, these two principles are not new; second language acquisition research has been assessing the ways input and interaction contribute to language proficiency for several decades. In the context of a lexical approach, however, input and interaction take on a somewhat different meaning.

With regard to input, Krashen (1981, 1982a, 1985) may have been the first to emphasize its importance, proposing that comprehensible input was essential for second language acquisition. Since then, much research has been devoted to exploring the role of input. Of particular interest is VanPatten's (1996, 2007) input processing theory, which proposes, in part, that learners focus most of their attention on content words rather than on subtle grammatical cues to understand meaning. Based on research exploring what learners attend to when processing input, VanPatten proposes a primacy of content words principle, which states that "learners process content words in the input before anything else" (2007, p. 117), and a lexical preference principle, which states that "learners will process lexical items for meaning before grammatical forms when they both encode the same information" (2007, p. 118). The following sentence illustrates the point that words carry more meaning than grammar:

> Yesterday Ann went to the movies.

The word *yesterday* makes the past tense (in this case of the verb *go*) redundant and therefore not essential to understanding the meaning of the sentence; the word *movies* is a place people go for entertainment, so the words *to the* are also superfluous. Ultimately, "yesterday Ann movies" communicates the same information as "yesterday Ann went to the movies." Rather than endorsing a lexical approach, however, VanPatten's input processing theory supports an approach to teaching grammar that is based on eliminating redundant words in a sentence to guide learners to focus on the grammatical morphemes that convey meaning (Lee & VanPatten, 2003; VanPatten, 1996, 2007; Wong, 2004). If, for example, the word *yesterday* were intentionally omitted from the sentence above, and learners were asked to determine when Ann went to the movies, they would have to focus on the past-tense *went* to understand that the event took place in the past. A lexical approach, on the other hand, would capitalize on learners' natural tendency to focus on redundant lexical information to understand the meaning of what they hear. In other words, rather than stripping meaning-bearing words away to intentionally force learners' attention on grammatical morphemes, a lexical approach would flood input with meaningful, redundant words and collocations.

Hulstijn cites research that supports the role of input for learning vocabulary. He notes that the kinds of oral and written tasks related to classroom language learning "require learners to process words elaborately and repeatedly" (2001, p. 272). He also points out that extensive reading is likely to contribute to incidental vocabulary learning. Abundant oral and written input with all of its naturally occurring redundancies allows learners in the classroom to hear and see words in their varying collocations and structural forms. Moreover, pedagogical approaches that focus on this kind of lexically rich input are likely to help students develop an increasing awareness of how words work together, thereby promoting the emergence of grammatical language.

Like input, interaction has been widely researched to assess its role in developing second language competence. In general, research has focused on the interaction between teachers and students, as well as between and among students (Antón, 1999; Atkinson, 2002; Blyth, 2002; Brooks & Donato, 1994; Gass, 1997; Pica, 1987, 1994; Pica, Young, & Doughty, 1987). These perspectives support the notion that interaction, regardless of the level of proficiency of the learners, promotes collaborative, meaning-based communication that leads to improved overall proficiency. In a description of how children learn their first language, Tomasello (2003) argues that the communicative act involves three elements: two interlocutors and the object of discussion. According to his theory, the communicative act revolves around a referent (an object, event, or idea) and involves directing attention and determining the intention of a speaker. He claims that this triadic interaction promotes children's use of short, communicative, and nonredundant utterances. Tomasello's notion about how children learn language in a triadic fashion has important applications to the second language learning context. Using Sarah as an example, we note that she engaged primarily in three-way communication involving herself, the merchant, and an object that served to direct her attention toward a thing (for example, *une courgette*) or an idea (such as where the jewelry merchant lived). Sarah's principal task was to direct the attention of her interlocutor and to determine his intention. During these interactions, her utterances were generally short and nonredundant. In a classroom setting, we might imagine a similar kind of interaction. For example, a teacher might refer to a movie and ask, "Do you want to see this movie tomorrow or next week?" A natural answer to this question would be "tomorrow" or "next week" rather than a complete, redundant sentence, such as "I want to see this movie tomorrow/next week." Although a one-word answer is not a complete, grammatical sentence, it is correct, appropriate, and wholly focused on the exchange of meaning. There is every reason to believe that this kind of interaction, which relies on the capacity to direct attention and understand intention, will become gradually more complex, especially when the subject (or object) of the triadic interaction becomes more interesting or compelling.

Another important consideration in a lexical approach involves the role that repetition plays in learning words and utterances. Although oral practice has traditionally been associated with the audiolingual method, research indicates that repeating and rehearsing new words and short phrases helps consolidate them in long-term memory (N. C. Ellis, 2001; Hulstijn, 2001). In the same way that repeating a new phone number aloud several times may help a person remember it, repeating and rehearsing the phonemes and syllables that make up a word or utterance promotes its retention in long-term memory. Moreover, the phoneme chunks and prosodic patterns of the second language become increasingly familiar through repetition. In a classroom setting, teaching strategies that encourage repetition of words and phrases can serve to reinforce a learner's ability to recall and use them. It is worth noting that rehearsing phrases that contain words in naturally occurring collocations would be more beneficial that focusing on individual isolated words.

To summarize, a lexical approach to foreign language teaching does not mean focusing uniquely on teaching vocabulary. Rather, in this context a lexical approach stresses the importance of input and interaction while capitalizing on the natural abilities of adult second language learners to perceive the ways words occur in patterns and how they function in face-to-face interaction. Such an approach involves four principal features:

1. Learners should be immersed in target language input that is filled with redundant lexical cues. Instead of stripping sentences of essential information or focusing on grammatical nuances, input should be highly contextualized and contain meaningful words and phrases.
2. Learners should have ample opportunities to repeat new words and phrases in varying combinations. Although oral/choral repetition may be associated with the audiolingual method, research confirms that it has an important effect on learning and recalling words.
3. Learners should be offered opportunities to engage in triadic (speaker-object/idea-speaker) rather than only dyadic (speaker-speaker) interactions so that a tangible referent is available as they try to understand the intention of the speaker. Even when discussing abstract ideas or concepts, having some kind of visual support (e.g., pictures, graphics, film clips) is beneficial.
4. Learners should be encouraged to express themselves in meaningful utterances rather than in grammatically accurate sentences. Although grammar and accuracy are ultimately important for full, proficient second language use, they should not be the central focus in oral production, especially in the earlier stages of the learning experience.

It is important to note that syntax is critical to real communication because it allows for the complex intricacies of language that enable people to develop similar cognitive structures without having shared experiences (Gyori, 1995). However, it is equally important to recognize that second language learners have a well-developed syntax in their first language that allows them to understand intuitively how language functions. Second language learners know that language is more than words and that real human communication involves more than naming objects. If they want to express complex ideas in the second language, they will be motivated to use their natural abilities to learn words and form progressively complex utterances. Finally, expecting adult second language learners to learn empty grammar rules is counterproductive, and maybe even unnatural; learning words and short utterances are the first steps to learning grammar.

Words and multicompetent second language learners

The idea that Sarah used her native language competence to learn and function in a second language exemplifies Cook's (1992, 2002a) notion of multicompetence. That is, she had the resources of two languages—her well-developed knowledge of English combined with her developing understanding of French—readily available, and she exploited all resources necessary to achieve her purposes. In particular, her native language competence helped her understand how people use words to communicate in face-to-face exchanges. She knew intuitively that words identify and describe things and that they can be linked together in short utterances. Moreover, she was probably aware (maybe even hyperaware) of what she was saying and was planning what she would say next. This kind of awareness is likely to promote and sustain successful functioning in a second language, especially among novice speakers.

As we have seen in the preceding chapters, a central characteristic of multicompetent second language learners is awareness of various features of second language development and use. This idea that awareness influences—and maybe even accelerates—second language learning (Herdina & Jessner, 2002) is particularly relevant with regard to learning and using words and collocations. Although there is considerable research on strategies for learning and teaching vocabulary, our intent here is to explore ways to foster learners' awareness about the role of words in second language development.

First, and above all, learners need to understand that people have the capacity to learn words for the rest of their lives; there seems to be no limit to the number of words a person can learn, both for passive recognition and active use. Although it can feel like a daunting task, learning words is part of what people do in their native language all the time. Moreover, learning synonyms in one's native language is not a radically different process from learning words in a second language. For example, when Sarah learned the French word *courgette* it was like learning a synonym for the English word *zucchini*. Learning *courgette* was, therefore, like adding any other word to her vocabulary. Even though it might take time for this new word to become part of her active vocabulary, with repeated exposure in a meaningful context she would be increasingly able to recall it and use it spontaneously. Whereas learning concrete words like *courgette* is like learning synonyms in one's native language, learning abstract words can pose a greater challenge because they rarely have a one-to-one correspondent.

For instance, if we imagine that Sarah wanted to describe the food she buys in the market as healthy (or healthful), she would quickly realize that healthy cannot be translated verbatim into French. Although *sain* is the first dictionary definition for healthy, the noun *santé* is more appropriate for expressing her meaning. More precisely, *santé* often co-occurs with other words in phrases, such *bon pour la santé* to describe something that is good for one's health (such as food) and *en bonne santé* to describe a healthy person. To express her meaning, therefore, Sarah would have to explore the nuances of what she wanted to say and rely on input and interaction with proficient speakers to guide her understanding and use of the word or expression. Learning abstract words in a second language involves recognizing that meaning is often veiled in linguistic and cultural conventions. Regardless of the kind of words they are trying to learn, the most important thing second language learners should understand is that people are able to learn countless numbers of words—regardless of language—throughout their lifetime.

In addition to exploring the nature of words and what it means to learn words in a second language, learners can be guided to consider the ways that words can stimulate grammatical language. In particular, they should be made aware that repeating and rehearsing new words and collocations in meaningful contexts and using them in interactions with teachers or peers can foster the ability to connect words and phrases in increasingly longer sequences with growing ease. By engaging in these kinds of activities and examining their effect on their own second language development, learners may perceive advantages of a lexical approach to second language learning that privileges words and phrases over empty grammar rules.

Finally, as we have said in previous chapters, promoting awareness about language and language learning is not typically included among foreign language classroom activities. Likewise, talking about words and collocations and their role in second language development is not generally part of the foreign language learning experience. Furthermore, these kinds of discussions would have to be conducted in the native language, especially for students in lower-level courses. Rather than being tangential, however, these discussions are likely to contribute to the kind of language awareness that is characteristic of multicompetent second language learners. In the previous chapters we determined that multicompetent second language learners have an awareness of the role of both first and second languages in bilingual functioning and a growing understanding that words are more resistant to loss than grammar; in this chapter we have broadened that understanding to include an awareness of the role that words and collocations play in second language learning and use.

→ YOUR VIEW 6

Interview second language learners at several different levels of proficiency to determine how they feel about learning vocabulary and grammar. Which do they consider more difficult? Why? Which do they consider more useful? Why?

Concluding Propositions

Proposition 4.1

People learn words in a second language with relative ease.

Listening to Sarah in the French market was remarkable mostly because it was not exceptional. Her utterances and interactions with the merchants were typical for a person her age and with her limited knowledge of French. She relied on natural adult language-learning strategies—namely, an ability to learn the words she saw and heard. She was able to name objects in her immediate surroundings and made references to people and events that were not present. There seemed to be no limit to the numbers of words and expressions she could learn. Although Sarah would have considered learning French grammar a challenge, she felt comfortable learning more words and expressions and was increasingly ready to navigate unfamiliar situations.

Like Sarah, students in a classroom setting are equipped to learn vast numbers of words. At the early stages of language learning, they are likely to rely heavily on words in their first language to process and retrieve words in the second language. Rather than try to avoid using the first language, students should explore their individual strategies for remembering new words in the second language. Moreover, it can be helpful to know that learning new words in a second language is not essentially different from learning new words in one's own language. Ultimately, students can benefit from understanding that their two languages can work in collaboration to increase their vocabulary in the second language.

Proposition 4.2

Words and short utterances are natural and normal in second language production.

In his well-known book, *The Language Instinct* (1994), Steven Pinker makes an important point about language functioning: "The languages of children, pidgin speakers, immigrants, tourists, aphasics, telegrams, and headlines show that there is a vast continuum of viable language systems varying in efficiency and expressive power." (p. 366). Although no one would want to suggest that second language learners (or teachers) should be satisfied with ungrammatical speech that is characterized by disconnected words and utterances, recognizing that there is genuine language functioning all along a continuum is essential. Words, short utterances, and full sentences are all valid kinds of speech. Moreover, learners demonstrate wide variability in their progress toward mastering a second language, and most adult learners attain a limited level of proficiency. Rather than describe success entirely in terms of grammatical accuracy, second language competence should take into account the number and variety of words and utterances in a learner's repertoire. In addition, the degree to which learners can comprehend grammatical language should carry as much weight as how much they can produce. Above all, it is essential to recognize that single- and multiple-word utterances, formulaic phrases, and appropriate collocations are the first indicators of grammatical speech.

Proposition 4.3

Multicompetent second language learners understand the role of words and short utterances in second language development.

Second language learners and teachers are often overly focused on grammar. Learning about the nature of words and exploring the ways that people learn many kinds of words throughout life can contribute to an understanding of the advantages of a lexical approach to second language learning. Furthermore, rather than conceiving of grammar as a symbolic system that must be learned explicitly, learners can imagine it as emerging gradually as more and more words and expressions become part of their vocabulary. Given oral and written input that is meaningful and contextualized, and given the opportunity to engage in triadic communication (speaker-object/idea-speaker), learners will try to understand the intention of others and respond appropriately. As learners communicate in the target language, they will produce short, often ungrammatical utterances made up of words and series of words. With time, and as communication necessitates, these utterances will be strung together to make increasingly complex utterances. In addition, being aware of this process can influence and accelerate it. Ultimately, multicompetence includes a growing awareness of the role of words in second language development.

Suggested Readings on the Evolution and Biology of Language

Bickerton, D. (1990). *Language and species.* Chicago: University of Chicago Press.

Briscoe, T. (2002). *Linguistic evolution through language acquisition.* New York: Cambridge UP.

Burling, R. (2005). *The talking ape.* New York: Oxford UP.

Givón, T., & Bertram F. (Eds.). (2002). *The evolution of language out of pre-language.* Philadelphia: John Benjamins.

Jackendoff, R. (2002). *Foundations of language: Brain, meaning, grammar, evolution.* New York: Oxford UP.

Pinker, S. (2007). *The language instinct.* New York: Harper Perennial Classics. (Original work published 1994. London: Penguin.

Puppel, S. (Ed.). (1995). *The biology of language.* Philadelphia: John Benjamins.

Tomasello, M. (2003). *Constructing a language: A usage-based theory of language acquisition.* Cambridge, MA: Harvard UP.

Researching Your Language Stories

1. Using the information that you got in *YOUR VIEW 4* and *YOUR VIEW 5*, design a questionnaire to assess whether teachers consider grammar or vocabulary more important for second language development.
   a. Give the questionnaire to several teachers who teach at different levels. Analyze and compare their answers.
   b. Observe the classes of the teachers who completed the questionnaire to determine if their answers correspond to your assessment from the observations. If possible, videotape the class session and analyze the teacher's talk to assess whether it emphasizes grammar over vocabulary, or vice versa, or neither.

[*YOUR VIEW 4: Interview several teachers who teach elementary-, intermediate-, and advanced-level foreign language students to determine how they feel about teaching grammar. Do they think learning grammar is difficult for their students? If so, why? How do they assess their students' feelings about learning grammar? To what degree do they consider teaching grammar to be a central part of their responsibility?*]

[*YOUR VIEW 5: Interview several teachers who teach all levels of language and literature to determine how they feel about teaching vocabulary. To what degree do they consider vocabulary to be an important part of second language learning? How do they assess their students' feelings about learning vocabulary? Do they consider grammar or vocabulary more important to the development of overall proficiency?*]

2. Using the information you collected from *YOUR VIEW 6*, devise a questionnaire to assess students' attitudes about learning vocabulary and grammar.
   a. Give the questionnaire to at least five students who are beginners, five students who are at the intermediate level, and five students who are in upper-level classes. Compare their answers to determine if level of proficiency changes their perceptions.
   b. Ask the five beginning-level students to meet with you individually. Make two vocabulary lists of eight items each on two separate sheets of paper. One list should include eight short phrases or collocations; the other list should include the same words but listed singly. (See the example below.) Make sure the items are unfamiliar to the students. Ask them which list would be easier to learn and why.

Sample Vocabulary Lists

Collocations	Individual Words
eat dinner	dinner
eat breakfast	to eat
take a bath	bath
take a shower	to take
go to bed	bed
go to work	to go

[YOUR VIEW 6: Interview second language learners at several different levels of proficiency to determine how they feel about learning vocabulary and grammar. Which do they consider more difficult? Why? Which do they consider more useful? Why?]

Notes

1. The speech of people who make repeated, systematic errors is often described as fossilized. The term *fossilization* refers to errors that become an enduring part of a speaker's interlanguage.
2. Muysken (1995) argues that no valid criterion has been established for distinguishing content morphemes and function morphemes. He suggests that there are at least four different possible criteria: (1) open (nouns and verbs) versus closed (pronouns) words; (2) words that are, or are not, paradigmatically organized—such as definite-indefinite or singular-plural; (3) the role words play in structuring a clause—central vs. peripheral; and (4) bound versus free morphemes.
3. In Calvin and Bickerton (2000), Bickerton describes pidgins as protolanguages and differentiates them from creole languages; pidgins are incomplete languages used by adults (often immigrants) trying to communicate in a second language, whereas creoles are fully grammatical languages spontaneously generated by the children of parents who spoke pidgin and containing elements of both languages. It is worth noting that Halliday uses the term *protolanguage* to describe child language development, defining it as "a systematic semiotic resource that develops before the mother tongue" (2004, p. 16).
4. Burling (2005, p. 17) cites evolutionary psychologists who support the idea that language evolved when early hominids needed it for social interaction.
5. Pinker's (1994) theories about language evolution are inspired by Chomsky's (1957, 1965) theories arguing that human beings are born with a language acquisition device, or an innate capacity to acquire language.
6. Bichakjian further believes that the Prague School (and particularly Jakobson) set linguistics on a distinctly essentialist track by arguing that "languages did not evolve . . . they had an essence which underwent a cycle of changes" (1995, p. 38).
7. Cangelosi and Domenico (2004) did a study to show how SBI (synthetic brain imaging) can provide credible models for different types of cognitive functioning, including language. They found that the left temporal neocortex plays a crucial role in lexical–semantic tasks related to the processing of nouns, whereas the processing of words related to actions (verbs) involves additional regions of the left dorsolateral prefrontal cortex. Their simulated studies provide some indication that nouns evolved in the brain before verbs.
8. According to Honjo (1999, p. 59), "Wernicke estimated the area that performs the semantic processing of language to be the posterior part of the left superior temporal gyrus near the angular gyrus. However, our PET [positron-emission tomography] studies suggested that this localization varies considerably among individuals. These results indicate that the dictionary of auditory language is distributed in a wide area in the left temporal lobe and that the perception of the meaning of language is accomplished by communication among these distant cortical areas."
9. See Chapter 3 for additional information on the sensitive period for language acquisition.

10. The merchant's goodwill clearly contributed to this positive and helpful interaction. Visitors to another culture cannot count on this kind of collaborative exchange with native speakers; cultures vary widely in their responsiveness to outsiders.

11. Herschensohn (2000) uses this argument to support the notion that universal grammar (UG) is available for second language acquisition.

12. Although the foreign language methods texts most often used, such as Hadley (2001), Shrum and Glisan (2005), and Lee and VanPatten (2003), do not talk explicitly about teaching grammar, their approaches are designed to promote increasing grammatical accuracy in the second language.

CHAPTER 5

"Eat, Ate, Eaten; Go, Went, Gone . . ."

OVERVIEW

Grammar may be one of the thorniest topics in foreign language teaching. Some teachers love thinking and talking about it, whereas others try to avoid it. Similarly, some students find it easy to learn the rules of a second language and enjoy tests that focus on grammatical accuracy, whereas others cringe at the thought of having to learn formulaic rules of any kind. At the heart of the issue, however, is not who likes grammar but rather how we conceive of grammar. If grammar is viewed as a set of static rules, both teachers and learners will go about the learning task with a particular goal in mind. If, on the other hand, grammar is viewed as emerging through use, the pedagogical implications would be quite different. In the end, the way grammar is viewed and taught can have a profound effect on second language development.

In Chapter 4 we reviewed the role of words and short utterances in the development of grammatical language, lending credence to the notion that teaching grammar rules devoid of meaningful content does not promote second language development. In this chapter, the "Snapshot" of Julien, a young French exchange student, exemplifies the experience of many second language learners who are able to recite rules of grammar effortlessly and yet are unable to apply them. Julien had mastered the present, past, and past perfect forms of vast numbers of English verbs, but this knowledge seemed to actually interfere with his ability to use the words in communication. The example of Julien is not used to suggest that grammar has no role in second language development. Quite the contrary, grammar has a critical role to play in moving learners along a continuum from words and short utterances to increasingly complex language that allows them to engage in higher order thinking and to share information about objects, events, and ideas. Grammar is essential to second language development, but rather than think of words and grammar as distinct orders of phenomena, we will consider them as being one integrated stratum within the linguistic system (Halliday, 2004).

In "Research Perspectives" we will further our understanding of how to deal with the challenges posed by grammar in the foreign language classroom by examining various definitions of grammar. Specifically, we will review learning theories of the 20th century that have guided pedagogical approaches and will explore current thinking about the role of grammar in second language teaching and learning. As we will see in "Perspectives for the Classroom," these theories and research challenge us to explore the implications of the notion that grammar is dynamic and emergent; they also challenge us to rethink pedagogical goals that are founded principally on developing grammatical accuracy in oral and written communication. The "Concluding Propositions" underscore the importance of teaching grammar in ways that foster the development of multicompetent second language learners.

SNAPSHOT

When our children were in their teens, we decided to host a 16-year-old French boy for six weeks during the summer. Very soon after Julien arrived, it became apparent that he would have significant challenges communicating in English. Although we all tried to engage him in conversation, he said very little. When asked if he ever spoke English at home in France, Julien shook his head, "No, . . . my mother . . . she want . . . she wants . . . I learn English." His answer was hesitant and awkward. To avoid putting him on the spot, we often made light conversation. Although Julien was usually silent, I realized he listened attentively and seemed to understand most of what we said. When I asked him what he had learned in English classes at school, he answered somewhat confidently, "verbs . . . *eat, ate, eaten* . . . *go, went, gone.*" We picked up on this topic of conversation and asked him if he could do that with more verbs. He claimed to know them all; when we quizzed him—*jump, run, laugh, find, cook*—he never missed one. Julien even knew the trickiest ones, such as *sing, sang, sung* and *bring, brought, brought,* reciting them like a recording. During the six weeks of Julien's stay, there was not a verb that tripped him up. By the end of his visit he was able to use words and short phrases like *let's go, whatever,* and *your turn,* but reciting verb forms remained everyone's favorite pastime.

Although Julien was mostly uninterested in giving me specific information about his English classes at school, he told me that classroom activities centered mainly on reviewing the homework for the day. He remembered having reading assignments about everyday life (in England), such as family, school, travel, and so forth. In class students worked on the vocabulary in the readings to clarify the meaning of the text and talked briefly about the topic. He said that the majority of class time was spent doing grammar exercises. When I asked what kinds of grammar exercises, he reported memorizing various rules and charts in his book and filling in blanks. He also remembered doing many translation exercises, both from French to English and vice versa.

Julien clearly had good memories of his English class and recalled that his teacher had visited the United States and loved American culture. In fact, Julien said he had the best teacher in his high school; however, this appreciation seemed personal rather than related to his teacher's ability to teach English. Above all, Julien knew that his teacher wanted his students to do well on the English portion of the national French exam, the *baccalauréat* that students take at the end of high school. To prepare for the written parts of the exam, the students worked hard on their English composition skills. The teacher told them that the best preparation for the oral portion of the English exam was to spend time in an English-speaking country. Julien was a good student, and following his teacher's advice, he signed up to spend the summer with us through the sister cities exchange program.

Thinking back on this experience with Julien, I remember being favorably impressed by his genuine interest in wanting to learn English. I also remember thinking he had many obstacles to overcome if he hoped to become a proficient speaker of English. I was never sure whether Julien was a poor language learner or simply a product of a teaching approach that (perhaps unintentionally) focused on knowing about English rather that knowing how to use English. When talking to a French colleague about Julien, she hardly hesitated before making the following statement about foreign language teaching in France: "J'avoue que pour aimer l'anglais il fallait vraiment en vouloir car tout ça manquait d'originalité et explique le mauvais niveau d'anglais de bien des français" (I have to admit that in order to like English one had to really want to work at it because the whole thing lacked in originality and explains the poor level of proficiency of many French people).[1] Although I have no interest in reinforcing any stereotypes about foreign language learning in France (in fact, many teachers there have begun to explore different approaches), I do think this remark sums up the relationship between teaching and learning a foreign language. That is, good students may be thwarted by a particular pedagogical approach and only through great effort be able to move beyond saying "go, went, gone." The story of Julien is common and not particular to the French educational setting. Students everywhere have similar experiences. If the story has a moral, it is that teaching matters.

→ YOUR VIEW 1

Find a student who has just returned from a study abroad experience. Ask or him or her to recall the first extended conversation he or she had alone with someone in the target culture. Try to assess what aspects of the interaction were most daunting: Comprehension? Speaking? Ask what aspects of the target language were easiest to recall and use and which were more difficult during that interaction. Finally, ask him or her which aspects of the second language improved most during the visit: Comprehension? Speaking? Reading? Writing? Grammar? Vocabulary? Cultural understanding?

RESEARCH PERSPECTIVES

Did Julien speak English? Clearly, English verb forms were well established in his long-term declarative memory[2] and were readily available for conscious recall. Moreover, conversations with him revealed that he was able to explain many rules of English grammar, that he could conjugate verbs in various tenses, and that he could list function words, such as subject pronouns (*I, you, he, she, it, we, you, they*), possessive adjectives (*mine, yours, his, hers, ours, yours, theirs*), and so forth. Although he had learned many lists and rules, he had great difficulty accessing these rules for spontaneous use. Knowing about English did not make Julien able to use English; most of the words and phrases that make language a tool for social interaction were missing in Julien's English repertoire.

This disassociation between knowing about a second language and being able to use it is a common experience for adult second language learners. The ensuing frustration not only discourages learners but often renders them silent, as described in the following account:

> In six years of high school and college Spanish, I rarely spoke a sentence outside my own language. I sat in the back corner of classrooms with my chin down, trying to memorize verbs. I struggled to learn the imperfect, the passive, the pluperfect, and the conjugations my teacher tried to explain by drawing a shoe on the chalkboard. These forms meant nothing more to me than flash cards and quizzes. They kept me silent. (Singer, 2004, p. 10)

Singer goes on to describe her experience teaching English as a second language in Costa Rica when a dove flew into her classroom window and died. She fully recognized her limitations in Spanish when she wanted to talk to her young students about this event: "I froze, trying to think of words to talk about death in a language that was not mine." What Singer had learned in her Spanish class was of little use to her when she and her young students stared down at the lifeless body of a gray bird gone astray.

Frustrations such as those described by Singer are familiar to most second language learners. Anyone who has spent time studying a second language in a classroom has felt the nearly physical sensation of being able to understand what has been said in the target language, but also the inability to formulate even a simple response. In other words, learners often experience a disconnection between what they know about the language and what they can actually do with the new language. Some applied linguists have used Chomsky's (1965) terms **linguistic competence**, or knowledge of the language system, and **linguistic performance**, or external evidence of language competence, or production to describe this phenomenon.[3] Although Chomsky used these terms to describe competence and performance in a person's native language, the terms have been used to explain the phenomenon in second language learning. Another way of characterizing this sense of disconnection between knowing and doing in a second language is Larsen-Freeman's (2003) notion of the inert knowledge problem:

> Knowledge that is gained in (formal lessons in) the classroom remains inactive or inert when put into service (in communication within and) outside the classroom. Students can recall the grammar rules when they are asked to do so but will not use them spontaneously in communication, even when they are relevant. (p. 8)

These terms describing the very real distinction between what a person knows and what he can do are essential to our thinking about the role of grammar in second language learning. So as to further our understanding of this problem of inert knowledge, we will explore definitions of grammar and the learning theories—both past and present—that have guided our thinking about how to teach grammar.

What is grammar?

Grammar is a common word, used regularly by people who talk about language. If asked, however, most people are unable to explain precisely what grammar is. In fact, any single definition of this word remains elusive. Taken in its broadest sense, we can say that grammar is the systematic account of the patterns of a language, including everything from its sounds to the arrangement of words in a sentence. Grammar is also generally distinguished from the lexicon, or the words in a language that can be found in a dictionary. Beyond this very broad definition, however, the word *grammar* is appropriated by different groups of people to describe a particular way they want to talk about language, and there is no single definition that people can agree on:

> Students, instructors, teacher trainers, and linguists all use the word "grammar," but they usually are referring to a range of concepts and constructs. Linguists even use the terms differently among themselves, depending on whether they consider their research to be theoretical or applied and whether their approaches and analyses are based in cognitive/psychological or syntactic/pragmatic frameworks. As a consequence, people often end up talking about dissimilar issues using comparable terminology, thus dooming discussions about grammar from the onset. (Katz & Blyth, 2008, p. 4).

In an effort to explain why discussions about grammar among foreign language teachers can be problematic, Katz and Blyth (2008) identify three different types of grammars: **prescriptive grammars**, or the standard and accepted rules for correct use of a particular language; **academic grammars**, used by linguists to describe the technical aspects of language, such as phonology, morphology, and syntax; and **pedagogical grammars**, or grammar books written for students. We might also make a contrast between prescriptive grammars that explain the rules of language in their idealized state and **descriptive grammars** that describe how people actually use language. Clearly these various kinds of grammars are designed for different audiences and have different purposes.

In addition to being difficult to define, the very nature of grammar is a subject for debate. For some, grammar may be viewed as a body of knowledge that can be learned and mastered. Foreign language teachers are often trained to think of grammar in these terms and to place great value on learning and practicing formal rules presented in textbooks or other pedagogical materials. Others may consider grammar as a dynamic system that develops organically through use rather than as a static subject to be learned. Although this view is relatively new, research exploring second language development as a dynamic process (de Bot, 2008; de Bot, Verspoor & Lowie, 2007; Herdina & Jessner, 2002; Jarvis & Pavlenko, 2008) is attracting increasing attention among applied linguists and foreign language teachers. Of particular interest is Larsen-Freeman's (2003) definition of grammar as a dynamic process rather than as a static product:

> One of my goals . . . was to deconstruct the conception of grammar as a static product that consists of forms that are rule governed, sentence-level, absolute, and constitute a closed system. I have suggested that, by viewing it solely this way, we have overlooked important qualities of grammar, such as that it is a dynamic process in which forms have meanings and uses in a rational, discursive, flexible, interconnected, and open system. (p. 142)

Ultimately, rather than describe grammar as something a person knows, she maintains that it is something a person does.

→ YOUR VIEW 2

Ask several people—students, teachers, and others—to define the word grammar. What experiences or knowledge informed their understanding of this word? Determine the similarities and differences in their definitions.

A historical view of approaches to teaching grammar

Some applied linguists argue that a teaching method may have limited effect on learning or that good learners are good learners despite the approach. The way grammar is taught in the foreign language classroom, however, may result in distinct ways of understanding grammar and using it meaningfully. During the past century in the United States, research in education and cognitive psychology has given rise to four fundamental theories about the nature of learning: learning as memorization, learning as habit formation, learning as a cognitive process, and learning as intersubjective activity. A review of these general learning theories underscores the degree to which they have influenced approaches to foreign language teaching in general and, by extension, the teaching of grammar.

The view of learning as memorization prevailed during the first half of the 20th century when educators believed that the mind was like a muscle that benefited from mental exercise. Although the Modern Language Association was founded in 1883, the study of modern foreign languages during that time was rare and students principally learned to read and translate Latin and Greek. This approach to teaching, called the grammar translation method, involved having students memorize grammar rules and learn poems and other texts by heart.[4] As the study of French and German gradually became popular during the first decades of the 20th century, teachers used the same approach as with classical languages.[5] That is, the focus of instruction was on grammar, and the primary goal of modern foreign language study was to read literary texts and to translate them into English. Although some teachers used the target language in the classroom—commonly referred to as the direct method—most teachers taught about the second language in English. Speaking the language was not among the main goals of study, largely because most American students had few opportunities to interact with people of other language groups. This approach resulted in a passive, although potentially extensive, knowledge of the target-language grammar.

In the post-World War II era behaviorist psychology gained increasing attention and gave rise to the view of learning as habit formation.[6] According to this view, learning was observable behavior shaped primarily by external conditions. The image often associated with this theory is that of a rat in a lab setting who learns to push a particular lever after being repeatedly rewarded with a food pellet. Studies of rats and other lab animals suggested that specific behaviors were learned by repeated stimulus and reward. This view of learning had a dramatic influence on classroom foreign language teaching, shifting the focus to rote oral practice and correction. This approach, called the audiolingual method (ALM), is often associated with the language laboratory, in which students could sit in sound-proofed cubicles listening and repeating audiotaped dialogues.[7] One of the hallmark features of the ALM was the use of drills to practice specific grammatical structures. Teachers were taught that drills,[8] or oral exercises, helped students internalize grammar rules. Rivers (1981) defined the purpose of oral drills as follows:

> The purpose of the drill is to concentrate the attention of the student on one structural problem at a time and to provide them with steady practice in handling this problem in various lexical contexts, without requiring them to focus attention on other details of the sequence. (p. 101)

In designing drills, teachers were to keep several fundamental principles in mind: Drills should be conducted orally/chorally until students are responding readily and accurately; they should be devoted to one specific structural pattern that has already been encountered; both the cue and the response should be in the foreign language; the cue should elicit only the desired response; each utterance should be short and complete; and drills should consist of eight to ten cue-response items. Table 5.1 gives examples of different kinds of drills designed to practice grammatical structures.

TABLE 5.1 Examples of Pattern Drills for Different Grammatical Structures

Replacement drill (object pronoun practice)

Teacher: I see the book.	Students: I see it.
Teacher: I see the woman.	Students: I see her.
Teacher: I see the men.	Students: I see them.

Transformation drill (negation practice)

Teacher: I am going to the airport.	Students: I am not going to the airport.
Teacher: I am going to the pharmacy.	Students: I am not going to the pharmacy.

Transformation drill (tense practice)

Teacher: I am going to the airport.	Students: I went to the airport.
Teacher: I am going to the pharmacy.	Students: I went to the pharmacy.

Restatement drill (imperative practice)

Teacher: Tell Mary to drink milk.	Students: Drink milk, Mary.
Teacher: Tell Jack to sit down.	Students: Sit down, Jack.

Restatement drill (interrogative practice)

Teacher: Ask me if Mary is here.	Students: Is Mary here?
Teacher: Ask me if Jack and Mary are here.	Students: Are Jack and Mary here?

Integration drill (relative pronoun practice)

Teacher: There is the dog. I love that dog.	Students: There is the dog that I love.
Teacher: There is the dress. I love that dress.	Students: There is the dress that I love.

(Examples based on Rivers, 1981, ch. 4)

Although there was widespread endorsement of this behaviorist approach for several decades, its popularity waned when foreign language teachers realized that it did not promote overall improvement of grammatically accurate speech. Although students were often able to recite memorized patterns with a good degree of accuracy, they were generally unable to use those grammatical structures in spontaneous, unstructured, meaningful interactions. In the end, the idea that learning grammar could be achieved through rote practice and memorization was proven to be limited in its scope.

Behaviorist notions about language learning faced serious challenges as teachers and scholars encountered Chomsky's linguistic theories,[9] giving rise to views of learning as a cognitive process. In simple terms, Chomsky did not believe that children learn or are taught their first language. He claimed that the unique and creative utterances of a young child could not possibly result from the often ungrammatical and incomplete language they hear. This argument, generally referred to as the poverty of the stimulus, proposed that complex cognitive functioning far exceeds behaviorist notions of conditioning and reward. Chomsky founded this argument on two theories: the existence of a **universal grammar** (UG), or the notion that all languages have similar fundamental principles and that individual languages each have specific parameters and grammatical rules, and of a **language acquisition device** (LAD), or the idea that every human is born with an innate ability to learn language. Although Chomsky's theories did not address second language learning, they revolutionized general thinking on the subject. Applied linguists began to wonder how a person learns the grammar of a second language if, as Chomsky suggested, language learning is a spontaneous cognitive process that takes place within the learner and not as a result of external stimuli. Specifically, linguists questioned whether the LAD remains operative for second language learning and, if so, whether learners can access UG.

These kinds of questions prompted research that focused on a cognitive understanding of second language learning. When Krashen published *Principles and Practice in Second Language Acquisition* in 1982, several of Chomsky's theories were articulated in terms that applied to the foreign language teaching/learning setting. In particular, the five hypotheses of his **monitor model** provoked debates that affected second language research and teaching. This model, summarized in Table 5.2, proposed that language acquisition occurs spontaneously and represents real language—as opposed to language learning that involves a conscious, rule-governed process[10]—that comprehensible input in the target language is essential to acquisition, and that learners acquire best when they have a positive attitude and are not anxious.

These five hypotheses gave rise to debates about how people learn grammar in a second language. Krashen's claims that language acquisition is a spontaneous and natural process that represents "real" language called into question the validity of language learning that involves conscious study of grammar rules. Research on the effectiveness of naturalistic (or implicit) versus instructed (explicit) grammar-teaching strategies in a classroom setting suggests that explicit attention to grammar produces measurable short-term results

TABLE 5.2 The Five Hypotheses of Krashen's Monitor Model

H1: Language acquisition and language learning are two different processes.

H2: Grammar is acquired in a predictable order in a natural setting.

H3: Learning functions only as an editor or monitor.

H4: Comprehensible input is essential for acquisition.

H5: Acquisition occurs when affective conditions are optimal.

(Scott, 1989, 1990) and can engage learners in thinking about grammar as a meaningful communication tool (Toth, 2004). Overall, most experimental studies that compare learning grammar under implicit and explicit conditions show a distinct advantage for the latter (Sanz & Morgan-Short, 2005). Nevertheless, the idea that language learning involves innate cognitive strategies continues to have a profound influence on the way grammar is taught. Teachers strive to create acquisition-rich classrooms in which students are exposed to as much comprehensible input as possible. In addition, they make every effort to speak exclusively in the target language, to avoid excessive explicit grammar instruction, and to devise activities that foster intrinsic motivation. Although many teachers endorse this view of language learning, some applied linguists consider it reductionist because cognition is viewed as a solitary process taking place within an autonomous language learning organism. In their view, this intrasubjective view disregards the role of external factors and underscores the validity of an internal bank of linguistic knowledge that may not have a direct connection to language performance (Atkinson, 2002).

The notion that learning a second language is an individual activity that involves innate cognitive skills faced criticism toward the end of the 20th century. In particular, the discovery of Vygotsky's (1962, 1978) work gave rise to an understanding of learning as intersubjective interaction, or as a process involving interaction between two or more people and not uniquely within an individual learner. Although Vygotsky was a developmental psychologist who died in the Soviet Union in 1934, his work has gradually attracted attention among psychologists and educators around the world. As in the case of Chomsky, Vygotsky's interest in children's cognitive development was applied to other disciplines, including second language learning.

Two theories proposed by Vygotsky are especially pertinent to considerations of how people learn a second language. The first is his notion that full cognitive development requires social interaction and that the range of skill a child develops with adult guidance or peer collaboration exceeds what can be attained alone. That is, he believed that a child's mental faculties develop as a result of his interaction with others. This understanding, referred to as the zone of proximal development, is based on the notion that there is a gap between a learner's current or actual level of development and a learner's emerging or potential level of development.

> In formulating the concept of the ZPD, Vygotsky was critical of psychological and educational practices which assess development and guide educational intervention solely on the basis of the level of individual, independent functioning. Instead, he insisted that two developmental levels of the individual must be taken into account: the actual developmental level, "established as a result of certain already completed developmental cycles," and the level of potential development, the level at which the individual functions with assistance from, or in collaboration with, more experienced members of society. . . . Specifically, then, the ZPD is "the distance between the

actual developmental level as determined by independent problem solving and the level of potential development as determined through problem solving under adult guidance or in collaboration with more capable peers." (Aljaafreh & Lantolf, 1994, pp. 465–483)

Second, Vygotsky believed that language is used to organize, manage, and alter mental activity. Rather than consider language as a vehicle for facilitating thoughts that are already present, he believed that language changes the flow and structure of mental functions. He described a particular kind of language—inner speech—that is evident when a person confronts a difficult cognitive, emotional, or social task. Aljaafreh and Lantolf (1994) summarize Vygotsky's views regarding the critical role of inner speech during a child's development:

> According to Vygotsky, the ontogenesis of mental functions is captured in the *genetic law of cultural development* as follows: "every function in the child's cultural development appears twice: first, on the social level, and later, on the individual level; first between people (inter-psychological), and then inside the child (intra-psychological)." Central to the evolution of external, or social, functions into internal, or mental, functions is the process of *internalization*, or more properly for sociocultural theory, *appropriation*. (p. 467)

In simpler terms, Vygotsky proposed that inner speech, or communication with the self, serves to mediate mental behavior and to solve problems for both children and adults.

These two ideas underscored the importance of classroom interaction in the target language—between and among learners, between teachers and learners, and within individual learners—for the development of grammatical language. Consequently, the benefits of talking to peers and to the teacher constitute essential elements of current approaches in the foreign language classroom. According to Brooks and Donato, "a Vygotskyan approach views speaking as the very instrument that simultaneously constitutes and constructs learners' interactions in the target language with respect to the target language itself, the task as it is presented and understood by the participants, the goal learners set for completing tasks, and their orientation to the task and to each other" (1994, p. 264). This understanding of second language learning views thinking and speaking as inseparable cognitive functions, suggesting that the learner and his linguistic tools must be viewed as a whole. It is worth noting that these Vygotskyan theories also underscore the importance of problem-solving activities as central components of classroom interactions. Research on the role of interaction among learners (Brooks & Donato 1994; Swain & Lapkin 1998), task-based activities (R. Ellis, 2003; Lee, 2000), and information-gap activities (Lee & VanPatten, 2003) has contributed to our understanding of the ways that learning grammar can be fostered through collaborative work among learners.

In summary, three of these learning theories—behaviorist, cognitivist, and sociocultural—have influenced the ways grammar is taught in the foreign language classroom. In many ways they continue to inform our thinking about the role of grammar in second language learning. However, rather than view these theories as manifestations of a swinging pendulum, with each one as a re-action to its predecessor, it is more useful to think of them as "a major river, constantly flowing, fed by many sources of water." (Mitchell & Vidal, 2001, p. 27)

→ YOUR VIEW 3

Review the basic principles of behaviorist, cognitivist, and sociocultural theories. Think back to your language-learning experiences and analyze which theory or theories guided the approach used by your teacher(s). List the aspects of each of these theories that you would like to include in your approach to teaching.

Current theories about the role of grammar in second language learning

During the past 50 years grammar has evolved from being the primary object of teaching and learning to being considered a natural result of input and interaction. This evolution in the role of grammar in the classroom has resulted from the changes in theories about learning in general as well as from applied linguists' interest in understanding the degree to which formal grammar instruction promotes second language learning. Studies of explicit and implicit grammar-teaching strategies (Scott, 1989, 1990; Terrell, 1991) have sought to compare the effectiveness of formal instruction with more naturalistic, immersion-like exposure to grammatical structures. Although the results of these studies suggest that explicit grammar-teaching strategies are more effective, the studies are limited because they focus on specific grammatical structures and only assess short-term learning conditions. In addition, explicit approaches to teaching grammar have generally been teacher centered and have involved either deductive or inductive presentations. **Deductive grammar teaching** entails moving from the statement of the rule to its application in an example; **inductive grammar teaching** involves moving from examples containing the targeted grammar structure to a formulation of the rule. Studies of traditional explicit approaches that focus primarily on linguistic forms have shown these approaches to be generally ineffective:

> In sum, research on traditional language teaching indicates that traditional language learners lack fluency; do not mentally represent their second language knowledge as explicit metalinguistic rules; do not learn what is taught and, if sometimes they do, later abandon the form in favor of another; and truly learn only what they are developmentally ready for. All in all, because traditional language teaching isolates linguistic form, provides no opportunities for the

development of fluency, misconstrues the notion of complexity, and ignores the existence and ordering of natural acquisition processes, it has not been an effective way to promote language acquisition. (Doughty, 1998, pp. 133–134)

Similarly, research suggests that implicit approaches that are communicative and input-based may not provide learners with enough guidance to acquire problematic elements of grammar (Katz & Blyth, 2008).

The advent of communicative approaches to language teaching in the 1980s and 1990s, which are still in favor today, renewed the debate regarding the role of grammar instruction. Initially based on Canale and Swain's (1980) model of communicative competence, communicative language teaching (henceforth CLT) de-emphasized the role of grammar in second language learning, relegating it to one of four principal competencies: grammatical competence (mastery of linguistic code), sociolinguistic competence (knowledge of social and cultural rules), discourse competence (ability to connect sentences coherently), and strategic competence (ability to use verbal and nonverbal communication strategies). Although the communicative competence model served as the theoretical foundation for CLT, and underscored the importance of thinking of communication as more than simply grammatical accuracy, it remained elusive to many foreign language teachers. In an effort to offer a more comprehensive description of the components of communicative competence, Celce-Murcia, Dörnyei, and Thurrell (1995) proposed a refined and expanded version of Canale and Swain's model to include five areas of competence: discourse, linguistic, actional, sociocultural, and strategic. In their view, this "construct was intended to serve as a fairly comprehensive checklist of language points as well as a content base in syllabus design that practitioners can refer to" (Celce-Murcia, Dörnyei, & Thurrell 1997, p. 144). Despite their slight differences, these models served to shift the focus of grammar as the object of study in and of itself to a view of grammar as one of several tools necessary for expressing meaning.

Although CLT is "best understood as a general approach rather than a specific teaching method" (Wesche & Skehan 2002, p. 216), there is a commonly held set of principles for classroom teaching at any level with any textbook. Table 5.3 lists many of the fundamental principles for CLT.[11]

The emphasis on the importance of meaningful and relevant comprehensible input, as well as on opportunities for learners to express personal meaning verbally and in writing, shifted the role of grammar from a central to a secondary concern. Communicative approaches to second language teaching stress the importance of what learners can do with language rather than what they know about language. As Celce-Murcia, Dörnyei, and Thurrell (1997) note:

> CLT highlights the primary goal of language instruction, namely, to go beyond the teaching of the discrete elements, rules, and patterns of the target language and to develop the learner's ability to take part in spontaneous and meaningful communication in different contexts, with different people, on different topics, for different purposes; that is, to develop the learner's communicative competence. (p. 149).

TABLE 5.3 General Principles for Communicative Language Teaching

✓ Use the target language at all times.

✓ Speak *to* the students rather than *at* the students.

✓ Encourage students to speak in the target language at all times.

✓ Create authentic, relevant, real-life learning materials and contexts.

✓ Work on four skills—listening, speaking, reading, and writing.

✓ Avoid practice activities (drills) that are repetitive or noncreative.

✓ Create opportunities for students to work on language functions, such as greeting, asking for information, expressing opinions, etc.

✓ Encourage students to express their own meaning.

✓ Create opportunities for students to work together in pairs and small groups.

✓ Avoid a focus on accuracy and give corrective feedback based on comprehensibility.

✓ Accommodate varied learning styles.

✓ Create a learning environment that is supportive and nonthreatening.

✓ Test the various dimensions of communicative competence and not just grammatical accuracy.

Although this approach to teaching may help learners develop higher levels of proficiency than previous approaches, there is a growing concern about the lack of grammatical accuracy in learners' sppech and writing.

> The dilemma that classroom second language learners and their teachers now face may be stated thus: Putting sole emphasis on forms is unsuccessful, since this approach results in learners who know about the second language but cannot use it. Putting sole emphasis on function and communications, while a far better approach in terms of high degree of fluency attained by learners, nonetheless places a taboo on attention to form that prevents them from becoming *accurate* and *precise* speakers. (Doughty, 1998, p. 140)

To address this concern, there has been renewed interest in rethinking the role of grammar in communicative language teaching. The term *focus on form*, or **FonF**, was first coined by Long (1991) and refers to a variety of teaching strategies that overtly draw learners' attention to a particular linguistic feature that arises during lessons having a principal focus on meaning. Adherents to this approach make an important distinction between a focus on *forms*, which refers to a focus on formal elements of a language in general, as opposed to a focus on *form*, which refers to attention "precisely to a linguistic feature as necessitated by a communicative demand" (Doughty & Williams, 1998, p. 3). Although there are no long-term studies of the effects of FonF, preliminary research suggests that it can have a positive influence on second language development among adults in classroom setting (Doughty, 1998). Moreover, FonF offers a compromise position for teachers who endorse CLT but who also recognize that adult second language learners in a classroom do not generally learn grammatical forms even in rich communicative contexts where the focus is strictly on meaning (Lightbown, 1998). As applied linguists continue to explore FonF, the essential questions that require further exploration include when to focus on form, what kinds of forms are best suited for this approach, and whether focus on form should be intentional on the part of a teacher or should arise spontaneously during student interaction (Doughty & Williams, 1998, p. 10).

Research investigating the effectiveness of various approaches to teaching grammar within a CLT framework suggests that focusing on the formal features of language can be beneficial. Swain and Lapkin (1998) studied learners engaged in **form-focused tasks**, or tasks that target the use of particular, predetermined structures in the second language. They concluded that learners working collaboratively on activities that draw their attention to grammatical forms engage in talk about the language they are producing, question their language use, and correct either their own or their peers' output. Studies of **consciousness-raising tasks**, or tasks in which the target language itself is the focus of activity, have indicated that when learners talk about a specific linguistic structure they discover how it works (Scott & de la Fuente, 2008). There is even a sense that these kinds of activities may be necessary to ensure the acquisition of certain grammatical features (R. Ellis, 2003, p. 150). **Input-processing instruction**, introduced by Lee and VanPatten (2003) is another kind of form-focused activity. In this approach, learners are presented with meaningful input that is tailored, or structured, to draw their attention to form. A particular grammatical structure is targeted in the input, and learners are required to respond in some way (see Table 5.4). Studies of the effects of input-processing instruction offer preliminary evidence that learners do acquire certain grammatical morphemes more effectively than with other approaches (VanPatten, 2007).

Ultimately, research on FonF, consciousness-raising, and input-processing shows that guiding learners to notice a grammatical form is more likely to result in learning than when they are left on their own to make form-meaning connections. Current thinking on CLT generally recognizes the importance of grammar instruction but emphasizes that grammar should be learned in meaningful contexts rather than as isolated rules.

→ YOUR VIEW 4

Read the following quotation from Diane Larsen-Freeman's 2003 book, Teaching Language: From Grammar to Grammaring. *Many foreign language teachers conceive of teaching as working on four skills: listening, speaking, reading, and writing. Analyze Larsen-Freeman's notion that grammar is a skill. Do you agree with her? In your view, how would this notion be put into practice in the foreign language classroom?*

"I think that it is more helpful to think of grammar as a skill rather than as an area of knowledge; this underscores the importance of students' developing an ability to do something, not simply storing knowledge about the language or its use. I have coined the term *grammaring* to highlight the skill dimension of grammar. I also find this term helpful in reminding us that grammar is not so fixed and rigid as the term *grammar* implies. It is far more mutable." (p. 13)

TABLE 5.4 Input-Processing Approach to Teaching Grammar[12]

Target structure: -ing
Context: Talking about free-time activities

Activity 1: Binary options

True/False listening exercise. Teacher reads at least six sentences aloud and students indicate True or False on a piece of paper. Sample sentences follow:

> I like sleeping late on Saturday.
> I do not like watching TV at night.
> I like eating pizza with friends.

Follow-up activity: Teacher leads discussion about students' preferences.

Activity 2: Selecting alternatives

Students work alone indicating their preferences (at least six items). Sample multiple-choice item follows:

> When I have free time I enjoy . . .
> _____ going out with friends.
> _____ watching TV.
> _____ reading a book.

Follow-up activity: In pairs, students compare their answers in preparation for Activity 3.

Activity 3: Supplying information

Students work in pairs to create a profile of their partner's free-time activities. Sample open-ended questions follow:

> Name of partner _____
> likes eating _____.
> loves drinking _____.
> enjoys watching _____.
> prefers going _____.

Activity 4: Elicit the rule
Draw students' attention to the targeted structure and elicit a rule.

PERSPECTIVES FOR THE CLASSROOM

The overview of learning theories and approaches to second language teaching in the previous section illustrates that learning outcomes may be directly related to how grammar is taught. That is, what learners can do with a second language may often result from the way their teachers present grammar. The story of Julien describes a second language learner who knew a good bit about English grammar but could not communicate meaningfully. Even though we don't know

Julien's English teacher, we can imagine from Julien's descriptions that grammar was a central focus of instruction. Moreover, it is likely that his teacher had a particular understanding of what it means to teach a second language and did his best to accomplish that goal. The following imaginary portrait of Julien's teacher serves to facilitate our understanding of how Julien might have been taught English grammar:

Table 5.5 Imaginary Portrait of a Teacher

The English teacher was a dynamic person who loved American culture. He talked endlessly in French about the United States and showed pictures that made the students want to travel there. Although he had a solid command of English grammar, he felt more at ease teaching about English than teaching in English. Therefore, when the students got down to serious business, they repeated words aloud and practiced grammar forms. Most of their work, both oral and written, required them to come up with a single correct answer. Students in the class rarely had an opportunity to talk spontaneously, and they did not have opportunities to speak English to their (equally deficient) classmates. They all believed that proficiency in English lay somewhere in the distant future, after years of grammar study.

Given this portrait, we can imagine that Julien did not hear much authentic English in real-life contexts, did not practice speaking with his peers, and was tested primarily on grammatical forms. In addition, this scenario underscores what is true for many foreign language teachers, namely, that teaching grammar rules constitutes the core of much classroom activity.

One of the significant contributions of communicative approaches to foreign language teaching has been to envision new ways to teach grammar. As discussed in the previous section, research suggests that teaching grammar explicitly can promote second language development when grammar is presented in meaningful contexts. For many proponents of CLT, this research has shed light on the validity of explicit grammar instruction, but more significantly, it has stressed the importance of how grammar is taught. In particular, it has informed our understanding of the importance of linking meaning to form. The imaginary portrait of Julien's teacher gives a concrete example of how teaching grammar devoid of meaningful contexts resulted in Julien's inability to use what he learned. Although research and practice in CLT have done much to further our understanding of the ways explicit grammar instruction can promote second language development, CLT perpetuates an understanding of grammar founded on the premise that there is a dichotomy between form and meaning. In this section I will suggest that the definition of CLT must be broadened to include an understanding of grammar as more than a means for achieving accurate, native-like personal expression. This new understanding, which principally views grammar as a dynamic system, serves as a backdrop for reconceptualizing the way we teach grammar. Ultimately, I will make the case that multicompetent second language learners are aware that grammar is not a subject to be learned but rather a way (or ways) of making meaning.

Rethinking communicative language teaching

The recent history of second language teaching in the United States can be viewed as an ongoing tension between form and meaning, or between how something is said (grammar) and what is said (content). In the 1980s proponents of CLT recognized that grammatical competence was only one dimension of communicative competence, and they sought to strike a balance between grammar and content. In particular, they emphasized the importance of teaching grammar in meaningful contexts rather than as isolated forms. In terms of learning goals, being able to use grammatical structures for oral and written communication took precedence over knowing about grammar. Although these functional goals of CLT served an important purpose for linking form and meaning. Although these functional goals of CLT served an important purpose for linking form and meaning, many teachers continue to struggle with how and when to teach grammar:

> There is no consensus among linguists and instructors as to how grammar should be taught or learned in the communicative classroom, and this uncertainty has been passed along to the textbook authors and the instructors. New and experienced instructors alike often struggle with the dilemma of whether to explain grammatical rules to their classes. (Katz & Blyth, 2008, p. 5)

As we saw in the previous section, explicit grammar instruction has seen a resurgence in communicative approaches; drawing on recent research, some applied linguists and teachers are designing tasks that focus primarily on meaning while drawing students' attention to form. Ironically, however, this attention to linguistic form implicitly reinforces the notion that grammar is a subject, or a body of knowledge that can be learned. Although learners within a communicative pedagogical framework may encounter grammatical structures in meaning-bearing, realistic contexts and may learn to apply these rules to express personal meaning, this focus perpetuates the notion that form and meaning are distinct. In other words, these new approaches to teaching grammar within the communicative framework have not fundamentally changed the way grammar is viewed and taught.

Even though CLT has done much to establish a sense of balance between grammar and communication, it has recently come under scrutiny. First and foremost, critics argue that communicative competence is a theoretical construct and that no one really knows what it might mean to be competent (Byrnes, 2006a). In addition, students who are products of CLT seem to have limitations that are not vastly different from students in the past when behaviorist approaches were in vogue. Furthermore, communicative approaches have not radically changed the content of what is taught at the elementary and intermediate levels of study; the familiar topics, such as food, clothing, and leisure activities, are still at the heart of what students learn. These utilitarian subjects prepare students to travel and exchange concrete information with speakers of the target language, but there is growing concern that students develop a superficial understanding of language and culture in general. Swaffar (2006) articulates the shortcomings of CLT in the following way:

> The pedagogy of communicative competence still reflects the strong structuralist leaning of its audiolingual predecessors—it focuses on student recall of information rather than on analysis of that information . . . without content and analytical thinking applied to that content, language competence, no matter how communicative, remains essentially self-referential. (pp. 247–249)

Even more important, the goals of CLT may not challenge students to think critically about complex issues such as the relationship between language and power or language and culture. Rather, CLT implicitly construes language as being functional and meaning as being constructed within and among learners. As Kramsch (2006) states:

> CLT had an ambitious agenda, based on a functional understanding of language (what language does rather than merely what it says), a dialogic view of the speech situations, and an ethnographic conception of the sociocultural context. It encompassed the use of both spoken and written language and the interaction between speakers and listeners, texts and their readers. . . . Not only has communicative competence become reduced to its spoken modality, but it has often been taken as an excuse largely to do away with grammar and to remove much of the instructional responsibility from the teacher who becomes a mere facilitator of group and pair work in conversational activities. (p. 250)

Although most applied linguists generally recognize the contributions of CLT, there is no question that its shortcomings center on the role of grammar and accuracy in personal expression. As it stands in current practice, students are taught grammatical forms in meaningful contexts so they can produce accurate and meaningful language. Grammar is, therefore, in the service of making meaning, and students are usually assessed according to their ability to generate meaningful language in increasingly accurate and complex ways. This learner-centered approach certainly has its merits; however, it is implicitly self-referential and assumes that learners not only want to, but are able to, meet these goals. As we have seen in previous chapters, working toward native-like proficiency is fundamentally unrealistic for most learners because they have widely varying abilities and few of them develop advanced-level proficiency. Clearly, we should preserve many of the dynamic dimensions of communicative approaches, such as rich and varied input and opportunities for interaction; however, we must re-envision how to teach grammar so that learners develop an awareness of how it functions to make meaning. In particular, we must avoid giving all our attention to form and accuracy in student output—both oral and written—and focus more on form in target language texts.

To understand how grammar functions to make meaning, the study of grammar must become significantly more text driven. That is, all media that are made up of words—journalistic writing, literature, film, vocal music—should be the principal sources for second language learning. Such an approach would expand the goals of CLT to include a focus on grammar that is descriptive in that it explores how grammar is used to express meaning, rather than uniquely prescriptive, or a static body of knowledge to be learned and used for personal reasons. Kramsch (2006) explains how such a descriptive approach may prepare students for our 21st-century world because it develops what she calls "symbolic competence":

> What is at stake in not only the communicative competence of nonnative speakers, but how they are to position themselves in the world, that is, find a place for themselves on the global market of symbolic exchanges. . . . It is no longer appropriate to give students a tourist-like competence to exchange information with native speakers of national languages within well-defined national cultures. They need a much more sophisticated competence in the manipulation of symbolic systems. . . . Symbolic competence does not do away with the ability to express, interpret, and negotiate meanings in dialogue with others, but enriches it and embeds it into the ability to produce and exchange symbolic goods in the complex global context in which we live today. (pp. 250–251)

Kramsch (2006) further argues that the study of literature is particularly well suited to developing symbolic competence because it fosters the production of complexity, tolerance of ambiguity, and the meaning of form.

Ultimately, communicative language teaching is being criticized because it may not prepare learners to function in a multicultural, multicultural world. Although it would be important to continue to foster the development of oral and written proficiency, communicative approaches should be broadened to include exposing students to target language texts to promote an understanding of how grammar makes meaning in many ways. Above all, we must avoid any approach that implicitly instills a sense that grammar is a subject that can be learned rather than an organic, dynamic tool that is shaped by what people do with it—people in power, creative people, suppressed people, and even people who are learning it.

→ YOUR VIEW 5

Read the list of strategies for communicative language teaching in Table 5.3 and create an imaginary portrait of a student who is taught according to these principles. Then, read Kramsch's definition of symbolic competence in the preceding quotations and create an imaginary portrait of a student who is exposed to this approach. Compare these two imaginary students and assess their similarities and differences.

Reconceptualizing grammar in the classroom

Given the preceding argument that grammar instruction should focus on the ways meaning is constructed in texts, we need to reassess our understanding of pedagogical grammar, or what teachers do in the classroom. Communicative approaches generally involve teaching grammar for personal expression; however, recent theories that conceive of language as a dynamic system that changes and evolves through use (de Bot, 2008; N. C. Ellis, 2003, 2008; Herdina & Jessner, 2002; Jarvis & Pavlenko, 2008; Larsen-Freeman, 2003; Tomasello, 2003) suggest that we need to view grammar instruction through a slightly different lens. In particular, grammar instruction has to account for the idea that grammatical language evolves through use. In Chapter 4 we explored a lexical approach founded on the idea that using words, collocations, and phrases during meaningful interaction promotes the development of increasingly complex speech. Larsen-Freeman (2003) has a similar view of language development, using the term *emergent grammar* to describe grammatical language that emerges out of discourse. She argues that if grammar is considered to be a set of fixed rules, with fixed exceptions, language will be understood as a body of knowledge to be mastered. Teaching grammar must avoid, therefore, a focus on learning to use prescribed grammar rules.

Applying this understanding of grammar as a dynamic system, or a set of intentions that evolve through use, can be challenging in the classroom. Textbooks and other teaching materials generally present grammar in metalinguistic terms (direct object, adjective, etc.), often alluding to the similarities and differences between English and the target language and providing examples of how the particular structure is used. As Negueruela (2008) notes, these textbook explanations reinforce a sense that grammar is a static subject to be learned:

> L2 grammatical explanations in most elementary and intermediate language textbooks are constructed both as a list of how to form various structures and a list of how to use these structures based on rules of thumb that attempt to explain their meaning and functionality. . . . Consequently, learners are forced to construct ad hoc—and sometimes inaccurate and incomplete—understandings of the target forms, their meaning, and their use. Furthermore, through these rules, grammar is constructed as an inert object that determines how language is to be used. (p. 160)

These kinds of grammar explanations can be helpful and may appeal to certain kinds of adult learners; however, they should not be the focus of instruction. Instead, teachers should balance activities that teach students to use grammar for personal expression with those that foster an awareness of how grammar is used to construe meaning in authentic oral and written texts.

It is worth reiterating that grammatical accuracy is an important consideration when defining goals within this new framework. Correct, native-like speech may no longer be viable as a primary goal of second language learning. Pratt (2003) argues that advanced competence in a foreign language does not necessarily mean advanced knowledge of the grammar of that language. Rather, "advanced competence involves the ability to conduct mature human relationships in the language. Whether these relationships are social, professional, or strategic, they involve knowledge far beyond the grammatical" (Pratt, 2003, p. 8). Given this understanding, learning goals must be reconceptualized to account for grammatical language meaning more than accurate language. In other words, "productive grammar practice should be seen as hypothesis-testing experimentation, where the primary goal is successful language rather than accurate language" (Kerr, 2008, p. 135). Because a correct form does not necessarily guarantee a correct meaning, goals—especially for novice learners—must be defined in terms of both form and meaning. Advanced-level learners who express interest in developing native-like proficiency should clearly work to develop accuracy in their oral and written language. In general, however, grammatical accuracy should not be a chief learning goal.

Rather than focus on grammar and accuracy, teachers must provide opportunities for students to develop awareness of how grammar is used in authentic texts. Maxim (2008) supports a genre-based approach to teaching grammar that is based on the notion that form is closely linked to meaning in textual environments. He points out that "the units of analysis for accessing language are not isolated sentences but rather texts, for it is within or as a text that language becomes meaningful" (Maxim, 2008, p. 173). Rather than teaching grammar through discrete rules, he argues that this approach is more appropriate because it exposes learners to grammar through a modeling of language in use. Similarly, Negueruela (2008) argues that teachers and students should adopt a "conceptual approach" to understanding grammatical structures. Using the example of teaching articles in Spanish, he states the following:

> For students, the goal is to develop a conceptualization about how Spanish organizes reality through its article system. . . . Within a conceptual approach, teachers and students have to become philosophers of language in the finest and most genuine sense of the word. This mindset might go against the pragmatic zeitgeist of current pedagogy. However, the intent of this type of thinking activity is not simply to understand language and explain it with empty and sophisticated verbalism, but rather to understand language with the intent of mastering complex new meanings through constructing new conceptualizations. (p. 162)

In a slightly different vein, Kerr (2008) proposes a corpus-based approach to teaching grammar based on the notion that lexical phrases are analyzable by rules of grammar and can serve as a springboard for language development. She advocates using word-searching tools to search for recurring lexical or grammatical forms. As an example, she describes looking for the word *since* in a text to explore the relation among its meaning, its use, and its grammatical function. She argues that this kind of data-driven learning introduces authentic language as the object of study, places the burden of responsibility on the student to discover how the language works, remedies the imbalance between teaching grammar and vocabulary (where grammar has gotten far more attention), and provides a vehicle for consciousness-raising activities (Kerr, 2008, p. 145). Kerr adds that "corpus linguistics seeks to discover the patterns that characterize language use—that is, the frequently occurring associations of language features, where the features in question may be lexical items or grammatical structures. Patterns studied may also involve the association of linguistic features with nonlinguistic features such as register, dialect, or time period" (2008, p. 130). Rejecting the grammar/vocabulary dichotomy, she claims that this approach raises learners' awareness of chunks and collocations; fixed expressions, such as social greetings; and other semifixed expressions, such as "what was really interesting" (2008, p. 134). Ultimately, she notes that "productive grammar practice should be seen as hypothesis-testing experimentation, where the primary goal is successful language rather than accurate language" (2008, p. 135).

The idea of an inquiry-driven approach to grammar teaching founded on the use of texts offers rich and varied possibilities. Dialogues from films, lyrics from songs, and informative and other kinds of texts on the Internet, as well as literary texts, offer models of real language that can engage students in analyses of form-meaning connections. The activities described in Table 5.6, based on one sentence taken from a literary text, illustrate how a teacher might guide elementary-level second language learners to explore word use and word order in the target language.

Although this inquiry-driven activity does not resemble a traditional grammar lesson, it can serve to help second language learners think creatively about what grammar does. Rather than see language as a set of prescribed rules, or as a mirror image of their language, this kind of text-based activity fosters in second language learners an understanding of grammar as a flexible tool that can be manipulated in a variety of ways to create meanings. Moreover, unlike classroom activities that are designed to help students use language for personal expression, these kinds of inquiry-driven activities may necessitate use of the native language. As we noted in Chapter 2, a language-use contract should specify the kinds of activities that are best suited for the target language and those that are not. For activities such as the one above, using the native language would help students engage in a sophisticated analysis of the various nuances of meaning in a text. Rather than take the place of communicative activities that develop functional use of the target language, however, these text-based activities should serve to complement them. In addition to preparing students to use the target language for utilitarian purposes, text-based, inquiry-driven activities cans serve to invigorate the intellectual content of foreign language courses, particularly at the lower levels of study. In the end, as Katz and

TABLE 5.6 Inquiry-Driven Grammar Activities Based on a Literary Text

Example taken from *Madame Bovary* by Gustave Flaubert (1857).

Emma Bovary is married to a doctor, Charles, whom she doesn't love. The following sentence describes Charles:

La conversation de Charles était plate comme un trottoir de rue, et les idées de tout le monde y défilaient, dans leur costume ordinaire, sans exciter d'émotion, de rire ou de rêverie.

[Charles's conversation was flat as a sidewalk, and the ideas of everyone paraded along it, in their everyday costume, without arousing emotion, laughter, or reverie.]

1) Words

Read the sentence aloud and guide students to look for words they know; do not let them focus on what they don't know. Have students work in pairs to look for familiar words. In the case of the model text, the words *conversation*, *plate*, *idées*, *costume*, *ordinaire*, *exciter*, and *émotion* should be familiar. Then ask them to look up these words in a bilingual dictionary and write their definitions in English.

– Choose one word in the text that is not likely to be familiar and that may indicate aesthetic or cultural nuances. In the case of the model text, the word *défilaient* is both a verb (*défiler*) and a noun (*un défilé*). Again, using the bilingual dictionary, have students look up the word and write the English definitions. They will find that the verb means "to walk in procession" but also "to unthread" or "to unstring." The noun means "a procession" or "a parade."

– If your classroom is set up with access to the Internet and a projection system, look up the word you have singled out and explore the ways it is used. In the case of *défilé*, a simple search reveals a *défilé militaire* ("military parade") with details about parades and national holidays. Another option is *défilés haute couture* showing people modeling designer clothes on a runway. On both of these sites the word refers to the English meaning "walking in procession" or "parade." Another site, however, invites the viewer to participate in a demonstration against child labor in developing countries where many cheap cotton clothes are made and sent to countries in the Western world. The term used on the site is *organiser un défilé de 'mode équitable'* or "organizing a demonstration for fashion that is based on equitable production of textiles."

2) Word Order

Ask students to return to the quotation from the novel and read it aloud. Then, ask them to determine which words are used to make order in the sentence. In the case of the model text, the words *et* ("and") and *sans* ("without") divide the sentence into three main parts:

La conversation de Charles était plate comme un trottoir de rue, / et les idées de tout le monde y défilaient, dans leur costume ordinaire, / sans exciter d'émotion, de rire ou de rêverie.

– Ask students to decide whether the parts of the sentence can be rearranged. In the case of the model text, the third part can be placed at the front of the sentence. Any other re-ordering disrupts the meaning because pronouns (*y* and *leur*) are displaced from their referents.

3) Reflection

Ask students to make notes about what they have learned in general about how words and word order make meaning.

– Ask students how an exercise like this helps them learn (1) that words can stand for different things in different contexts and (2) that word order within a clause is often fixed.

Blyth note, "instructors need to have an open mind as to what constitutes 'grammar instruction'" (2008, p. 3).

→ YOUR VIEW 6

Think about the distinction between learning to use grammar for personal communication vs. developing an awareness of how grammar is used in authentic texts, both oral and written. To what degree do you think inquiry-driven, text-based activities that are carried out in the first language constitute teaching grammar? Given that there is no prescribed set of materials for such an approach, what kinds of texts might you choose?

Grammar and multicompetent second language learners

The story about Julien offers an example of a second language learner who was a disempowered second language user. More than likely, his teacher unintentionally taught English in such a way as to give rise to an understanding of grammar as a body of knowledge to be learned. Therefore, rather than being able to use English for meaningful communication, Julien possessed a seemingly vast storehouse of inert grammatical knowledge. He was, in a very real sense, locked into a static system of rules. Moreover, he did not have the kinds of resources that we have come to identify with multicompetent second language learners. In particular, he did not have an awareness about the nature of language or the ways that grammar is a dynamic system that evolves and changes with use. Multicompetent second language learners, in contrast, come to understand that learning grammar is a process, that grammatical language emerges through use, and that native-speaker accuracy is not the chief goal.

One of the principal attributes of the multicompetent learner is the ability to reflect on the learning process. According to Negueruela (2008), second language development is a conceptual process. He claims that "language-awareness activities should focus on teaching grammar based on concepts that explain language meaning (versus a grammar of morphology or a grammar of syntax)" (2008, p. 152). Moreover, the problem-solving skills that adults bring to the second language learning task are suited to these kinds of awareness activities. As N. C. Ellis notes, "adult learners have sophisticated formal operational means of thinking and can treat language as an object of explicit learning, that is, of conscious problem-solving and deduction" (2003, p. 72). When learners engage in consciousness-raising activities they develop an awareness of both the function of a particular form and an understanding of grammar as fluid and dependent on context.

Larsen-Freeman (2003) argues that grammar rules can empower students when they understand that rules are not arbitrary or sterile:

The final problem [with grammar rules] is not a linguistic one. It is political, having to do with the distribution and the withholding of power. It can be asked, "Who owns the rules?" "Who makes them up?" The answer to these questions is not "language students." This is a problem if we truly want our students to feel that they own the language. I think one solution to this problem is to help language students understand the internal logic of the language they are studying so that they will be free to express the meaning that they want in accurate and appropriate ways. (p. 51)

Larsen-Freeman further states that we, as foreign language teachers, "must work to change what students think grammar is" (2003, p. 153). To achieve that goal, we must offer students opportunities to explore different ways of thinking about grammar. Ultimately, promoting learners' awareness about grammar fosters the characteristics I associate with being multicompetent second language learners:

1. Multicompetent second language learners learn to ask questions about grammar. These questions revolve around how a structure is formed, when and why it is used, and what it means (see Chapter 4 of Larsen-Freeman, 2003 for more details regarding the three-part pie chart of form, meaning, and use). Because the answers to these questions are not always concretely evident, they can lead to discussions that draw on critical thinking skills for both learners and teachers.

2. Multicompetent second language learners formulate flexible and diverse hypotheses about grammar. For example, we can imagine that when Julien was learning verb forms (*eat, ate, eaten*), he was formulating hypotheses that English is a set of predetermined, prescriptive rules that must be learned and mastered. If Julien had had opportunities to hear or read English in many contexts, to focus on form in meaningful contexts, and to reflect on how grammar functions in texts, he might have learned to hypothesize about the many different ways that grammar is used to make meaning in English.

3. Multicompetent second language learners view grammar mistakes in a positive way. As Larsen-Freeman (2003, p. 154) notes, mistakes can be gifts to all members of a class if they are viewed by both teachers and learners as ways to further explore how the new language functions.

4. Multicompetent second language learners recognize that, although knowing a grammar rule may feel comforting, it is not sufficient for understanding the complexities of the ways that grammar makes meaning.

Finally, grammar may be a thorny topic, but it can also be the most fun part of teaching a foreign language. If teachers and learners understand that it can be counterproductive to learn empty rules and that they should concentrate on generating hypotheses about how rules operate to make meaning in a specific context, they will move toward becoming empowered second language users.

Concluding Propositions

Proposition 5.1

Knowing and doing may be both divergent and convergent in second language development.

Many language learners describe the often-frustrating divergence between what they know about a second language and what they can do with that language. This distinction may be a neurological one related to how information is stored in long-term memory, or it may be related to the different ways the brain processes what learners hear and understand. Regardless of the reasons, for many learners knowing and doing are divergent processes, and learners should be made aware that this phenomenon is a natural and normal part of the second language learning process. Learners should also be made aware, however, that knowing and doing can converge. The idea that language, and by extension grammar, is a dynamic system that evolves and emerges with use suggests that what a learner knows and does can coincide and converge. This emergent view of grammar underscores the notion that language acquisition and language use are dynamic and that "real-time performance or practice is simultaneous with changes in underlying competence. From this perspective, through language use, language changes; through language use, language is acquired" (Larsen-Freeman, 2003, p. 113). In the end, when it comes to second language use, what a learner knows and does can both diverge and converge.

Proposition 5.2

Teaching grammar matters.

It is comforting to think that, to varying degrees, people learn what they are taught. It may be disconcerting, however, to think that the way a particular subject is taught may have a life-long effect on the mental representation the learner develops of that subject. During the grammar-translation era, students were taught grammar structures in paradigms—verb conjugations, tenses, pronouns, and so forth. The point of instruction was to arm students with a sort of internalized grammar reference book so that they could read and translate texts. During the audiolingual era, students were required to listen to tapes and memorize dialogues. The point of instruction was to provide students with a native-like pronunciation and responses to what they might hear in predictable situations. During the communicative language teaching era—which is alive and thriving today—learners hear and read comprehensible, authentic language and learn to generate creative and meaningful speech. Although there have been many derivative teaching methods, these three primary approaches have shaped the language-learning experience of the 20th century. The learning outcome from each of these approaches has been different, and for each there have been strengths and shortcomings. In the future, language teachers will need to reconsider the ways they teach grammar, questioning specifically how learners benefit from certain approaches and why. In particular, they must avoid fostering the development of inert knowledge and promote an understanding of grammar as a dynamic, emergent system.

Proposition 5.3

Multicompetent learners are aware that grammar is more than rules.

Grammar has traditionally been considered a body of knowledge to be learned. As a result, many second language learners have been led to believe that mastering the grammar will result in native-like, accurate speech and writing. However, knowing a grammar rule does not guarantee a learner can use it. To promote multicompetent learners, goals must be defined in terms that reflect an understanding of grammar as a dynamic, emergent system rather than a static, rule-governed subject. In Larsen-Freeman's words, "grammar acquisition may first be characterized as a period of lexicalization, in which learners use prefabricated sequences or chunks of language, followed by a period of syntacticization, in which learners are able to infer a creative rule-governed system" (2003, p. 83). In addition to being aware that grammar emerges through use, multicompetent learners have a growing ability to reflect on the ways grammar works in texts of all kinds (e.g., literary, journalistic, visual) and are willing to explore how each utterance, each sentence, and each paragraph convey subtle and powerful messages. Moreover, when learners understand that meaning is fluid and that grammar is a tool for expressing meaning, the particularities of any single language can teach them about language in general. Multicompetent second language learners are aware that what a translator may say, or what a newspaper article may proclaim, is entirely context-driven. As a result, multicompetent learners are open-minded with regard to language and meaning and possess a tolerance for ambiguity when encountering unfamiliar cultures and peoples.

Suggested Readings on Approaches to Teaching Grammar

Doughty, C., & Williams, J. (Eds.). (1998). *Focus on form in classroom second language acquisition.* New York: Cambridge UP.

Hinkel, E., & Fotos, S. (Eds.). (2002). *New Perspectives on grammar teaching in second language classrooms.* Mahwah, NJ: Lawrence Erlbaum.

Katz, S. L., & Watzinger Tharp, J. (Eds.). (2008). *Conceptions of L2 grammar: Theoretical approaches and their application in the L2 classroom.* AAUSC Issues in Language Program Direction. Boston: Heinle.

Larsen-Freeman, D. (2003). *Teaching language: From grammar to grammaring.* Boston: Heinle.

Lee, J., and Valdman, A. (Eds.). (1999). *Form and meaning: Multiple perspectives.* AAUSC Issues in Language Program Direction. Boston: Heinle.

Researching Your Language Stories

1. Explore how several teachers who claim to teach within a CLT framework—both
   novice and experienced teachers—teach grammar.
   a. Using the checklist in Table 5.3, first determine the degree to which these teach-
      ers follow the general principles of CLT.
   b. Ask each teacher how they teach grammar. You might ask if they rely on guide-
      lines in the textbook or in other teaching materials, whether they favor inductive
      or deductive approaches, if they design their own form-focused tasks, and so
      forth.
   c. Analyze the differences and similarities in the ways these teachers conceive
      of their approaches to teaching grammar. If possible, observe several of them to
      determine if their teaching reflects their perceptions.

2. Using the model in Table 5.5, select a short text and design an inquiry-driven, text-
   based grammar lesson.
   a. Show your lesson to an experienced teacher who claims to teach within a com-
      municative framework. Determine what this teacher thinks about this approach.
   b. Repeat the above activity with a novice teacher.

Notes

1. My colleague, Maïté Monchal, whose English is superb, made this statement.
2. See Chapter 3 for an overview of declarative and procedural long-term memory
   systems.
3. Chomsky (1965) defined grammatical competence in terms of language of an
   ideal speaker-hearer at a single instant in time and did not take into account
   things like working memory, errors of performance, or other features of an individual speaker.
4. Chapter 3 of Hadley's *Teaching language in context* (2001) presents a brief but
   thorough review of this method.
5. After a German submarine sank the *Lusitania* off the coast of England in 1915,
   the study of German declined dramatically and the United States entered a
   40-year-long period of isolationism.
6. B. F. Skinner, author of *Science and human behavior* (1953), is the psychologist
   most often associated with behaviorist theories.
7. Learning in this lab setting could be observed and evaluated by teachers. Very
   quickly, high schools and colleges across the United States invested in building
   language labs, lending credence to this scientific method. In fact, the quality of a
   foreign language program was often based on its investment and use of a language lab. The first language laboratory was installed at Louisiana State University
   in 1947.
8. The military word *drill* is associated with an intensive language program called the
   Army Specialized Training Program, designed to prepare American soldiers for
   combat in the World War II. This program identified bright and willing young men
   to train for 9 months, 12 hours each day, with native speakers in small group settings.
9. Chomsky's first book, *Syntactic structures* (1957) introduced linguists to cognitive
   theories that revolutionized thinking about language. He expanded on his theories

in his subsequent books, *Aspects of the theory of syntax* (1965) and *Reflections on language* (1975).

10. Interestingly, Paradis's work in neurolinguistics (*A neurolinguistic theory of bilingualism,* 2004) leads him to believe that the acquisition/learning distinction is essential to an understanding of second language acquisition because he considers the two processes to require different brain systems.

11. These principles are among those endorsed by proponents of proficiency-oriented foreign language teaching. In her book *Teaching language in context* (2001) Hadley offers detailed descriptions of how to promote communicative competence. Wesche and Skehan (2002) offer a similar list of features that characterize CLT.

12. Table 5.4 shows my own interpretation of an input-processing approach to teaching grammar.

CHAPTER 6

"I spoke French to a Japanese woman!"

OVERVIEW

Multilingual is a word that is increasingly used to describe our 21st-century world. In historically unprecedented ways, people are coming in contact with others who speak different languages and inhabit different cultural spaces. This contact may be face-to-face or it may occur virtually through a variety of technologies. Regardless, multilingual, multicultural encounters are a fact in our globalized world. The challenge to foreign language teachers in the United States is, therefore, greater than ever. We must continue to explore all possible means to make the classroom a place where learners can encounter the target culture in compelling ways. We must also use the foreign language classroom to empower learners to function with confidence across languages and cultures.

Relating her experience studying a foreign language, Ruth Simmons, President of Brown University, states the following:

> I wanted to understand how one could be empowered to foster international, intercultural, and interracial accord, and language study helped me understand better the important role that education could play in achieving such goals. . . . No matter how deeply we study or experience a culture, whether dimensions of our own or another, we will always experience that culture more meaningfully if we absorb the intellectual and cultural values that are evident in how a culture has chosen to express itself. (Simmons, 2004, p. 684)

She goes on to say that foreign language study is both an intellectual exercise and a psychological experience; it is also, and above all, a "test of one's self-identity" (p. 684).

Simmons further notes that, although many students embrace the value of multiculturalism, they do not often see the connection between that value and studying a foreign language. She attributes this lack of understanding to foreign language curricula that do not seem to respond to students' perceived needs, stating that "many students may not recognize the potential of foreign language study to shape their outlook on living in society because traditional language and literature study (in spite of many recent efforts to reconfigure and broaden the courses of study) may still seem too removed from the practical issues with which societies concern themselves today" (2004, p. 686).

This statement certainly challenges the foreign language teaching profession to make our courses relevant, but not in the ways we may have traditionally construed relevance. That is, foreign language teaching that centers on promoting the development of utilitarian language use for personal expression does not necessarily prepare students to live and work in a multilingual, multicultural global world. Simmons argues that standing "outside one's language and culture is one of the most destabilizing and yet exhilarating experiences one can have" (2004, p. 687); however, these kinds of experiences do not come from working tirelessly to achieve correct, native-like oral and written expression. In this final chapter of *Double Talk* we will explore a fundamentally new way of thinking about teaching and learning to demonstrate that the foreign language classroom can be a place where learners gain inside perspectives on the products and practices of people who live in another place and speak another language.

The "Snapshot" of Sharon describing her encounter with a Japanese woman in the south of France serves to illustrate that oral proficiency played little, if any, role in her memorable multilingual experience. French was the only language these two people knew in common, and they succeeded in communicating in spite of the fact that they were both barely proficient in French. This language story sets the stage for exploring an approach to foreign language teaching founded on literacy rather than on language proficiency. In "Research Perspectives" we will explore ways current practice may reinforce cultural isolationism rather than foster multiculturalism. We will also examine the implicit goals of communicative approaches to foreign language teaching in order to call into question the central role of oral proficiency. A review of current theories exploring the development of literacy in a second language challenges commonly held goals for foreign language learning, as outlined in the "Perspectives for the Classroom." I will propose a dynamic teaching-learning approach that calls for a rethinking of the role of the teacher, as well as a fully reconceptualized curriculum organized around goals designed to promote multicompetent second language learning. In addition to outlining specific dimensions of this "inverted curriculum" I will review assessment criteria for multicompetent learners. The "Concluding Propositions" summarize key concepts that have been outlined throughout *Double Talk*.

SNAPSHOT

When I met Sharon . . . house, she immediately began talking to me about her trip to France several years before. Her fondest memory, she told me, was speaking French to a Japanese woman in Nice. It was the highlight of the trip—a moment she would never forget. Because I had begun to listen more intentionally to the language stories I hear so frequently, I asked her to tell me more about this chance meeting with a Japanese woman. Her story sounded like multilingual magic, and she later agreed to send it to me via e-mail:

> *Several years ago, I had the opportunity to help chaperone the high school's French Club student trip to Paris and Rome. Although I'd taken four or five years of French between high school and college, it had been about 25 years since I'd spoken any French at all. I was concerned I wouldn't be able to keep up—both with the students I was traveling with and the country!*
>
> *I borrowed a set of French tapes and began to listen to them whenever I was driving in the car. Little by little, pieces of the language came back—but just a bit. I was quite sure I would find myself sorely lacking in the communication department. After a few days in Paris, our group ventured south by train and by bus and spent a couple of days in Nice, which turned out to be my favorite city of all.*
>
> *Our second day there found me on my own for the day as we'd given the students a free day. I began exploring and found myself down by the marina. A Japanese woman approached me and began a conversation. It quickly became apparent that she was struggling with her French, as was I. But you know, we did it! To my surprise, we were actually able to communicate! We exchanged the normal pleasantries; she said she was looking for a bank. I believe she was asking "ou est un banque"? Maybe? I had passed one a couple of blocks back on the right and I have some recollection of referring to the bank being "au droit" (I think that's on the right, right?). She may have asked me if I lived there (God only knows how I understood THAT because I couldn't phrase that in French at this moment!)—but I seem to recall saying "j'ai american" or something . . . to which she responded something like "j'ai japanese"?*
>
> *We were both struggling a bit . . . but between the stumbling over the words and a few hand gestures, we got there and laughed with each other. For instance, even though I did know the word jambs she gestured to her legs when she used it. She told me she was staying in a place "up the hill" behind where we were standing and her "jambs" hurt because she been walking up and down the hill to get into town. We were struggling in our attempts to communicate. Why I even remember jambs is beyond me. There were lots of pauses as we tried to retrieve the right words . . . then we chuckled at our "ah-hah" moments. Should I say we "comprendez-ed"?*
>
> *Who could have known that this short moment of my ten-day trip would turn out to be the highlight and the memory of which I am most fond?*

Listening to Sharon's story, and then reading her description of the event, was striking because of the obvious joy that lay at the heart of the experience. Neither she nor the Japanese woman she met on the street in Nice spoke French and yet they managed to communicate briefly. Their common knowledge of

French—however limited—allowed them to transcend the boundaries of language and culture and to create a sense of solidarity in an unfamiliar country. Clearly, anyone who knows French will immediately find the errors in Sharon's rendition of this event: *banque* is feminine (*une banque*); *où* (where) has an accent on the *u*; *jambe* (leg) is missing the *e*; and she meant to say "je suis américaine" (I am American) rather than "j'ai" (I have). At the end, her joke to me about understanding (*comprendez-ed*) is a wonderful example of word play, no doubt pronounced "comprendayed." In Sharon's memory, this cross-cultural connection was exhilarating, empowering, and memorable.

→ YOUR VIEW 1

What elements, in your view, contributed to making the interaction described above such a positive and memorable experience? Can this kind of experience be replicated in a classroom setting during a conversation activity between students? In your opinion, could students experience this feeling of success or triumph after completing a listening comprehension exercise? After completing a reading or writing task?

RESEARCH PERSPECTIVES

The experience Sharon describes is remarkable chiefly because her brief interaction in French with a person of another culture was a powerful and positive experience. In fact, she states that that encounter was the highlight of her 10 day trip to France. The essence of this positive multilingual experience can be described as occupying a "third space," as discussed in Chapter 1. This symbolic space is neither that of a person's first language/culture nor that of the target language/culture, but rather a uniquely individual realm between the two. In other words, Sharon and the Japanese woman she met were able to display multiple cultural memberships, thereby identifying themselves and each other as neither French, nor American, nor Japanese, but as multilingual and cross-cultural. This experience, however fleeting, served as a site of identity construction that defined and empowered Sharon to such a degree that it remained vivid 10 years later. In fact, the strength of the memory may be related to the fact that the encounter helped her shape a new, multicultural identity.

Sharon's story describes the kind of experience people often have in an immersion setting; the chance encounter was unscripted and served to convey and share information. This is not the kind of experience we can easily duplicate in the foreign language classroom. That is, the classroom is rarely a place where learners who know each other interact and experience the "aha" moment that Sharon describes. This is not to say that the classroom is an unnatural environment; rather, it is a very particular kind of environment that can offer very particular kinds of learning experiences. In this final chapter we will explore the idea that authentic texts, both oral and written, can offer learners encounters with the target language and culture that are memorable and that promote an identity as an empowered, multicultural second language user.

Isolationism reconsidered

The global world of the 21st century is, by anyone's definition, politically and economically interconnected. Furthermore, people everywhere are increasingly linked to each other via an array of digital technologies. In large part, isolationism is a thing of the past. However, the foreign language classroom in the United States has maintained a kind of isolationist thinking that merits our consideration. Although students are generally exposed to a wide variety of materials that offer them a peek at the world beyond the classroom, the kinds of activities that characterize communicative language teaching (CLT) may unintentionally promote an insular view. Magnan (2007) crafts a convincing argument that foreign language teaching as it is currently conceived within the CLT framework encourages personalized activities that reinforce learners' cultural isolation. She states that most textbooks used in the United States encourage students to talk about themselves with their classmates:

> This practice introduces three problems for language learning: (a) talk about self generally does not elicit the analytical language that collegiate language departments consider pertinent to their intellectual missions; (b) too much talk about self perpetuates self-referential notions of language and culture, preparing students to present an egocentric view when abroad; (c) talk with U.S. classmates fosters a U.S. frame of reference and discourse, although the words to express them are foreign. . . . If activity is regulated in the classroom by instructional tasks, then CLT, with its dominant practice of personalized pair work, encourages Americanized thinking and learning outcomes that remain American in character. (Magnan, 2007, pp. 250–251)

This isolation, in turn, promotes a self-serving use of the target language rather than a means for reaching across linguistic and cultural boundaries.

   Kramsch's (1998a, 2009) notion of "thirdness" serves as a way of re-envisioning foreign language teaching to avoid promoting an isolationist perspective. In Chapter 1 we explored Kramsch's (1998a) notion of a multilingual identity that resides in a third space between the native language and the target language. We proposed that multilingual classrooms that value all languages—including English—can help learners develop multilingual identities and display multiple cultural memberships. In addition to being a symbolic site for identity construction, Kramsch's notion of thirdness is an educational principle in a plurilingual, pluricultural world—a stance, or "a way of seeing the relation of language, thought and culture" (2009). This third space is conceived as one in which learners grow into another speech community and find their places as "intercultural speakers" (2009). In this kind of a space language learning is not an activity that involves a primarily self-referential use of the target language.

Rather, language learning is an exploration of the learners' culture(s) and language(s) (first space) as well as an exploration of the target culture and language (second space), both of which help learners develop intercultural competence (third space) that informs their language use. As such, learners are engaged in interactions with a larger cultural context, which in turn requires them to use language to do more than describe their food preferences or leisure activities. Referring to the intercultural language learning (ILL) movement in Australia, Kramsch states that "ILL pedagogy helps students construct this Third Place by making connections between the L1/C1 [first language/first culture] and the L2/C2 [second language/second culture]; communicating across linguistic and cultural boundaries and identifying and explaining those boundaries; critically reflecting on their own intercultural behaviors and their own identity; and taking responsibility for contributing to successful communication across languages and cultures" (2009, p. 244).

This view of foreign language teaching reaches beyond the boundaries of the classroom to a heterogeneous, symbolic third space in which "meaning does not reside in language alone. Linguistic meaning is created in relation to diverse symbol systems (icons, space, color, gesture, or other representational systems) and modalities of communication (writing, sound, visuals, touch, and body), not to speak of diverse languages. If we need a grammar or rules for this mode of communication, it is to be a grammar of multimodality—that is, it will contain rules that account for how language meshes with diverse symbol systems, modalities of communications, and ecological resources to create meaning" (Canagarajah, 2007, p. 932). To that end, foreign language pedagogy must privilege authentic encounters through texts—both oral and written—that offer learners experiences that encourage the development of interpretive strategies that will serve them outside the classroom.

Beyond orality[1]

Learning to speak a foreign language may be one of the main goals for students in a foreign language classroom. Many students believe that access to the target culture lies primarily in being able to speak the language well enough to communicate with native speakers outside the classroom. However, as we have seen in previous chapters, adults (beyond the sensitive period for language learning) may have significant difficulty learning to speak a foreign language. The leap from using single words and utterances to stringing them together in meaningful sentences is often challenging. Within a relatively short period of time, the classroom learning experience can feel like an avalanche of new grammatical concepts and structures that are increasingly difficult to use for oral communication. In fact, many foreign language programs inundate students with most of the grammatical features of the target language in the first two or three years and expect them to learn to use them well enough to carry on (at least) a simple conversation. This expectation is, however, practically unattainable; most people cannot learn to speak another language well after two, three, or even four years of classroom study. Yet, in spite of the fact that we know learning to speak a second language can be difficult, it remains our top priority and chief learning goal.

Learning to speak has been a central pedagogical goal for several decades. The audiolingual method of the 1960s and 1970s focused chiefly on spoken language; in fact, students were often deprived of the written word until they had mastered a structure orally. Likewise, communicative approaches to language teaching from the 1980s to the present also privilege speaking over other language skills. Maxim (2003) crafts a persuasive argument that by favoring the development of verbal abilities, communicative language teaching may actually limit students' opportunities to develop advanced language abilities:

> In the typical programmatic progression for undergraduate FL [foreign language] learners, the first two years of instruction emphasize spoken language use in [a] primarily interactive and familiar setting while adhering to an underlying linguistic syllabus. At the end of these two years, learners are presumed to be in command of the language and therefore ready for upper level instruction where courses have a specific content focus and are by nature more text-based. . . . Perhaps a more appropriate framework for FL departments would be one that reflects the intellectual learning goals that define them as legitimate academic units and support the long-term nature of FL learning up through advanced levels of instruction. (pp. 182–183)

In addition to proposing that learning goals should be broadened to include the development of competencies other than speaking, Maxim notes that most textbooks follow the principles of CLT and therefore present a fundamentally oral approach to learning.

Communicative approaches were also influenced by the American Council on the Teaching of Foreign Languages (ACTFL) proficiency guidelines, first published in 1986. These guidelines were intended to help teachers assess proficiency in all four skills—reading, writing, listening, and speaking—however, "only the speaking guidelines have had a major impact on foreign language instruction" (Liskin-Gasparro, 1999, p. 311). Moreover, the Oral Proficiency Interview (OPI), which is designed to provide a reliable means for assessing how well a person speaks a language, has also influenced the ways foreign language teachers think about the role of speaking in overall language development. Even though there is a corresponding writing proficiency test that describes functional ability according to four main levels—Novice, Intermediate, Advanced, and Superior—it has not had as much influence on classroom teaching as the OPI. In the end, even though the proficiency guidelines were designed as an assessment tool, the guidelines for evaluating oral proficiency have had considerable influence on classroom teaching practice. Although teachers may attend to developing proficiency in listening, reading, and writing, they are likely to be most concerned about moving their students along the scale from Novice-level to Intermediate on the ACTFL scale for oral proficiency, and possibly to Advanced-level oral proficiency.

Learning to speak the target language should certainly be among the goals for foreign language study; however, we should de-emphasize it and shift our attention to other kinds of learning goals for several reasons. First, as we have already noted, speaking a foreign language is difficult for most people. It is a complex undertaking involving many processes that have yet to be fully explained. In fact, speaking in one's native language is only marginally understood. As described by de Bot, Lowie, and Verspoor (2005), monolingual speech involves a complex series of processes:

> When you want to say something, do you first form a concept and then find a word, or do you first find the word? Once you have found words, how and at what stage are they put in the right order? At what point do you begin to actually pronounce each word?—after you have mentally constructed a whole sentence or as each word or series of words that belong together have been formed?" (pp. 39–40)[2]

Obviously, this process is even more complex in a foreign language. Various models of bilingual (and multilingual) speech production seek to explain how people access words in their two languages. However, there is little agreement as to whether a person has one lexicon or separate lexicons for each language (de Bot, Lowie & Verspoor, 2005; de Groot, 1993; Fabbro, 1999; Kroll & Sunderman, 2003; Paradis, 2004). Research in bilingual speech production also explores the complex ways that a person's two languages interact while speaking (Herdina & Jessner, 2002; Jarvis & Pavlenko, 2008). (See Chapter 2 for a review of bilingual language processing.)

A second, related reason for shifting our focus away from speaking is that teaching students to produce more than imitative, formulaic speech is difficult. In other words, communicating meaningfully and successfully with proficient speakers of another language can be a challenging task. As Blyth (1999) points out, "one of the major obstacles to the teaching of pragmatically conditioned word order, or any other 'form' of the spoken language, lies in the evanescent nature of speech itself. Naturally occurring speech is fleeting, making it exceedingly difficult to represent accurately" (p. 186). Moreover, Blyth observes that oral language is often taught using written language rather than real-life examples of authentic interaction. He argues that modern technology has much to offer in dealing with this problem: "If pedagogical sentential grammars were largely made possible by the technology of the printing press, then perhaps the grammar of oral interaction will finally become possible thanks to the development of multimedia technology" (Blyth, 1999, p. 188).

Another important consideration, mentioned by Swaffar and Arens (2005), involves the fact that speaking and listening "occur within real-world constraints" (p. 33) and are "immediacy tasks that restrict the learner's ability to use prior knowledge and cognitive processes" (p. 33). By contrast, reading and writing are recursive tasks that allow people to reread and reconsider (Kern, 2003; Swaffar & Arens, 2005). Moreover, these recursive tasks "foster analysis and reflection about the processes of producing and interpreting meaning through language (Kern, 2003, p. 6) and should, therefore, be given more attention in the foreign language classroom.

Finally, because language learning in general and speaking, in particular, have been the principal goals at the elementary and intermediate levels of study, foreign language learning is often perceived as a skill and not as real academic pursuit. As Shohamy (2006) so aptly states, "because language teaching was not related to a discernible intellectual domain, FL teaching has not been regarded as a prestigious activity within the academy" (p. 194). As a result, those responsible for teaching language are often ghettoized within foreign language departments and treated like second-class citizens. In fact, the language/literature divide frequently discussed by language teachers and applied linguists (see, for example, Scott & Tucker, 2001) is not surprising because all too often teaching language is not, pre and post an intellectual endeavor. That is, language teaching frequently involves fostering the development of oral skills that are dependent on individual talent rather than on intellectual engagement. In other words, some students are inherently capable of imitating new sounds and of learning to speak a foreign language, whereas others are poorly suited for those endeavors; nevertheless, their successes are likely to be measured primarily by their ability to use the target language to express personal meaning. Pinning our professional reputations on our ability to teach students to speak the target language—a skill that some can master and others cannot—is potentially risky. Rather than trying to argue that teaching students to speak a foreign language has academic merit, we should think seriously about whether this endeavor is, pre and post valid.

→ YOUR VIEW 2

Find two or three textbooks in your target language published within the past 5 years. Read the introductory materials and assess the degree to which learning to speak the target language is a principal goal. Look at the in-class activities and determine how many of them involve speaking in the target language. Review the homework exercises and assess the degree to which they serve to prepare the learner to engage in oral interactions in class. Likewise, note how often the activities in the ancillary materials (audio, video, computer exercises) serve to prepare students to speak. Overall, how do the textbooks compare with regard to their focus on speaking?

Literacy and foreign language learning

Making speaking a central goal of foreign language learning is, questionable. As noted earlier, it can lead to an excessive focus on language use for expressing personal meaning, which may prevent students from engaging in other activities that can prepare them for higher-order critical thinking. Instead of focusing on speaking, students should be involved in exploring texts—both oral and written—that promote critical inquiry. Recent attention to promoting literacy in foreign language education attests to a shift in thinking among applied linguists (Byrnes, 2005; Byrnes & Sprang, 2003; Kern, 2003; Kern & Schultz, 2005; Maxim, 2003; Swaffar, 2003; Swaffar & Arens, 2005; Walther, 2007). Kern (2003) offers an expansive yet coherent definition of literacy and proposes that it should be an organizing principle for foreign language curricula:

> What I mean by "literacy," then, is more than reading and writing as skills or as prescribed patterns of thinking. It is about relationships between readers, writers, texts, culture, and language learning. It is about the variable cognitive and social practices of taking and making textual meaning that provide students access to new communities outside the classroom, across geographical and historical boundaries. It involves an awareness of how acts of reading, writing, and conversation *create* and *shape* meanings, not merely transfer them from one individual or group to another. It is precisely because literacy is not monolithic, but variable and multiple, tied to the various sociocultural practices of a given society, that is of key importance in our teaching of language and culture. (p. 3)

This notion that literacy includes reading, writing, and speaking is especially pertinent to a rethinking of foreign language teaching because it integrates communicative approaches with analytic, text-based approaches. In Kern's view, oral communication does not "take a back seat in a literacy-based approach" (2003, p. 4) but rather is enhanced by reading and writing. In fact, he argues that literacy involves a broad range of written and oral language use particularly when learners are engaged in reading, discussing, and writing. Above all, Kern argues that literacy involves active thinking. He states that "words are always embedded in linguistic and situational contexts, reading and writing involve figuring out relationships between words, between larger units of meaning, and between texts and real or imagined worlds" (2003, p. 5).

Like Kern, Swaffar and Arens (2005) propose that literacy should be at the heart of foreign language education. They believe that foreign language departments have a unique role to play in academic institutions because they contribute to the development of cross-cultural literacy: "The intellectual charge of a foreign language program, regardless of its specific content focus, is to teach students how a language other than their native tongue produces and distributes knowledge within communicative frameworks" (p. 5). Furthermore, they argue that this kind of teaching cannot be done by colleagues in English or history:

> In this vision, FL departments represent the only segment in the humanities that empowers students to become readers, listeners, or viewers that are able to identify how cultural production in a foreign language is transacted and managed and how foreign language speakers contact and influence one another in cultural and multicultural frameworks. FL departments teach students to transact such differences across cultures, as producers of discourses, texts, and other artifacts (practices, gestures, and the like) that bridge their own identities into other cultures. In other words, they teach students to become agents of culture across hegemonic lines. (Swaffar & Arens, 2005, p. 5)

In this view, foreign language teachers have a unique responsibility for promoting cross-cultural literacy.

One of the most interesting features of Swaffar and Arens's (2005) approach to developing literacy is their idea of multiple language use. They propose that students should have opportunities to read texts on a particular topic in both English and the target language because they believe that this strategy can help learners overcome language difficulties while also leading them to make comparisons and connections with the target culture. They note that the "L1 text can orient the reader to a text's topic and point of view more effectively (more pleasurably, more in tune with cultural comparisons) than can other kinds of language aids (e.g., dictionaries), because it focuses the reader's attention on appropriate connections of language and cultural elements, on culturally similar or dissimilar patterns between the two texts" (Swaffar & Arens, 2005, p. 63). They also encourage the use of tasks that have students compare short texts in English and in the target language to help them become aware of the similarities and differences in both form and content of different kinds of texts. These comparisons are likely to lead to an awareness of cultural, textual, and linguistic differences and ultimately to intercultural knowledge. In the end, Swaffar and Arens argue that this approach through multiple literacies can promote a view of foreign language students as "literate adult learners rather than as form-deficient students" (2005, p. 16).

Byrnes has been a leading voice in the field for more than a decade because of her work on the Developing Multiple Literacies curriculum at Georgetown University.[3] This initiative has attracted attention for its innovative 4-year undergraduate program designed to promote literate nonnative users of German. Byrnes's view of language as a social semiotic is at the core of her view of literacy:

> I believe the contemporary scene allows for a decidedly different viewpoint, namely the possibility of considering language as a culturally embedded form of human meaning-making, of semiosis, in short, of language as a social semiotic. By that I mean taking knowledge to be intricately linked to the language patterns of situated language use, where the use of language is a way of knowing and a way of being that is historical in origin and directly related to social action. (Byrnes & Kord, 2001, p. 40)

She argues that understanding the nature of language as a social semiotic puts meaning-making at the heart of language use that, among other things, calls for a "reconsideration of the nature of interlanguage development, understood not as an additive progression toward native-like norms, but as working toward a multicompetence that, at the college level, is best described in terms of multiple literacies" (Byrnes & Kord, 2001, p. 42). Ultimately, Byrnes (2005) challenges the validity of foreign language programs that offer "content-indifferent language courses" and "language-indifferent content courses" (p. 287). Although Byrnes recognizes that there is no clear proposal regarding the kind of content that would be best suited to developing literacy, she favors content-based instruction (CBI) that de-emphasizes personal communication in favor of developing literacy through language and content: "The almost exclusive focus on oral language use that approximates real-world interactive and transactional language, coupled with the ambivalent stance toward explicit teaching, leaves little room for developing the kinds of literate capacities that are so much in demand for CBI and any advanced learning" (Byrnes, 2005, p. 294).

→ YOUR VIEW 3

Read the following quotation from Janet Swaffar and Katherine Arens's 2005 book, Remapping the Foreign Language Curriculum: An Approach Through Multiple Literacies. *In this book they argue that literacy, as defined in the quotation below, should be the principal goal of foreign language learning. In your opinion, should this view serve as a guiding principle for foreign language programs in the United States? If so, how would it change the way foreign languages are taught?*

"Literacy describes what empowers individuals to enter societies; to derive, generate, communicate, and validate knowledge and experience; to exercise expressive capacities to engage others in shared cognitive, social, and moral projects; and to exercise such agency with an identity that is recognized by others in the community." (p. 2)

PERSPECTIVES FOR THE CLASSROOM

The discussion of literacy in the preceding section underscores the idea that we need to carefully rethink approaches to teaching foreign language that focus on developing oral proficiency for self-referential kinds of communication. Although Sharon's story of meeting a Japanese woman in Nice is not directly linked to what we might call literacy, it serves to underscore that oral proficiency was not what made her experience successful or memorable. In fact, her French might well have been in the Novice Low range on the ACTFL oral proficiency scale. What Sharon did have, however, was a life-long interest in France and experience looking at French travel books, magazines, and Web sites. Most of the material she read was in English; however, she admitted to having fun trying to read little snippets of French prose from time to time. Even though she found reading in French challenging, she expressed surprise at how much she remembered and could understand. She also remarked that during her trip she was especially interested in trying to read museum brochures, signs and advertisements in shop windows, and descriptions of various food items in outdoor markets. These kinds of activities are, in my view, experiences of literacy. Drawing on her life experiences and ability to read, Sharon was engaged in the often thrilling experience of discovering and interpreting another language and culture.

Although there is no question that being in the target culture makes this kind of experience more immediate, the classroom can also offer compelling literacy encounters through texts. In fact, our work as teachers should focus on ways to offer our students literacy experiences in the classroom that stimulate their interest in the target language and culture. Moreover, we must recognize that oral proficiency in a second language is not necessarily a measure of a person's ability to develop what Swaffar and Arens (2005) have termed "multiple literacies." In the end, foreign language students should leave their course of study with some sense that they encountered the target culture in memorable ways. As Walther notes, "no matter what reasons students may have for studying a foreign language and culture, it is crucial that they received the kind of education that will make them truly literate users of language and better interpreters of the world around them" (2007, p. 13).

Drawing on this notion that literacy should be at the core of our teaching, we will explore ways to rethink foreign language teaching and to reconceptualize the foreign language curriculum. In so doing I will bring together all of the principles that have been discussed in *Double Talk*. Ultimately, I will describe ways to assess multicompetent second language learning.

Rethinking foreign language teaching

As we have seen throughout this book, approaches to foreign language teaching have changed and evolved over time. Research in cognition, psychology, and sociology have, at different points in history, modified our understanding of learning and, by extension, shaped our pedagogical approaches (see Chapter 5). There is every reason to believe that this process will go on; new theories and discoveries will continue to transform our conceptions of teaching and learning. What will not change, however, is that people will always have experiences with other languages and, therefore, unique language stories to tell. In *Double Talk* we have explored a variety of real-life language stories to help frame our understanding of realistic goals for classroom foreign language learners. Rather than offer a set of fixed principles about teaching, these stories highlight the importance of listening to what we hear. That is, second language use outside the classroom—among native and nonnative speakers, among incipient and proficient bilinguals—can inform classroom practice. Social, economic, and political changes in our multilingual, multicultural world will require different kinds of language use, so we must continue to listen to the language-learner stories we hear outside the classroom in order to inform our practice.

This idea that language stories from beyond the classroom walls can serve to ground practice implicitly rules out any discussion of methods or techniques.[4] Rather, it means we need to engage in continuous analysis and examination of our beliefs about language, language learning, and language use. Reflecting critically about our assumptions will then shape our teaching practice. Given this view, foreign language teaching and learning are fundamentally dynamic in nature; they are nonlinear, often unpredictable, and highly context sensitive, and they change over time. In other words, teaching and learning are a dynamic system of beliefs and practices that are interconnected and mutually informing. Accordingly, the classroom is a privileged learning environment in which language and knowledge emerge; it is not a setting in which teachers and learners should try to emulate naturalistic, immersion-like foreign language learning. In other words, the classroom is not an unnatural place for language learning, but rather an entirely natural context for engaging with authentic materials from the target culture(s). Ultimately, teachers, learners, and texts—oral and written—are variables that interact dynamically in a complex system that must be viewed holistically.

In this dynamic teaching-learning system the teacher's role must be reconceptualized. Taking a historical view of teaching, Kumaravadivelu (2003) states that teachers have been considered passive technicians who were conduits of information and reflective practitioners who facilitated learning. He argues in favor of a new view of the foreign language teacher as a transformative intellectual who is an agent of change. Similarly, Lee and VanPatten (2003) oppose the idea of a teacher with an "Atlas complex" who is an authoritative transmitter of knowledge, proposing instead that teachers should explore ways "in which instruction can work *in unison with* acquisitional processes rather than *against* them" (p. 23). Both of these views are particularly well conceived because they focus on learners and the learning process rather than on teaching as a performative act. Within a dynamic teaching–learning system, learners and learning are also core concerns; the difference, however, is that in this dynamic system teachers are learners and, conversely, learners are teachers. In other words, the relationship between teaching and learning is dynamic, and teachers and learners participate mutually in the learning process.

In Chapter 1 we explored the idea that language learning affects learners' identities (Norton & Toohey, 2002). We also considered the notion that language, culture, and mind interactively shape each other such that learners' first and second (and more) languages constitute multiple representations of the world (Watson-Gegeo, 2004). Given the dynamic teaching–learning theory proposed above, the classroom can be viewed as a site of identity construction for both teachers and learners. In other words, teachers and learners are "speaking and interacting in between spaces, across multiple languages or varieties of the same language" and performing "cultural acts of identity" (Kramsch, 1998a, p. 70). In this sense, a teacher's identity is not fixed but is perpetually changing and adapting to account for new ways of thinking and being. Like learners, therefore, teachers have evolving multilingual identities that reside in a symbolic third space between languages and cultures.

This idea that both teachers and students are learners may seem threatening because it appears to give them equal standing in the classroom. On the contrary, however, this view places a teacher in the position of demonstrating what it means to be a life-long learner who continues to think of herself as shaped and changed by new encounters with the target language and culture. More specifically, in a literacy-based approach to teaching, in which texts of all kinds are the point of encounter with the target culture(s), a teacher can model how she observes, conceptualizes, and interprets a text; she can also help students articulate their interpretations (in both English and the target language) in ways that are more coherent and informed. Defined in this way, being a learner is an integral part of a teacher's multilingual identity. The authority of this teacher-learner lies in her ability to present herself as an experienced learner who is continually exploring how to live with difference and ambiguity.

In keeping with this dynamic teaching-learning approach, there are three guiding principles for the teacher:

1. The teacher respects nonnative language use. Whether or not the teacher a native speaker of the target language, she recognizes that learners have wide variability in their ability to achieve native-like speech. Moreover, the teacher is familiar with Cook's (1999, 2001) notion of the L2 user who uses another language at any level for any purpose, and seeks to articulate learning goals that promote second language use. Furthermore, the teacher should avoid what Pavlenko (2002) calls "gate keeping practices" that allow some learners in and leave others out. Teachers must imagine that all students are able to become second language users and that it is counterproductive to single out students who experience difficulty developing oral proficiency. Furthermore, the teacher encourages learners to explore their identities in relation to the target language and culture, taking into consideration the learners' native languages and cultures. Ultimately, the teacher must respect the learner as an individual and as a member of the learning setting in which he is located, and not as a person seeking to be somebody else in a different setting.

2. The teacher recognizes that *language use* refers to more than speaking. In the context of our discussion about developing literacy, the word *use* must be broadened to include listening, reading, writing, and speaking. Therefore, rather than spending the majority of class time on activities designed to promote oral proficiency, students must have frequent opportunities to read and reflect. This idea fits well with the communication standard as outlined in the *Standards for Foreign Language Learning in the 21st Century* (1999/2006), which includes three communicative modes: interpersonal, interpretive, and presentational. Although the interpersonal and presentational modes refer principally to oral language use, the interpretive mode involves being able to "understand and interpret written and spoken language on a variety of topics."[5] Kern's (2003) literacy-based curriculum is founded on the idea that learners should be prepared to interpret multiple forms of language use, both oral and written. Scott and Huntington's (2006) research also underscores the ways that reading—in this case a poem—can promote the development of the interpretive mode. Furthermore, the teacher recognizes that language use can also mean using English. Rather than promote exclusive use of the target language, the teacher helps students engage in productive uses of English (see Chapter 2 for details regarding a language-use contract).

3. The teacher is aware that talking about target language texts is a preferable way to prepare students for target culture encounters than talking about oneself. As noted previously, communicative approaches to language teaching have privileged self-referential speech. In other words, students have been encouraged to talk about themselves—their likes and dislikes, leisure-time activities, studies, family, and friends, and so forth. Within this framework, many classroom activities involve using targeted grammar structures and vocabulary to talk to peers about topics related to personal interests. In a curriculum that privileges encounters with authentic oral and

written texts, students are encouraged to listen, read, reflect, and react. In other words, they talk about texts and any talk about themselves relates mainly to their thoughts and feelings about texts.

Rather than being fixed prescriptions for what classroom teaching involves, these principles outline ways of thinking about teaching and learning. As such, classroom practice should emerge organically, regardless of the teaching materials that are being used. Kramsch describes "a third culture pedagogy" that "leaves space for mischievous language play, carnivalesque parody, simulation and role-play and the invention of fictitious, hybrid identities that put into question NS [native speaker] claims on authenticity" (2009, p. 238). She further proposes that this third culture pedagogy "uses any method that 'works': communicative activities but also the memorization of vocabulary, poems, or prose; real-world tasks but also dictation, translation and the transcription of audio-recordings or written texts. Exercises in communicative fluency in the L2, but also observation and reflection in the L1" (2009, p. 239). In other words, placing learning at the center of a dynamic teaching-learning venture can offer memorable encounters with the target language and culture.

It is worth noting that the subject of a teacher's level of proficiency in the target language is cause for some debate. Liskin-Gasparro (1999) believes that foreign language teachers should be proficient speakers, noting that "it is one of the great ironies of the late 20th century that initiatives to improve the linguistic proficiency of beginning foreign language teachers exist side-by-side in state legislatures with language policy measures that discourage the development and maintenance of bilingualism" (p. 285). She argues that a proficiency level of Advanced on the ACTFL scale is the appropriate standard to set for beginning teachers, although it is a difficult standard to meet given that very few students can achieve this level by learning in a classroom. "Without a significant linguistic immersion experience, it is a rare language major who will graduate from college with an oral proficiency rating of Advanced" (1999, p. 288). Although Liskin-Gasparro makes a valid point, the reality is that many teachers are not highly proficient speakers of the target language. In a dynamic teaching–learning approach as outlined above, texts, rather than teachers, are at the center. That is, the teacher serves as a model for inquiry-driven learning. Therefore, the contributions of teachers who may not measure up on the proficiency scale remain valid and potentially compelling.

→ YOUR VIEW 4

Interview several teachers, both novice and experienced, to determine how they view their role as foreign language teachers. Do they think of themselves as orchestrating classroom activities? As facilitators for student learning? Do they consider their knowledge of the target language and culture important features of their identity as teachers? Do they consider themselves to be learners of the target language and culture? What are their views of the three guiding principles for the teacher outlined above?

Reconceptualizing the curriculum

In this final chapter of *Double Talk* it is important to reiterate that the real-life language stories offer us new ways of thinking about language use. However, they also offer us new ways of envisioning curricular goals. Of particular importance is relinquishing the long-held goal of creating expert, native-like second language speakers. Such a shift in priorities would mean, above all, that we would no longer spend the first two years of classroom study focusing on developing the linguistic skills necessary to speak and write accurately in complete sentences. More specifically, this would mean that grammar would not be a principal focus of instruction. Instead, students should be given abundant and varied opportunities to read and interpret oral and written texts—target language texts as well as those written in other languages familiar to the students—that are available to them in a variety of media. In other words, the focus of learning during the first two years of study should be on developing literacy.

This proposed change of focus for the first two years is grounded in two principal theories. First, as we saw in Chapters 4 and 5, learning words and short utterances may be more likely to promote complex language use than learning grammar rules. The idea that learning words and collocations should take precedence over learning grammar rules is based on the notion that language acquisition occurs through language use (de Bot, 2008; N. C. Ellis, 2003, 2008; Herdina & Jessner, 2002; Jarvis & Pavlenko, 2008; Larsen-Freeman, 2003). In other words, rather than thinking of grammar as a subject to be learned, it is viewed as a system that emerges through use. R. Ellis (2002) offers a particularly coherent argument for not teaching grammar in the early stages of language learning:

> An assumption of traditional approaches to grammar is that it should be taught from the very beginning stages of a language course. This assumption derives from behaviorist learning theory, according to which learning consists of habit formation. Learners must be taught correct habits from the start to avoid the unnecessary labor of having to unlearn wrong habits in order to learn the correct ones later. . . . There are, in fact, some very obvious reasons for not teaching grammar to beginners. First, as the immersion studies have shown . . . , learners do not need grammar instruction to acquire considerable grammatical competence. Learners with plentiful opportunities to interact in the L2 are likely to acquire basic word order rules and salient inflections without assistance. For example, L2 learners who have never received instruction are able to acquire the rules for ordering elements in the English noun phrase. . . . Of course, not all learners will acquire these features . . . some learners will fossilize early. But, many learners will go quite a long way without any attempt to teach them grammar. In other words, up to a point, the acquisition of a grammar takes place naturally. If grammar teaching is to accord with how learners learn, then it should not be directed at beginners. Rather, it should await the time that learners have developed a significantly varied lexis to provide a basis for rule

extraction. In crude terms this is likely to be at the intermediate-plus stages of development. There is a case, therefore, for reversing the traditional sequence focusing initially on the development of vocabulary and the activation of the strategies for using lexis in context to make meaning and only later seeking to draw learners' attention to the rule-governed nature of language. (pp. 22–23)

A second reason for shifting the focus of instruction toward literacy during the first two years is that most students are capable of interacting with target-language texts before they have mastered the grammatical system. If one of our main goals is to expose students to a new language and culture, it is unreasonable to think that focusing principally on learning the language achieves that purpose. As Walther (2007) notes, "learning how to speak a foreign language in and of itself no more guarantees this larger knowledge and understanding than does learning how to pass a test" (p. 8). She endorses an ecological model that views language "as a living entity that cannot be divorced from its uses in culturally and historically situated activity" (p. 10) and argues that language emerges "from social activity in communities of practice" (p. 10). Of particular interest is Walther's idea that language learning should be relational or organic as opposed to linear, and that learning should be situated in contexts of social practice. To that end, she believes that lower-level foreign language courses must offer more than input output models of information exchange:

> The ecological perspectives . . . offer opportunities for broadening or extending our practices in a way that will bring our lower-level courses more into line with the larger questions of history, language, and culture that engage our discipline and with the educational mission of the university in helping students negotiate their identities in an increasingly multicultural environment. (Walther, 2007, p. 12)

Ultimately, Walther supports an approach that expands the contents and contexts of traditional textbooks, moves beyond utilitarian role-play that engages students in mundane activities like ordering food in restaurants, gives more attention to collaborative projects that move students beyond classroom activities (such as virtual museums and service-learning projects), and focuses more attention on literature and the creative arts.

Table 6.1 outlines a reconceptualized curriculum in which the first two years are devoted to relevant, text-based explorations of the target language and culture. This model is based on the idea that grammar should be the focus of study at more advanced levels and that beginning students are capable of engaging with authentic, target language texts. Furthermore, it is founded on the notion that students will be motivated to continue their study of the target language and that this motivation, combined with their experience interacting with texts, promotes life-long multicompetent second language learning.

This inverted curriculum, with a text-based approach during the first two years of study, changes what it means to study a foreign language at an advanced level. In particular, it means that foreign language study beyond the second year

TABLE 6.1   Reconceptualized Curriculum for First Two Years of Foreign Language Study

First two years	Goals	Approach	Outcome
Traditional goals	1. Proficiency in listening, speaking, reading, writing 2. Grammatical competence 3. Knowledge about target culture(s)	1. Target language input 2. Interaction about topics of personal interest related to everyday life 3. Focus on sentence grammar 4. Discussion of culture in target language	1. Good language learners identified 2. 20% of students continue study of target language 3. Rapid attrition of grammatical knowledge and verbal skills 4. Sense of self as deficient language learner
Goals for promoting multicompetent second language learners	1. Growing ability to read and interpret a variety of target-language texts (oral and written) as well as pertinent texts in English 2. Developing awareness of bilingualism and L2 use 3. Increasing sensitivity to the ways culture is expressed and perceived in texts	1. Target language input (oral and written) representing diverse genres 2. Interaction in both target language and English about oral and written texts 3. Focus on words and utterances in oral and written texts 4. Discussion of bilingualism and second language development	1. All learners identified as L2 users at some level 2. 50% of students continue study of target language 3. Maintenance of reading and interpretive abilities 4. Sense of self as L2 user

involves expanding and refining vocabulary knowledge, developing linguistic accuracy in speaking and writing, and working with increasingly complex oral and written texts. As we saw in the preceding sections, the recent interest in advanced language learning has drawn attention to the importance of literacy (Byrnes & Maxim, 2003; Byrnes, Weger-Guntharp, & Sprang, 2006; Swaffar & Arens, 2005). The value of this attention lies precisely in the fact that it shifts our concentration away from a central focus on developing oral proficiency and general linguistic competence in the target language. However, this attention to developing literacy should also inform our research and teaching at the lower levels of foreign language study. There is no question that research is needed to assess this kind of reconceptualized curriculum, both at the early and later stages of study. This is especially true given that there is very little research to inform our understanding of what it means to function at an advanced level, as Byrnes (2006b) points out:

> Just what we mean by "advanced L2 abilities," how they are acquired either naturalistically or in tutored settings, and what environmental influences might hinder or help their development at different ages and in different settings, is remarkably constricted in its scope and vision, remarkably neglected in second language acquisition (SLA) research, and treated at a remarkably experiential level in educational practice. (p. 1)

Ultimately, this inverted curriculum targets all learners, not just good language learners. It is founded on the notion that all students can be multicompetent second language learners who become what Cook (2002b) calls multicompetent L2 users.

In an article addressing the complexities of language use in multilingual communities, Canagarajah (2007) argues for a pedagogy that reflects how language is used in the world. Although he discusses English language use by nonnative speakers of English, the fundamental principles echo various features of this reconceptualized curriculum for developing multicompetent second language learners:

> Pedagogy can be refashioned to accommodate the modes of communication and acquisition seen outside the classroom. . . . Students would develop language awareness (to cope with the multiple languages and emergent grammars of contact situations), rather than focusing only on mastering the grammar rules of a single variety. In a context of plural forms and conventions, it is important for students to be sensitive to the relativity of norms. Therefore, students have to understand communication as performative, not just constitutive. That is, going beyond the notion of just construction [of] prefabricated meaning through words, they will consider shaping meaning in actual interactions and even reconstructing the rules and conventions to represent their interests, values, and identities. In other words, it is not what we know as much as the versatility with which we can do things with language that defines proficiency. Pedagogical movements such as learner strategy training and language awareness go some way toward facilitating such instructional strategies. (Canagarajah, 2007, p. 936)

→ YOUR VIEW 5

The reconceptualized curriculum with its goals for developing multicompetent second language learners described in Table 6.1 does not make reference to pedagogical materials that a teacher might use. How might existing textbooks and testing materials be used within this framework? In what ways do the National Standards for Foreign Learning in the 21st Century support this approach? What kinds of texts might you choose to engage learners in the first and second years of study?

Assessing multicompetent second language learners

The inverted curriculum outlined in the previous section is organized around goals designed to promote multicompetent second language learners. Practically speaking, the outline offers concrete ways of thinking about goals and classroom activities. What is more elusive, however, is understanding how we might assess learning in this kind of framework. As Norris states, "good assessment calls for more than creation of accurate testing tools" (2006, p. 173); he believes that why we assess must drive any consideration of how we assess. Norris further recommends that assessment be an integral part of curricular design and that all members of the teaching community be able to interpret and use them. Given the principles outlined in *Double Talk*, an essential question should guide any thinking about assessment: What does it mean to be a multicompetent second language learner? Although we are just beginning to explore what this means, Table 6.2 includes criteria that can serve to organize the development of assessment tools.

Above all, assessment of the multicompetent second language learner must account for the variability of nonnative speech. In other words, learner language in all its various forms must be valued. In a discussion of advanced-level proficiency (ALP), Shohamy (2006) addresses the issue of learner language:

> Traditionally, the construct of ALP, like all other language proficiency levels, has been based on a monolingual construct of language whereby "other" languages, especially the L1 of the learners, had no place and no role to play in the learning of the language; in fact, they constituted an unacceptable, even illegitimate, intrusion by "foreign elements" into learners' and bilinguals' speech. Furthermore, the posited progression and hierarchy assumed that the higher the proficiency level, the less learners engaged the L1 as they reached for the goal of being like "the native speaker." Recent research, however, shows an important role for L1 in L2 proficiency at all levels. (p. 195)
>
> Multiple levels of correctness as well as flexible criteria of correctness that reflect the specific context and goals are appropriate. Worded negatively, we could say that rigid "native speaker" correctness criteria no longer apply; worded positively, an explicit focus on content and message intentions is appropriate. (p. 202)

In a recent e-mail exchange with Vivian Cook, he commented that "the multicompetence flag is waving" throughout *Double Talk*. This statement could not be truer. His notion of the multicompetent mind and the corresponding notion of the L2 user are foundational principles in *Double Talk* from beginning to end. In my view, these notions offer us a fundamentally new way to conceptualize what it means to teach and learn foreign languages in a 21st-century world. In particular, I have proposed that his theory of multicompetence can be operationalized in the American foreign language classroom setting through the correlated notion of a multicompetent second language learner. This new theoretical construct is, to my mind, a well-founded way to reconceptualize foreign language teaching in the United State and to offer a dynamic and compelling vision for the future.

TABLE 6.2 Assessment Criteria for Multicompetent Second Language Learners

The multicompetent second language learner . . .

- distinguishes between native language use and L2 use.
- articulates ways that his or her multilingual identity is evolving.
- recognizes acceptable uses of English in the classroom.
- familiarizes him-or herself with features of bilingual and multilingual language use, such as code-switching, and other cross-linguistic phenomena.
- alternates between English and the target language in appropriate ways.
- engages in intentional learning of words and collocations.
- develops a personal approach to language use that supports the emergence of grammatical language.
- seeks out appropriate target-language texts (oral and written) that contribute to classroom discussion.
- reflects critically about oral and written target-language texts.
- asks increasingly informed questions about the target language and culture.
- identifies strategies for second language maintenance.
- exhibits traits of a multilingual, multicultural citizen, such as appreciation of diversity, tolerance for ambiguity, awareness of human rights issues, and so forth.

→ YOUR VIEW 6

One of the principal characteristics of multicompetent second language learners, as we have described them in Double Talk, *is having language awareness. Read the following quotation from Ingeborg Walther's 2007 article entitled* Ecological Perspectives on Language and Literacy: Implications for Foreign Language Instruction at the Collegiate Level *and determine the degree to which the questions she poses address the assessment criteria outlined in Table 6.2.*

"How often do we involve students in a critical reflection about how language reflects other voices as well as their own or about how people's interpretation and production of texts is contingent on their own social scripts? Or, to put it somewhat differently, how often do we get students to reflect about how language works to achieve particular effects in particular contexts?." (Walther, 2007, p. 12)

Concluding Propositions

Proposition 6.1

Oral proficiency is not sufficient for multicultural understanding.

For several decades foreign language teachers have endorsed communicative approaches that center on developing oral proficiency. Being able to speak the target language has been a central learning goal. The reason for this nearly exclusive focus on oral skills lies in the assumption that being able to talk to people who speak another language grants a person access to the target language and culture. Consequently, most classroom activities are designed to promote communicative competence so that students can learn to talk to people from the target culture about everyday topics. However, this approach is likely to promote self-referential, isolationist thinking, and oral proficiency may not be the key to multicultural understanding. The challenge faced by foreign language teachers, therefore, involves balancing the utilitarian goals of communicative approaches with the intellectual goals that are increasingly considered essential to the development of global citizenship in the 21st century.

Proposition 6.2

Literacy promotes multicompetent second language learning.

Rather than focus on oral proficiency and grammar, we should make literacy the chief consideration from the first stages of language learning. Learners do not need to achieve advanced-level functioning in the target language to be able to engage in text-based, target language activities. Instead, we should assume that they are capable of reading and interpreting a variety of target language texts, both oral and written. Furthermore, they should have opportunities to read pertinent texts in English, or other languages they may know, to promote cross-cultural and cross-linguistic awareness. Multicompetent second language learners are defined in terms of their growing sensitivity to the ways culture is expressed and perceived by both members of the target language communities and by those in other language communities. Cook (2000c) asserts that teaching involves changing students' minds and promoting their cognitive flexibility. To do this, he argues, teachers must first recognize that students have minds. This view of students implicitly means that teachers must believe that students are capable of learning to read target language texts and to reflect about them critically from the earliest stages of language study.

In an approach to foreign language teaching that centers on literacy, teachers as well as students are learners. In other words, both teachers and students are involved in selecting, reading, interpreting, and talking about texts. Because there is no prescribed subject to be learned, knowledge emerges from interactions. This dynamic teaching-learning approach means that, like their students, teachers are multicompetent second language learners. What distinguishes them from their students is their experience as language learners and their ability to model what it means to be life-long learners who shape and are shaped by text-based encounters with the target culture.

Proposition 6.3

Multicompetent second language learners become literate second language users.

Cook's (2002a) term *L2 user* helps to frame second language learning as students becoming proficient L2 users rather than deficient native speakers. The goal of becoming an second language user who stands between two languages, capable of using the resources of both, is more realistic than goals requiring learners to achieve native-like proficiency in the target language. In *Double Talk* we have proposed that the foreign language classroom serves to prepare multicompetent second language learners to become proficient second language users. In fact, the classroom environment is an ideal setting in which to explore one's emerging multilingual identity, to learn about language use of all kinds, to identify ways to maintain second language use, and to think critically about texts of all kinds. These classroom activities help learners develop the awareness and the skills necessary to become literate second language users who are empowered to interact with people of other languages and cultures around the world.

Suggested Readings on 21st-Century Approaches to Second/Foreign Language Teaching

Byrnes, H., Weger-Guntharp, H. D., & Sprang, K. (Eds.). (2006). *Educating for advanced foreign language capacities.* Washington, DC: Georgetown UP.

Johnson, M. (2004). *A philosophy of second language acquisition.* New Haven, CT: Yale UP.

Kumaravadivelu, B. (2003). *Beyond methods: Macrostrategies for language teaching.* New Haven, CT: Yale UP.

Kumaravadivelu, B. (2006). *Understanding language teaching: From method to post-method.* Mahwah, NJ: Lawrence Erlbaum Associates.

Swaffar, J., & Arens, K. (2005). *Remapping the foreign language curriculum: An approach through multiple literacies.* New York: The Modern Language Association.

Researching Your Language Stories

1. Using the information that you got from *YOUR VIEW 4*, design a questionnaire to assess how teachers describe their role in the classroom. If possible, focus your questions on issues related to their identity as foreign language teachers.

   a. Give the questionnaire to several teachers who teach different languages. Analyze and compare their answers. Note, in particular, whether there are predictable response patterns based on the age of the teachers, the length and kinds of teaching experiences, the teachers' national origin, and the languages they teach.

   b. Give the same questionnaire to pre-service teachers. Determine the degree to which identity as a foreign language teacher is related to preconceived notions about teaching, to experiences as foreign language students, to pre-service teaching materials, and so forth.

c. Compare the questionnaires of teachers who are currently teaching and those who are preparing for careers as foreign language teachers. What do their answers indicate about teacher preparation? Is the issue of identity relevant for those preparing to teach?

[YOUR VIEW 4: Interview several teachers, both novice and experienced, to determine how they view their role as foreign language teachers. Do they think of themselves as orchestrating classroom activities? As facilitators for student learning? Do they consider their knowledge of the target language and culture important features of their identity as teachers? Do they consider themselves learners of the target language and culture? What are their views of the three guiding principles for the teacher outlined above?]

2. Review the goals outlined in the following Five Cs of the *Standards*. These standards were developed as guidelines for teachers and are, therefore, open to interpretation.

a. Discuss these standards with several teachers (pre-service, novice, or experienced) who have not read *Double Talk*. Try to assess how they understand and use (or not) the *Standards*.

b. Discuss these standards with people who have read *Double Talk*. Try to assess ways that *Double Talk* helps or hinders understanding of these standards.

c. Imagine that you are being interviewed for a teaching position and have been asked about the *Standards*. How would you describe the ways they inform your teaching practice?

THE FIVE Cs OF THE *STANDARDS*

Communication: Communicate in languages other than English.

1.1 Students engage in conversations, provide and obtain information, express feelings and emotions, and exchange opinions.

1.2 Students understand and interpret written and spoken language on a variety of topics.

1.3 Students present information, concepts, and ideas to an audience of listeners or readers on a variety of topics.

Cultures: Gain knowledge and understanding of other cultures.

2.1 Students demonstrate an understanding of the relationship between the practices and perspectives of the culture studied.

2.2 Students demonstrate an understanding of the relationship between the products and perspectives of the culture studied.

Connections: Connect with other disciplines and acquire information.

3.1 Students reinforce and further their knowledge of other disciplines through the foreign language.

3.2 Students acquire information and recognize the distinctive viewpoints that are only available through the foreign language and its culture.

Comparisons: Develop insight into the nature of language and culture.

4.1 Students demonstrate understanding of the nature of language through comparisons of the language studied and their own.

4.2 Students demonstrate understanding of the concept of culture through comparisons of the cultures studied and their own.

Communities: Participate in multilingual communities at home and around the world.

5.1 Students use the language both within and beyond the school setting.

5.2 Students show evidence of becoming life-long learners by using the language for personal enjoyment and enrichment.

Notes

1. This notion is taken from Kern and Schultz's (2005) article in which they argue for an integrative approach to research on reading and writing in second language acquisition.

2. To explain the complexity of involved in speaking, Levelt (1989) proposed a model that is generally accepted one for a monolingual speaker. According to Levelt's model, the production of speech takes place in three stages, the Conceptualizer, the Formulator, and the Articulator. See Chapter 2 for a discussion of bilingual speaking models.

3. See the following Web site for additional information on the program in German at Georgetown University: http://www1.georgetown.edu/departments/german/programs/undergraduate/curriculum/36465.html

4. Richards and Rodgers (2001) summarize the American applied linguist Edward Anthony's definitions of approach, method, and technique: "According to Anthony's model, approach is the level at which assumptions and beliefs about language and language learning are specified; method is the level at which theory is put into practice and at which choices are made about the particular skills to be taught, the content to be taught, and the order in which the content will be presented; technique is the level at which classroom procedures are described" (p. 18).

5. This definition is taken from the generic overview of the Five Cs of the *Standards*.

SUMMARY OF CONCLUDING PROPOSITIONS

Proposition 1.1

Monolingualism is an inadequate term for describing 21st-century language use.

Proposition 1.2

Multilingual classrooms empower second language learners.

Proposition 1.3

Multicompetent second language learners become successful second language users.

Proposition 2.1

Code-switching is a normal and natural occurrence among people who speak more than one language.

Proposition 2.2

Code-switching can play a constructive role in the foreign language classroom.

Proposition 2.3

Multicompetent second language learners are aware of what it means to be bilingual.

Proposition 3.1

Second language loss is a normal and natural occurrence.

Proposition 3.2

Words are more resistant to loss than grammar in second language learning.

Proposition 3.3

Multicompetent second language learners are aware of the relationship between language development and language loss.

Proposition 4.1

People learn words in a second language with relative ease.

Proposition 4.2

Words and short utterances are natural and normal in second language production.

Proposition 4.3

Multicompetent second language learners understand the role of words and short utterances in second language development.

Proposition 5.1

Knowing and doing may be both divergent and convergent in second language development.

Proposition 5.2

Teaching grammar matters.

Proposition 5.3

Multicompetent second language learners are aware that grammar is more than rules.

Proposition 6.1

Oral proficiency is not sufficient for multicultural understanding.

Proposition 6.2

Literacy promotes multicompetent second language learning.

Proposition 6.3

Multicompetent second language learners become literate second language users.

GLOSSARY OF TERMS

Academic grammar: a term used by linguists to describe the technical aspects of language, such as phonology, morphology, and syntax.

Affective filter: one of the five hypotheses in Krashen's monitor model; it states that acquisition occurs when affective conditions are optimal.

Aphasia: loss or impairment of speech resulting from brain injury or disease.

Bilingual: a term used to describe a person who knows and uses two languages, usually the first, or native, language and a second one.

Borrowing: a term used to describe the conscious introduction of words from one language into another.

Broca's area: an area of the brain named for 19th-century physician Pierre Paul Broca; this area is located in the left frontal lobe and is responsible for articulated language.

Chunk: a term used to refer to words or morphemes that are combined into a single unit as a result of frequent repetition.

Closed class words: a category of words that is limited and contains a finite number of words, including pronouns, prepositions, and conjunctions; see also **function word**.

Code-switching (CS): a language behavior of bilingual speakers characterized by the alternation between two languages.

Collocation: lexical units that habitually go together, such as *tomorrow morning* or *blond hair*.

Consciousness-raising tasks: tasks in which the target language itself is the focus of activity; designed to help students discover and raise awareness of how a specific structure works by talking about the linguistic form as an object.

Content word (morpheme): a word with a lexical, dictionary meaning (e.g., *house, big, happily*); open class words with limitless possibilities for increase.

Critical period hypothesis: a hypothesis (Lenneberg, 1967) that linguistic development must occur between birth and around age 12 (at puberty), a period after which human beings are incapable of acquiring language.

Cross-linguistic influence (CLI): the influence of a person's knowledge of one language on that person's knowledge or use of another language.

Declarative memory: also referred to as explicit memory; includes learned knowledge that can be consciously retrieved and verbalized; declarative memory consists of semantic memory (facts, concepts, general knowledge; related to the meaning of things) and episodic memory (events and personal history; experiential knowledge of the self).

Deductive grammar teaching: a teaching strategy that progresses from stating the rule to showing its application in an example.

Descriptive grammar: a study of the way people use the grammar of a particular language; in contrast to **prescriptive grammar**, which refers to the standard and accepted rules for correct usage in a particular language.

Dialect: a distinct variety of a language often spoken in a specific area.

Embedded language: a term that refers to the secondary language in bilingual code-switching, as opposed to the dominant language, or the **matrix language**.

Explicit memory: see **declarative memory**.

FonF: an acronym for *focus on form*; refers to a variety of teaching strategies that overtly draw learners' attention to a particular linguistic feature that arises during lessons that have a principal focus on meaning.

Form-focused tasks: tasks that target the use of particular, predetermined features of the second language.

Fossilization: errors that become an enduring part of a speaker's **interlanguage**; permanent stabilizing of a language at a stage short of success.

Function word (morpheme): a word with a grammatical meaning (i.e., *the*, *him*, *which*); function words are closed class words with limited numbers that rarely change.

Grammar: a general term referring to a set of rules that describe the structure and patterns of a language; the study of classes of words and their functions and relations in a sentence. See also **prescriptive grammar** and **pedagogical grammar**.

Heritage learner: a learner who is studying the language of his or her family or community of origin.

Holophrase: an utterance consisting of a single meaning unit; in child language "takaba" (take a bath) might act as a single word having a single conceptual meaning; in adult language, "I would like" can have a single meaning to express desire or need for something.

Implicit memory: see **procedural memory**.

Inductive grammar teaching: a teaching strategy that progresses from giving examples to stating the rule.

Input: the language a learner hears or reads.

Input-processing instruction: a grammar teaching strategy that involves presenting learners with meaningful **input** designed to draw their attention to a particular form.

Interaction: face-to-face or written communication between or among people.

Interference: incorrect structures in the new language that mirror structures in the native language. See **negative transfer**.

Interlanguage: a term coined by Selinker (1972) that refers to a "hypothesized separate linguistic system based on the observable output which results from a learner's attempted production of a target language norm" (p. 117); generally understood as a system of rules in the mind of a person learning a second language, which is intermediate between that of his or her native language and that of the one being learned.

L2 user: a description of a person who knows and uses another language at any level for any purpose.

Language Acquisition Device (LAD): Language acquisition device; this term was proposed by Chomsky (1965) to describe an innate "organ" that serves to construct native language grammar in children.

Lemma: a term that refers to a lexical-conceptual structure that represents the speaker's communicative intention; it is broader than the term *word*.

Lexeme: a word considered as a lexical unit (e.g., *dog* and *dogs* are the same lexeme; similarly *eat*, *ate*, *eaten* are the same lexeme with varying morphological forms).

Lexical meaning: a meaning for an individual unit; a dictionary meaning.

Lexicon: the individual words that make up a language.

Linguistic competence: a term used to refer to a person's internalized knowledge of language.

Linguistic performance: a term used to refer to external evidence of language competence, or language use.

Long-term memory: as opposed to **short-term memory**; considered to involve **declarative memory** and **procedural memory**.

Matrix language: a term that refers to the dominant language in bilingual code-switching, as opposed to the secondary language, or the **embedded language**.

Metalinguistic awareness: the ability to articulate an understanding about language or the grammatical structure of language.

Metapragmatic awareness: the ability to articulate an understanding of the pragmatic aspects of language, or the ways that language is used in actual communication.

Monitor model: a model of second language acquisition (Krashen, 1981) that includes five hypotheses about second language acquisition: (1) Language acquisition and language learning are two different processes; (2) grammar is acquired in a predictable order in a natural setting; (3) learning functions only as an editor or monitor; (4) comprehensible input is essential for acquisition; (5) acquisition occurs when affective conditions are optimal.

Monolingual: a term used to describe a person who knows and uses only one language, usually his or her first, or native language.

Morpheme: a unit smaller than a smaller than a word that has grammatical meaning as opposed to lexical meaning (e.g., in the word *dogs,* the -s is a morpheme indicating plurality).

Multicompetence: the knowledge of two languages in one mind; coined by Cook (1991), this term accounts for an individual's knowledge of language that includes both first language competence and a developing understanding of a second language.

Multilingual: a term used to describe a person who knows and uses more than two languages.

Nativist theories: theories that consider language an inborn and uniquely human capacity.

Negative transfer: errors in the second language caused by interference from the first language; see **interference**.

Open class words: a category of words that includes nouns, verbs, adjectives, and adverbs; this class can be considered limitless in that new words can be added; see also **content word (morpheme)**.

Oral Proficiency Interview (OPI): a formal method for assessing a person's oral proficiency originally designed for use by the U.S. government and adapted for educational use by the American Council on the Teaching of Foreign Languages.

Output: a term used to describe what a learner says in the target language; as opposed to **input**, or what a learner hears or reads.

Pedagogical grammar: grammar rules written for students.

Prescriptive grammar: the standard and accepted rules for correct use of a particular language; in contrast with **descriptive grammar**, which refers to the study of the way people use the grammar of a particular language.

Procedural memory: also called nondeclarative memory or implicit memory; refers to a type of learning or knowledge that is not available for conscious recall; it depends on the repeated execution of a task and generates automatic behavior.

Proficiency: a term used to describe what learners can do with a target language in speaking, listening, reading, and writing. The *ACTFL Proficiency Guidelines* describe novice, intermediate, advanced, and superior proficiency in listening, speaking, reading, and writing.

Register: a linguistic variety, either written or spoken, that a person uses with a particular group; certain formal settings (ceremonial, academic, etc.) generally require a formal register of language as opposed to a casual setting among friends where the register would be less formal.

Sensitive period: a term used in the context of child language acquisition to refer to a developmental period characterized by a greater receptivity for acquiring language; see also **critical period hypothesis**.

Short-term memory: also called working memory; holds information for short periods of time.

Sociocultural theories: in the context of language acquisition/learning, these theories emphasize the importance of learning as a collaborative activity between and among people.

Syntax: the study of the way words are put together to form phrases, clauses, and sentences.

Transfer: see **cross-linguistic influence**; **interference**.

Uptake: a term that refers to what a student actually learns after being exposed to input.

Universal Grammar (UG): this term was proposed by Chomsky (1957, 1965) to describe a set of principles and parameters of grammar that is inherited genetically.

Wernicke's area: an area of the brain named for 19th-century physician Carl Wernicke; this area is located in the left temporal lobe and accounts for comprehension of sounds and words.

Word: a sound-meaning unit; see also **open class words, closed class words, content word**, and **function word**.

REFERENCES

ACTFL Proficiency Guidelines (1986, 2001). Hastings-on-Hudson, NY: American Council on the Teaching of Foreign Languages.

Aitchison, J. (1995). Chimps, children, creoles: The need for caution. In S. Puppel (Ed.), *The biology of language* (pp. 1–17). Philadelphia: John Benjamins.

Aljaafreh, A., & Lantolf, J. P. (1994). Negative feedback as regulation in second language learning in the zone of proximal development. *The Modern Language Journal, 78,* 465–483.

Andersen, R. W. (1982). Determining the linguistic attributes of language attrition. In R. D. Lambert & B. F. Freed (Eds.), *The loss of language skills* (pp. 83–118). Rowley, MA: Newbury House.

Antón, M. (1999). The discourse of a learner-centered classroom: Socio-cultural perspectives on teacher-learner interaction in the second-language classroom. *The Modern Language Journal, 83,* 303–318.

Appel, R., & Muysken, P. (1987). *Language contact and bilingualism.* London: Arnold.

Atkinson, D. (1993). Teaching in the target language: A problem in the current orthodoxy. *Language Learning Journal, 8,* 2–5.

Atkinson, D. (2002). Toward a sociocognitive approach to second language acquisition. *The Modern Language Journal, 86,* 525–545.

Auer, J. C. P. (2000). A conversation analytic approach to code-switching and transfer. In L. Wei (Ed.), *The bilingualism reader* (pp. 166–187). New York: Routledge. (Reprinted from *Codeswitching,* pp. 187–214, by M. Heller, Ed., 1988, Berlin: Mouton de Gruyter.)

Bateman, B. E. (2008). Student teachers' attitudes and beliefs about using the target language in the target language classroom. *Foreign Language Annals, 41,* 11–28.

Beatty, J. (2001). *The human brain: Essentials of behavioral neuroscience.* Thousand Oaks, CA: Sage Publications, Inc.

Belz, J. A. (2002). Identity, deficiency, and first language use in foreign language education. In C. Blyth (Ed.), *The sociolinguistics of foreign-language classrooms* (pp. 209–248). AAUSC Issues in Language Program Direction, Boston: Heinle.

Berko-Gleason, J. (1982). Insights from child language acquisition for second language loss. In R. D. Lambert & B. F. Freed (Eds.), *The loss of language skills* (pp. 13–23). Rowley, MA: Newbury House.

Bialystok, E. (1999). Cognitive complexity and attentional control in the bilingual mind. *Child Development, 70,* 636–644.

Bichakjian, B. H. (1995). Essentialism in language: A convenient, but fallacious premise. In S. Pupple (Ed.), *The biology of language* (pp. 33–59). Philadelphia John Benjamins.

Bickerton, D. (1990). *Language and species.* Chicago: University of Chicago Press.

Bley-Vroman, R. (1990). The logical problem of foreign language learning. *Linguistic Analysis, 20*, 3–49.

Blom, J. P., & Gumperz, J. J. (1972). Social meaning in structure: Code switching in Norway. In J. J. Gumperz & D. Hymes (Eds.), *Directions in sociolinguistics* (pp. 407–434). New York: Holt, Rinehart and Winston.

Blyth, C. (1999). Toward a pedagogical discourse grammar: Techniques for teaching word-order constructions. In J. Lee & A. Valdman (Eds.), *Form and meaning: Multiple perspectives* (pp. 183–229). AAUSC Issues in Language Program Direction. Boston: Heinle.

Blyth, C. (Ed.). (2002). *The sociolinguistics of foreign-language classrooms.* AAUSC Issues in Language Program Direction. Boston: Heinle.

Bongartz, C., & Schneider, M. L. (2003). Linguistic development in social contexts: Study of two brothers learning German. *The Modern Language Journal, 87*, 13–37.

Briscoe, T. (2002). *Linguistic evolution through language acquisition.* New York: Cambridge University Press.

Brooks, F. B., & Donato, R. (1994). Vygotskyan approaches to understanding foreign language learner discourse during communicative tasks. *Hispania, 77*, 262–274.

Burling, R. (2005). *The talking ape.* New York: Oxford, UK: Oxford University Press.

Bybee, J. (2002). Sequentiality as the basis of constituent structure. In T. Givón & B. F. Malle (Eds.), *The evolution of language out of pre-language* (pp. 109–134). Philadelphia: John Benjamins.

Byrnes, H. (2005). Content-based foreign language instruction. In C. Sanz (Ed.), *Mind and context in adult second language acquisition* (pp. 282–302). Washington, DC: Georgetown University Press.

Byrnes, H. (2006a). Perspectives. *The Modern Language Journal, 90*, 244–246.

Byrnes, H. (2006b). Locating the advanced learner in theory, research, and educational practice: An introduction. In H. Byrnes, H. D. Weger-Guntharp, & K. Sprang (Eds.), *Educating for advanced foreign language capacities* (pp. 1–14). Washington, DC: Georgetown University Press.

Byrnes, H., & Kord, S. (2001). Developing literacy and literary competence: Challenges for foreign language departments. In V. M. Scott & H. Tucker (Eds.), *SLA and the literature classroom: Fostering dialogues* (pp. 35–73). AAUSC Issues in Program Direction. Boston: Heinle.

Byrnes, H., & Maxim, H. H. (Eds.). (2003). *Advanced foreign language learning: A challenge to college programs.* AAUSC Issues in Language Program Direction. Boston: Heinle.

Byrnes, H., & Sprang, K. A. (2003). Fostering advanced L2 literacy: A genre-based cognitive approach. In H. Byrnes & H. H. Maxim (Eds.), *Advanced foreign language learning: A challenge to college programs* (pp. 47–85). AAUSC Issues in Language Program Direction. Boston: Heinle.

Byrnes, H., Weger-Guntharp, H. D., & Sprang, K. (Eds.). (2006). *Educating for advanced foreign language capacities.* Washington, DC: Georgetown University Press.

Calvin, W. H., & Bickerton, D. (2000). *Lingua ex machina: Reconciling Darwin and Chomsky with the human brain*. Cambridge, MA: MIT Press.

Canagarajah, S. (2007). Lingua franca English, multilingual communities, and language acquisition. *The Modern Language Journal, 91*, 923–939.

Canale, M., & Swain, M. (1980). Theoretical bases of communicative approaches to second language teaching and testing. *Applied Linguistics, 1*, 1–47.

Cangelosi, A., & Domenico, P. (2004). The processing of verbs and nouns in neural networks: Insights from synthetic brain imaging. *Brain Language, 89*, 401–408.

Celce-Murcia, M., Dörnyei, Z., & Thurrell, S. (1995). Communicative competence: A pedagogically motivated model with content specifications. *Issues in Applied Linguistics, 6*, 5–35.

Celce-Murcia, M., Dörnyei, Z., & Thurrell, S. (1997). Direct approaches in L2 instruction: A turning point in communicative language teaching? *TESOL Quarterly, 31*, 141–152.

Chavez, M. (2002). The diglossic foreign-language classroom: Learners' views on L1 and L2 functions. In C. Blyth (Ed.), *The sociolinguistics of foreign-language classrooms* (pp. 163–208). AAUSC Issues in Language Program Direction. Boston: Heinle.

Chomsky, N. (1957). *Syntactic structures*. The Hague, The Netherlands: Mouton.

Chomsky, N. (1965). *Aspects of the theory of syntax*. Cambridge: MIT Press.

Chomsky, N. (1975). *Reflections on language*. New York: Pantheon Books.

Chomsky, N. (1980). *Rules and representations*. New York: Columbia University Press.

Cook, V. (1991). *Second language learning and language teaching*. New York: Arnold.

Cook, V. (1992). Evidence for multicompetence. *Language Learning, 42*, 557–591.

Cook, V. (1999). Going beyond the native speaker in language teaching. *TESOL Quarterly, 33*, 185–209.

Cook, V. (2001). Using the first language in the classroom. *The Canadian Modern Language Review, 57*, 402–423.

Cook, V. (Ed.). (2002a). *Portraits of the L2 user*. Clevedon, UK: Multilingual Matters.

Cook, V. (2002b). Background to the L2 user. In V. Cook (Ed.), *Portraits of the L2 user* (pp. 1–28). Clevedon, UK: Multilingual Matters.

Cook, V. (2002c). Language teaching methodology and the L2 user perspective. In V. Cook (Ed.), *Portraits of the L2 user* (pp. 327–343). Clevedon, UK: Multilingual Matters.

Cook, V. (Ed.). (2003). *Effects of the second language on the first*. Clevedon, UK: Multilingual Matters.

Cook, V. (2007). Multicompetence: Black hole or wormhole for SLA research? In Z.–H. Han (Ed.), *Understanding second language process* (pp. 16–26). Clevedon, UK: Multilingual Matters.

Cook, V. (in press). The relationship between first and second language acquisition revisited. In E. Macaro (Ed.), *The Continuum companion to second language acquisition*. London: Continuum.

de Bot, K. (2000). A bilingual production model: Levelt's 'speaking' model adapted. In L. Wei (Ed.), *The bilingualism reader* (pp. 420–442). New York: Routledge. (Reprinted from *Applied Linguistics*, 1992, *13*, 1–24.)

de Bot, K. (1993). Word production and the bilingual lexicon. In R. Schreuder & B. Weltens (Eds.), *The bilingual lexicon* (pp. 191–214). Philadelphia: John Benjamins.

de Bot, K. (2002). Cognitive processing in bilinguals: Language choice and code-switching. In R. B. Kaplan (Ed.), *The Oxford handbook of applied linguistics* (pp. 287–300). New York: Oxford University Press.

de Bot, K. (2008). Introduction: Second language development as dynamic process. *The Modern Language Journal, 92*, 166–178.

de Bot, K., & Hulsen, M. (2002). Language attrition: Tests, self-assessments and perceptions. In V. Cook (Ed.), *Portraits of the L2 User* (pp. 251–274). Clevedon, UK: Multilingual Matters.

de Bot, K., Lowie, W., & Verspoor, M. (2005). *Second language acquisition: An advanced resource book*. New York: Routledge.

de Bot, K., Verspoor, M., & Lowie, W. (2007). A dynamic systems theory approach to second language acquisition. *Bilingualism: Language and Cognition, 10*, 7–21.

de Groot, A. M. B. (1993). Word-type effects in bilingual processing tasks: Support for a mixed-representational system. In R. Schreuder & B. Weltens (Eds.), *The bilingual lexicon* (pp. 27–51). Philadelphia: John Benjamins.

Dewaele, J.-M. (2006). Expressing anger in multiple languages. In A. Pavlenko (Ed.), *Bilingual minds: Emotional experience, expression and representation* (pp. 118–151). Clevedon, UK: Multilingual Matters.

Dewaele, J.-M., & Pavlenko, A. (2003). Productivity and lexical diversity in native and non-native speech: A study of cross-cultural effects. In V. Cook (Ed.), *Effects of the second language on the first* (pp. 120–141). Clevedon, UK: Multilingual Matters.

Doughty, C., & Williams, J. (Eds.). (1998a). *Focus on form in classroom second language acquisition*. New York: Cambridge University Press.

Doughty, C., & Williams, J. (1998b). Issues and terminology. In C. Doughty & J. Williams (Eds.), *Focus on form in classroom second language acquisition* (pp. 1–11). New York: Cambridge University Press.

Doughty, C. (1998). Acquiring competence in a second language. In H. Byrnes (Ed.), *Learning foreign and second languages: Perspectives in research and scholarship* (pp. 128–156). New York: The Modern Language Association.

Doughty, C. J., & Long, M. H. (Eds.). (2003). *The handbook of second language acquisition*. Malden, MA: Blackwell.Ellis, R. (1994). *The study of second language acquisition*. Oxford, UK: Oxford University Press.

Ellis, N. C. (2001). Memory for language. In P. Robinson (Ed.), *Cognition and second language instruction* (pp. 33–68). Cambridge, UK: Cambridge University Press.

Ellis, N. C. (2003). Constructions, chunking, and connectionism: The emergence of second language structure. In C. J. Doughty & M. H. Long (Eds.), *The handbook of second language acquisition* (pp. 63–103). Malden, MA: Blackwell.

Ellis, N. C. (2008). The dynamics of second language emergence: Cycles of language use, language change, and language acquisition. *The Modern Language Journal, 92,* 232–249.

Ellis, R. (1994). *The study of second language acquisition.* Oxford: Oxford University Press.

Ellis, R. (2002). The place of grammar instruction in the second/foreign language curriculum. In E. Hinkel & S. Fotos (Eds.), *New perspectives on grammar teaching in second language classrooms.* Mahwah, NJ: Lawrence Erlbaum.

Ellis, R. (2003). *Task-based language learning and teaching.* New York: Oxford University Press.

Ellwood, C. (2008). Questions of classroom identity: What can be learned from codeswitching in classroom peer group talk? *The Modern Language Journal, 92,* 538–557.

Fabbro, F. (1999). *The neurolinguistics of bilingualism: An introduction.* East Sussex, UK: Psychology Press.

Fabbro, F. (2002). The neurolinguistics of L2 users. In V. Cook (Ed.), *Portraits of the L2 user* (pp. 199–220). Clevedon, UK: Multilingual Matters.

Forster, K. I., & Jiang, N. (2001). The nature of the bilingual lexicon: Experiments with the masked priming paradigm. In J. L. Nicol (Ed.), *One mind, two languages: Bilingual language processing* (pp. 72–83). Malden, MA: Blackwell.

Gass, S. (1997). *Input, interaction and the second language learner.* Mahwah, NJ: Lawrence Erlbaum.

Gass, S., & Mackey, A. (2007). Input, interaction, and output in second language acquisition. In B. VanPatten & J. Williams (Eds.), *Theories in second language acquisition: An introduction* (pp. 175–199). Mahwah, NJ: Lawrence Erlbaum.

Genesee, F. (2000). Early bilingual language development: One language or two? In L. Wei (Ed.), *The bilingualism reader* (pp. 327–343).New York: Routledge. (Reprinted from *Journal of Child Language,* 1989, *16,* 161–179.)

Genesee, F. (2001). Bilingual first language acquisition: Exploring the limits of the language faculty. *Annual Review of Applied Linguistics, 21,* 153–168.

Genesee, F. (2002). Portrait of the bilingual child. In V. Cook (Ed.), *Portraits of the L2 user* (pp. 170–196). Clevedon, UK: Multilingual Matters.

Giauque, G. S., & Ely, C. M. (1990). Code-switching in beginning foreign language teaching. In R. Jacobson & C. Faltis (Eds.), *Language distribution issues in bilingual schooling* (pp. 174–184). Philadelphia: Multilingual Matters.

Gill, J. H. (1997). *If a chimpanzee could talk and other reflections on language acquisition.* Tucson, AZ: University of Arizona Press.

Gitsaki, C. (1999). *Second language lexical acquisition: A study of the development of collocational knowledge.* Bethesda, MD: International Scholars Publications.

Givón, T., & Malle, B. F. (Eds.). (2002). *The evolution of language out of pre-language.* Philadelphia: John Benjamins.

Gomes de Matos, F. (2002). Second language learners' rights. In V. Cook (Ed.), *Portraits of the L2 user* (pp. 305–323). Clevedon, UK: Multilingual Matters.

Grosjean, F. (1998). Exploring the recognition of guest words in bilingual speech. *Language and Cognitive Processes, 3*, 233–274.

Grosjean, F. (2000). Processing mixed language: Issues, findings, and models. In L. Wei (Ed.), *The bilingualism reader* (pp. 443–469). New York: Routledge. (Reprinted from *Tutorials in bilingualism*, pp. 225–254, by A. M. de Groot & J. F. Kroll, Eds., 1997, Mahwah: NJ, Lawrence Erlbaum.)

Grosjean, F. (2001). The bilingual's language modes. In J. L. Nicol (Ed.), *One mind, two languages: Bilingual language processing* (pp. 1–22). Malden, MA: Blackwell.

Gyori, G. (1995). Animal communication and human language: Searching for their evolutionary relationship. In S. Puppel (Ed.), *The biology of language* (pp. 99–126). Philadelphia: John Benjamins .

Hadley, A. O. (2001). *Teaching language in context* (3rd ed.). Boston: Heinle.

Halliday, M. A. K. (2004). On grammar as the driving force from primary to higher-order consciousness. In G. Williams & A. Lukin (Eds.), *The development of language* (pp. 15–44). London: Continuum.

Hamers, J. F., & Blanc, M. H. A. (2000). *Bilinguality and bilingualism* (2nd ed.). Cambridge, UK: Cambridge University Press.

Herdina, P., & Jessner, U. (2002). *A dynamic model of multilingualism: Perspectives of change in psycholinguistics.* Clevedon, UK: Multilingual Matters.

Hernandez, A. E., Dapretto, M., Mazziotta, J., & Bookheimer, S. (2001). Language switching and language representation in Spanish-English bilinguals: An fMRI study. *NeuroImage, 14*, 510–520.

Herschensohn, J. (2000). *The second time around: Minimalism and L2 acquisition.* Philadelphia: John Benjamins.

Hildebrand-Nihlson, M. (1995). From proto-language to grammar: The psychological considerations for the emergence of grammar in language evolution. In S. Puppel (Ed.), *The biology of language* (pp. 127–145). Philadelphia: John Benjamins.

Hinkel, E., & Fotos, S. (Eds.). (2002). *New perspectives on grammar teaching in second language classrooms.* Mahwah, NJ: Lawrence Erlbaum.

Honjo, I. (1999). *Language viewed from the brain.* Basel, Switzerland: Karger.

Hulstijn, J. H. (2001). Intentional and incidental second language vocabulary learning: A reappraisal of elaboration, rehearsal and automaticity. In P. Robinson (Ed.), *Cognition in second language instruction* (pp. 258–286). Cambridge, UK: Cambridge University Press.

Hyltenstam, K., & Abrahamsson, N. (2003). Maturational constraints in SLA. In C. J. Doughty & M. H. Long (Eds.), *The handbook of second language acquisition* (pp. 539–588). Malden, MA: Blackwell.

Illes, J., Francis, W. S., Desmond, J. E., Gabrieli, J. D., Glover, G. H., Poldrack, R., et al. (1999). Convergent cortical representation of semantic processing in bilinguals. *Brain and Language, 70*, 347–363.

Jackendoff, R. (2002). *Foundations of language: Brain, meaning, grammar, evolution.* New York: Oxford University Press.

Jacobson, R. (Ed.). (2001). *Codeswitching worldwide II*. New York: Mouton.

Jarvis, S., & Pavlenko, A. (2008). *Crosslinguistic influence in language and cognition*. New York: Routledge.

Jessner, U. (2003). A dynamic approach to language attrition in multilingual systems. In V. Cook (Ed.), *Effects of the second language on the first* (pp. 234–246). Clevedon, UK: Multilingual Matters.

Jiang, N. (2004). Semantic transfer and its implications for vocabulary teaching in a second language. *The Modern Language Journal, 88*, 416–431.

Johnson, M. (2004). *A philosophy of second language acquisition*. New Haven, CT: Yale University Press.

Katz, S. L., & Watzinger-Tharp, J. (Eds.). (2008). *Conceptions of grammar: Theoretical approaches and their application in the L2 classroom*. AAUSC Issues in Language Program Direction. Boston: Heinle.

Katz, S. L., & Blyth, C. S. (2008). What is grammar? In S. L. Katz & J. Watzinger-Tharp (Eds.), *Conceptions of grammar: Theoretical approaches and ther application in the L2 classroom* (pp. 2–14). AAUSC Issues in Language Program Direction. Boston: Heinle.

Kern, R. G. (2003). Literacy and advanced foreign language learning: Rethinking the curriculum. In H. Byrnes & H. H. Maxim (Eds.), *Advanced foreign language learning: A challenge to college programs* (pp. 2–18). AAUSC Issues in Language Program Direction. Boston: Heinle.

Kern, R. & Schultz, J. M. (2005). Beyond orality: Investigating literacy and the literary in second and foreign language instruction. *The Modern Language Journal, 89*, 381–392.

Kerr, B. J. (2008). Applications of corpus-based linguistics to second language instruction: Lexical grammar and data-driven learning. In S. L. Katz & J. Watzinger-Tharp (Eds.), *Conceptions of grammar: Theoretical approaches and their application in the L2 classroom* (pp. 128–150). AAUSC Issues in Language Program Direction. Boston: Heinle.

Kim, K. H. S., Relkin, N. R., Lee, K.-M., & Hirsch, J. (1997). Distinct cortical areas associated with native and second languages. *Nature, 388*, 171–174.

Koike, D., & Liskin-Gasparro, J. (2002). Privilege of the nonnative speaker meets practical needs of the language teacher. In C. Blyth (Ed.), *The sociolinguistics of foreign-language classrooms* (pp. 263–266). AAUSC Issues in Language Program Direction. Boston; Heinle.

Kramer, A. (2006). Teachers' use of English in communicative German language classrooms: A qualitative analysis. *Foreign Language Annals, 39*, 435–450.

Kramsch, C. (1998a). *Language and culture*. New York: Oxford University Press.

Kramsch, C. (1998b). The privilege of the intercultural speaker. In M. Byram & M. Fleming (Eds.), *Language learning in intercultural perspective: Approaches through drama and ethnography* (pp. 16–31). Cambridge, UK: Cambridge University Press.

Kramsch, C. (2002). The privilege of the non-native speaker. In C. Blyth (Ed.), *The sociolinguistics of foreign-language classrooms* (pp. 251–262). AAUSC Issues in Language Program Direction. Boston: Heinle.

Kramsch, C. (2006). From communicative competence to symbolic competence. *The Modern Language Journal, 90*, 249–252.

Kramsch, C. (2009). Third culture in language education. In V.J. Cook & L. Wei (Eds.), *Contemporary applied linguistics volume I* (pp. 233–254). London: Continuum.

Kramsch, C., & Whiteside, A. (2007). Three fundamental concepts in second language acquisition and their relevance in multilingual contexts. *The Modern Language Journal, 91*, 907–922.

Krashen, S. (1981). *Second language acquisition and second language learning.* New York: Pergamon.

Krashen, S. (1982a). *Principles and practice in second language acquisition.* New York: Pergamon.

Krashen, S. (1982b). Accounting for child-adult differences in second language rate and attainment. In S. Krashen, R. C. Scarcella, & M. H. Long (Eds.), *Child-adult differences in second language acquisition* (pp. 202–226). Rowley, MA: Newbury House.

Krashen, S. (1985). *The input hypothesis: Issues and complications.* London: Longman.

Krashen, S., Long, M. H., & Scarcella, R. C. (1982). Age, rate, and eventual attainment in second language acquisition. In S. Krashen, R. C. Scarcella, & M. H. Long (Eds.), *Child-adult differences in second language acquisition* (pp. 161–172). Rowley, MA: Newbury House.

Kroll, J. F. (1993). Accessing conceptual representations for words in a second language. In R. Schreuder & B. Weltens (Eds.). *The Bilingual Lexicon* (pp. 53–81). Philadelphia: John Benjamins.

Kroll, J. F., & Tokowicz, N. (2001). The development of conceptual representation for words in a second language. In J. L. Nicol (Ed.), *One mind, two languages: Bilingual language processing* (pp. 49–71). Malden, MA: Blackwell.

Kroll, J. F., & Sunderman, G. (2003). Cognitive processes in second language learners and bilinguals: The development of lexical and conceptual representations. In C. J. Doughty & M. H. Long (Eds.), *The handbook of second language acquisition* (pp. 104–129). Malden, MA: Blackwell.

Kumaravidevelu, B. (2003). *Beyond methods: Macrostrategies for language teaching.* New Haven, CT: Yale University Press.

Kumaravidevelu, B. (2006). *Understanding language teaching: From method to postmethod.* Mahwah, NJ: Lawrence Erlbaum.

Lacorte, M., & Canabal, E. (2002). Interaction with heritage learners in foreign language classrooms. In C. Blyth (Ed.), *The sociolinguistics of foreign-language classrooms* (pp. 107–129). AAUSC Issues in Language Program Direction. Boston: Heinle.

Lambert, R. D., & Freed, B. F. (Eds.). (1982). *The loss of language skills.* Rowley, MA: Newbury House.

Lantolf, J. P. (2002). Sociocultural theory and second language acquisition. In R. B. Kaplan (Ed.), *The Oxford handbook of applied linguistics* (pp. 104–114). New York: Oxford University Press.

Lantolf, J. P., & Thorne, S. L. (2006). *Sociocultural theory and the genesis of second language development.* Oxford, UK: Oxford University Press.

Larsen-Freeman, D. (1997). Chaos/complexity science and second language acquisition. *Applied Linguistics, 18*, 141–165.

Larsen-Freeman, D. (2003). *Teaching language: From grammar to grammaring.* Boston: Heinle.

Larsen-Freeman, D. (2007). Reflecting on the cognitive-social debate in second language acquisition. *The Modern Language Journal, 91*, 773–787.

Larsen-Freeman, D., & Cameron, L. (2008). Research methodology on language development from a complex theory perspective. *The Modern Language Journal, 92*, 200–213.

Lee, J. (2000). *Tasks and communicating in language classrooms.* New York: McGraw-Hill.

Lee, J., & Valdman, A. (Eds.). (1999). *Form and meaning: Multiple perspectives.* AAUSC Issues in Language Program Direction. Boston: Heinle.

Lee, J., & VanPatten, B. (2003). *Making communicative language teaching happen* (2nd ed.). New York: McGraw-Hill.

Lenneberg, E. (1967). *Biological foundations of language.* New York: Wiley and Sons.

Levelt, W. J. M. (1989). *Speaking: From intention to articulation.* Cambridge, MA: MIT Press.

Levine, G. S. (2003). Student and instructor beliefs and attitudes about target language use, first language use, and anxiety: Report of a questionnaire study. *The Modern Language Journal, 87*, 343–364.

Levine, G. S. (2004). Co-construction and articulation of code choice practices in foreign language classrooms. In C. M. Barrette & K. Paesani (Eds.), *Language program articulation: Developing a theoretical foundation* (pp. 110–130). AAUSC Issues in Language Program Direction. Boston: Heinle.

Li, C. N. (2002). Missing links, issues, and hypotheses in the evolutionary origin of language. In T. Givón & B. F. Malle (Eds.), *The evolution of language out of pre-language* (pp. 83–106). Philadelphia: John Benjamins.

Liebscher, G., & Dailey-O'Cain, J. (2004). Learner code-switching in the content-based foreign language classroom. *The Canadian Modern Language Review, 60*, 501–525.

Lightbown, P. M. (1998). The importance of timing in focus on form. In C. Doughty & J. Williams (Eds.), *Focus on form in classroom second language acquisition* (pp. 177–196). New York: Cambridge University Press.

Liska, J. (1995). Ritual/representation as the semiogenetic precursor of hominid symbol use. In S. Puppel (Ed.), *The biology of language* (pp. 157–172). Philadelphia: John Benjamins.

Liskin-Gasparro, J. (1999). Issues for foreign language departments and prospective teachers. In P. Franklin, D. Laurence, & E. B. Welles (Eds.), *Preparing a nation's teachers: Models for English and foreign language programs.* New York: The Modern Language Association.

Long, M. H. (1981). Input, interaction, and second language acquisition. In H. Winitz (Ed.), *Native language and foreign language acquisition* (pp. 259–278). New York: New York Academy of Sciences.

Long, M. H. (1991). Focus on form: A design feature in language teaching methodology. In K. de Bot, R. Ginsberg, & C. Kramsch (Eds.), *Foreign language research in cross-cultural perspective* (pp. 39–52). Philadelphia: John Benjamins.

Long, M. H. (1996). The role of the linguistic environment in second language acquisition. In Ritchie, W. C. & Bahtia, T. K. (Eds.), *Handbook of second language acquisition* (pp. 413–468). New York: Academic Press.

Mackey, W. F. (2000). The description of bilingualism. In L. Wei (Ed.), *The bilingualism reader* (pp. 26–56). New York: Routledge. (Reprinted from *Canadian Journal of Linguistics*, 1982, 7, 51–85.)

Magnan, S. S. (2007). Reconsidering communicative language teaching for national goals. *The Modern Language Journal, 91*, 249–251.

Martin-Jones, M. (1995). Code-switching in the classroom: Two decades of research. In L. Milroy & P. Muysken (Eds.), *One speaker, two languages: Cross-disciplinary perspectives on code-switching* (pp. 90–111). New York: Cambridge University Press.

Matthiessen, C. M. I. M. (2004). The evolution of language: A systemic functional exploration of phylogenetic phases. In G. Williams & A. Lukin (Eds.), *The development of language* (pp. 45–90). London: Continuum.

Maxim, H. H. (2003). Expanding visions for collegiate advanced foreign language learning. In H. Byrnes & H. H. Maxim (Eds.), *Advanced foreign language learning: A challenge to college programs* (pp. 180–193). AAUSC Issues in Language Program Direction. Boston: Heinle.

Maxim, H. H. (2008). Developing advanced formal language abilities along a genre-based continuum. In S. L. Katz & J. Watzinger-Tharp (Eds.), *Conceptions of grammar: Theoretical approaches and their application in the L2 classroom* (pp. 172–188). AAUSC Issues in Language Program Direction. Boston: Heinle.

McLaughlin, J., Osterhout, L., & Kim, A. (2004). Neural correlates of second-language word learning: Minimal instruction produces rapid change. *Nature Neuroscience, 7*, 703–704.

Meisel, J. M. (2000). Early differentiation of languages in bilingual children. In L. Wei (Ed.), *The bilingualism reader* (pp. 344–369). New York: Routledge. (Reprinted from *Bilingualism across the lifespan*, pp. 13–40, by K. Hyltenstam & L. Obler, Eds., 1989, Cambridge: Cambridge University Press.)

Meisel, J. M. (1994). Code-switching in young bilingual children: The acquisition of grammatical constraints. *Studies in Second Language Acquisition, 16*, 413–439.

Milroy, L., & Muysken, P. (Eds.). (1995). *One speaker, two languages: Cross-disciplinary perspectives on code-switching*. Cambridge, UK: Cambridge University Press.

Mitchell, C. B., & Vidal, K. E. (2001). Weighing the ways of the flow: Twentieth century language instruction. *The Modern Language Journal, 85*, 26–38.

Muysken, P. (1995). Code switching and grammatical theory. In L. Milroy & P. Muysken (Eds.), *One speaker, two languages: Cross-disciplinary perspectives on code-switching* (pp. 177–198). Cambridge, UK: Cambridge University Press.

Myers-Scotton, C. (1993a). *Social motivations for codeswitching.* New York: Oxford University Press.

Myers-Scotton, C. (1993b). *Duelling languages.* New York: Oxford University Press.

Myers-Scotton, C. (1995). A lexically based model of code-switching. In L. Milroy & P. Muysken (Eds.), *One speaker, two languages: Cross-disciplinary perspectives on code-switching* (pp. 233–256). Cambridge, MA: Cambridge University Press.

Myers-Scotton, C. (2000). Code-switching as indexical of social negotiations. In L. Wei (Ed.), *The bilingualism reader* (pp. 137–165). New York: Routledge. (Reprinted from *Codeswitching*, pp. 156–186, by M. Heller, Ed., 1988, Berlin: Mouton de Gruyter.)

Myers-Scotton, C., & Jake, J. L. (2000). Matching lemmas in a bilingual language competence and production model: Evidence from intrasentential code-switching. In L. Wei (Ed.), *The bilingualism reader* (pp. 281–320). New York: Routledge. (Reprinted from *Linguistics*, 1995, *33*, 981–1024.)

Negueruela, E. (2008). A conceptual approach to promoting L2 grammatical development: Implications for language program directors. In S. L. Katz & J. Watzinger-Tharp (Eds.), *Conceptions of grammar: Theoretical approaches and their application in the L2 classroom* (pp. 151–171). AAUSC Issues in Language Program Direction. Boston: Heinle.

Nichols, P. C., & Colón, M. (2000). Spanish literacy and the academic success of latino high school students: Codeswitching as a classroom resource. *Foreign Language Annals, 33*, 498–511.

Norris, J. M. (2006). Assessing advanced foreign language learning and learners. In H. Byrnes, H. D. Weger-Guntharp, & K. Sprang (Eds.), *Educating for advanced foreign language capacities* (pp. 167–187). Washington, DC: Georgetown University Press.

Norton, B., & Toohey, K. (2002). Identity and language learning. In R. B. Kaplan (Ed.), *The Oxford handbook of applied linguistics* (pp. 115–123). New York: Oxford University Press.

Obler, L. K. (1982). Neurolinguistic aspects of language loss as they pertain to second language attrition. In R. D. Lambert & B. F. Freed (Eds.), *The loss of language skills* (pp. 60–79). Rowley, MA: Newbury House.

Odlin, T. (2002). Language transfer and cross-linguistic studies: Relativism, universalism, and the native language. In R. B. Kaplan (Ed.), *The Oxford handbook of applied linguistics* (pp. 253–261). New York: Oxford University Press.

Odlin, T. (2003). Cross-linguistic influence. In C. J. Doughty and M. H. Long (Eds.), *The handbook of second language acquisition* (pp. 436–486). Malden, MA: Blackwell.

Oxford, R. L. (1982). Technical issues in designing and conducting research on language skill attrition. In R. D. Lambert & B. F. Freed (Eds.), *The loss of language skills* (pp. 119–137). Rowley, MA: Newbury House.

Paradis, M. (2004). *A neurolinguistic theory of bilingualism.* Philadelphia: John Benjamins.

Patkowski, M. S. (1982). The sensitive period for the acquisition of syntax in a second language. In S. Krashen, R. C. Scarcella, & M. H. Long (Ed.), *Child-adult differences in second language acquisition* (pp. 52–63). Rowley, MA: Newbury House.

Pavlenko, A. (2002). Poststructuralist approaches to the study of social factors in second language learning and use. In V. Cook (Ed.), *Portraits of the L2 user* (pp. 277–302). Clevedon, UK: Multilingual Matters.

Pavlenko, A. (Ed.). (2006). *Bilingual minds: Emotional experience, expression and representation*. Clevedon, UK: Multilingual Matters.

Pavlenko, A. (2006a). Bilingual selves. In A. Pavlenko (Ed.), *Bilingual minds: Emotional experience, expression and representation* (pp. 1–33). Clevedon, UK: Multilingual Matters.

Perdue, C. (2002). Development of L2 functional use. In V. Cook (Ed.), *Portraits of the L2 user* (pp. 123–146). Clevedon, UK: Multilingual Matters.

Petersen, J. (1988). Word-internal code-switching constraints in a bilingual child's grammar. *Linguistics, 26,* 479–493.

Pica, T. (1987). Second language acquisition, social interaction, and the classroom. *Applied Linguistics, 8,* 3–21.

Pica, T. (1994). Research on negotiation: What does it reveal about second language learning conditions, processes and outcomes? *Language Learning, 44,* 493–527.

Pica, T., Young, R., & Doughty, C. (1987). The impact of interaction on comprehension. *TESOL Quarterly, 21,* 737–758.

Pinker, S. (1994, 2007). *The language instinct.* London: Penguin.

Poplack, S. (2000). Sometimes I'll start a sentence in Spanish *y termino en español:* Toward a typology of code-switching. In L. Wei (Ed.), *The bilingualism reader* (pp. 221–256). New York: Routledge. (Reprinted from *Linguistics,* 1979/1980, *18,* 581–618.)

Pratt, M. L. (2003). Building a new public idea about language. *ADFL Bulletin, 34(3),* 5–9.

Pulvermüller, F. (2002). *The neuroscience of language: On brain circuits of words and serial order.* Cambridge, UK: Cambridge University Press.

Puppel, S. (Ed.). (1995). *The biology of language.* Philadelphia: John Benjamins.

Richards, J. C., & Rodgers, T. S. (2001). *Approaches and methods in language teaching.* Cambridge, UK: Cambridge University Press.

Rivers, W. (1968/1981). *Teaching foreign language skills.* Chicago: University of Chicago Press.

Rodriguez-Fornells, A., Rotte, M., Heinze, H.-J., Nösselt, T., & Münte, T. F. (2002). Brain potential and functional MRI evidence for how to handle two languages with one brain. *Nature, 415,* 1026–1029.

Saffran, E. M., & Sholl, A. (1999). Clues to the functional and neural architecture of word meaning. In C. M. Brown & P. Hagoort (Eds.), *The Neurocognition of language* (pp. 241–272). Oxford, UK: Oxford University Press.

Sanz, C., & Morgan-Short, K. (2005). Explicitness in pedagogical interventions: Input, practice, and feedback. In C. Sanz (Ed.), *Adult second language acquisition* (pp. 234–263). Washington, DC: Georgetown University Press.

Savage-Rumbaugh, E. S., & Rumbaugh, D. M. (1993). In K. R. Gibson & T. Ingold (Eds.), *Tools, language and cognition in human evolution* (pp. 86–108). Cambridge, MA: Cambridge University Press.

Savage-Rumbaugh, S., Shanker, S. G., & Taylor, T. J. (1998). *Apes, language and the human mind*. Oxford, UK: Oxford University Press.

Scott, V. M. (1989). An empirical study of explicit and implicit teaching strategies in foreign language education. *The Modern Language Journal, 73*, 14–22.

Scott, V. M. (1990). Explicit and implicit grammar teaching strategies: New empirical data. *The French Review, 63*, 779–89.

Scott, V. M., & Tucker, H. (Eds.). (2001). *SLA and the literature classroom: Fostering dialogues*. AAUSC Issues in Language Program Direction. Boston: Heinle.

Scott, V. M., & Huntington, J. A. (2006). Literature, the interpretive mode, and novice learners. *The Modern Language Journal, 91*, 3–14.

Scott, V. M., & de la Fuente, M. J. (2008). What's the problem? L2 learners' use of L1 during consciousness-raising, form-focused tasks. *The Modern Language Journal, 92*, 100–112.

Selinker, L. (1972). Interlanguage. *International Review of Applied Linguistics, 10*, 209–231.

Sharwood Smith, M. A. (1989). Crosslinguistic influence in language loss. In K. Hyltenstam & L. K. Obler (Eds.), *Bilingualism across the lifespan* (pp. 185–201). Cambridge, UK: Cambridge University Press.

Shohamy, E. (2006). Rethinking assessment for advanced language proficiency. In H. Byrnes, H. D. Weger-Guntharp, & K. Sprang (Eds.), *Educating for advanced foreign language capacities* (pp. 188–208). Washington, DC: Georgetown University Press.

Shrum, J. L., & Glisan, E. W. (2005). *Teacher's handbook: Contextualized language instruction* (3rd ed.). Boston: Heinle.

Simmons, R. J. (2004). America's relationship with the world. How can languages help? *The French Review, 77*, 682–687.

Simon, D.-L. (2001). Towards a new understanding of codeswitching in the foreign language classroom. In R. Jacobson (Ed.), *Codeswitching worldwide II* (pp. 311–342). New York: Mouton de Gruyter.

Singer, J. (2004). La Paloma. *Orion*, March/April, 10-.

Smillie, D. (1995). Biological and cultural factors in the evolution of language. In S. Puppel (Ed.), *The biology of language* (pp. 265–276). Philadelphia: John Benjamins.

Snow, C. E., & Hoefnagel-Höhle, M. (1982). The critical period for language acquisition: Evidence from second language learning. In S. Krashen, R. C. Scarcella, & M. H. Long (Eds.), *Child-adult differences in second language acquisition* (pp. 93–111). Rowley, MA: Newbury House.

Standards for foreign language learning in the 21st century. (1996/1999). New York: ACTFL and the National Standards in Foreign Language Education Project.

Storch, N., & Wigglesworth, G. (2003). Is there a role for the use of the L1 in an L2 setting? *TESOL Quarterly, 37*, 760–770.

Sunderman, G., & Kroll, J. F. (2006). First language activation during second language lexical processing: An investigation of lexical form, meaning, and grammatical class. *Studies in Second Language Acquisition, 28*, 387–422.

Swaffar, J. (2003). A template for advanced learner tasks: Staging genre reading and cultural literacy through the précis. In H. Byrnes & H. Maxim (Eds.), *Advanced foreign language learning: A challenge to college programs* (pp. 19–45). AAUSC Issues in Language Program Direction. Boston: Heinle.

Swaffar, J. (2006). Terminology and its discontents: Some caveats about communicative competence. *The Modern Language Journal, 90*, 246–249.

Swaffar, J., & Arens, K. (2005). *Remapping the foreign language curriculum: An approach through multiple literacies.* New York: The Modern Language Association.

Swain, M. (1998). Focus on form through conscious reflection. In C. Doughty & J. Williams (Eds.), *Focus on form in classroom second language acquisition* (pp. 64–81). New York: Cambridge University Press.

Swain, M., & Lapkin, S. (1998). Interaction and second language learning: Two adolescent French immersion students working together. *The Modern Language Journal, 82*, 320–337.

Terrell, T. D. (1991). The role of grammar instruction in a communicative approach. *The Modern Language Journal, 75*, 52–63.

Tomasello, M. (2002). The emergence of grammar in early child language. In T. Givón & B. F. Malle (Eds.), *The evolution of language out of pre-language* (pp. 309–328). Philadelphia: John Benjamins.

Tomasello, M. (2003). *Constructing a language: A usage-based theory of language acquisition.* Cambridge, MA: Harvard University Press.

Tomasello, M., & Call, J. (1997). *Primate cognition.* Oxford, UK: Oxford University Press.

Toribio, J. A. (2001). On the emergence of bilingual code-switching competence. *Bilingualism: Language and Cognition, 4*, 203–231.

Toth, P. D. (2004). When grammar instruction undermines cohesion in L2 Spanish classroom discourse. *The Modern Language Journal, 88*, 14–30.

Train, R. W. (2002). The (non)native standard language in foreign language education: A critical perspective. In C. Blyth (Ed.), *The sociolinguistics of foreign-language classrooms* (pp. 3–39). AAUSC Issues in Language Program Direction. Boston: Heinle.

Turnbull, M., & Arnett, K. (2000). Teachers' use of the target and first languages in second and foreign language classrooms. *Annual Review of Applied Linguistics, 22*, 204–218.

Ullman, M. T. (2004). Contributions of memory circuits to language: The declarative/procedural model. *Cognition, 93*, 231–270.

Ullman, M. T. (2005). A cognitive neuroscience perspective on second language acquisition: The declarative/procedural model. In C. Sanz (Ed.), *Mind and context in adult second language acquisition: Methods, theory, and practice* (pp. 141–178). Washington, DC: Georgetown University Press.

Van Geert, P. (2008). The dynamic systems approach in the study of L1 and L2 acquisition: An introduction. *The Modern Language Journal, 92,* 179–199.

VanPatten, B. (1996). *Input processing and grammar instruction: Theory and research.* Norwood, NJ: Ablex.

VanPatten, B. (2007). Input processing in adult second language acquisition. In B. VanPatten & J. Williams (Eds.), *Theories in second language acquisition* (pp. 115–135). Mahwah, NJ: Lawrence Erlbaum.

Verspoor, M., Lowie, W., & van Dijk, M. (2008). Variability in second language development from a dynamic systems perspective. *The Modern Language Journal, 92,* 214–231.

Viorica, M., Spivey, M., & Hirsch, J. (2003). Shared and separate systems in bilingual language processing: Converging evidence from eyetracking and brain imaging. *Brain and Language, 86,* 70–82.

Vygotsky, L. S. (1962). *Thought and language.* Cambridge, MA: MIT Press.

Vygotsky, L. S. (1978). *Mind in society: The development of higher psychological processes.* Cambridge, MA: Harvard University Press.

Walther, I. (2007). Ecological perspectives on language and literacy: Implications for foreign language instruction at the collegiate level. *ADFL Bulletin, 38(3) & 39(1),* 6–14.

Warford, M. K. (2007). L1 vs. L2 in the foreign language classroom: New findings. *NECTFL Review, 60,* 50–60.

Wartenburger, I., Heekeren, H. R., Abutalebi, J., Cappa, S. F., Villringer, A., & Perani, D. (2003). Early setting of grammatical processing in the bilingual brain. *Neuron, 37,* 159–170.

Watson-Gegeo, K. A. (2004). Mind, language, and epistemology: Toward a language socialization paradigm for SLA. *The Modern Language Journal, 88,* 331–350.

Webb, J. B., & Miller, B. L. (Eds.). (2000). *Teaching heritage language learners.* New York: American Council on the Teaching of Foreign Languages.

Wei, L. (Ed.). (2000a). *The bilingualism reader.* New York: Routledge.

Wei, L. (2000b). Dimensions of bilingualism. In L. Wei (Ed.), *The bilingualism reader* (pp. 3–25). New York: Routledge.

Wei, L., Milroy, L., & Pong, S. C. (2000). A two-step sociolinguistic analysis of code-switching and language choice: The example of a bilingual Chinese community in Britain. In L. Wei (Ed.), *The bilingualism reader,* (pp. 188–209). New York: Routledge. (Reprinted from *International Journal of Applied Linguistics,* 1992, *2(1),* 66–83.)

Weltens, B., & Grendel, M. (1993). Attrition of vocabulary knowledge. In R. Schreuder & B. Weltens (Eds.), *The bilingual lexicon* (pp. 135–156). Philadelphia: John Benjamins.

Wesche, M. B., & Skehan, P. (2002). Communicative, task-based, and content-based language instruction. In R. B. Kaplan (Ed.), *The Oxford handbook of applied linguistics* (pp. 207–228). New York: Oxford University Press.

Wilkerson, C. (2008). Instructors' use of English in the modern language classroom. *Foreign Language Annals, 41*, 310–320.

Williamson, S. G. (1982). Summary chart of findings from previous research on language loss. In R. D. Lambert & B. F. Freed (Eds.), *The loss of language skills* (pp. 207–223). Rowley, MA: Newbury House.

Wong, W. (2004). *Input enhancement: From theory and research to the classroom.* New York: McGraw-Hill.

INDEX